MARGARET A. BERRY, B.A., M.Ed. ▪ PATRICIA S. MORRIS, B.A., M.L.S.

STEPPING INTO RESEARCH!

A COMPLETE RESEARCH SKILLS ACTIVITIES PROGRAM FOR GRADES 5–12

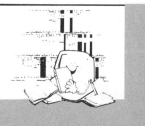

Illustrated by J. Payne

THE CENTER FOR APPLIED RESEARCH IN EDUCATION
Business & Professional Division
A division of Simon & Schuster
West Nyack, New York 10995

**THE CENTER FOR APPLIED
RESEARCH IN EDUCATION**
Business & Professional Division
A division of Simon & Schuster
West Nyack, New York 10995

10 9 8 7 6 5 4

Library of Congress Cataloging-in-Publication Data

Berry, Margaret A.
    Stepping into research : a complete research skills activities
program for grades 5–12 / Margaret A. Berry, Patricia S. Morris ;
illustrated by J. Payne.
        p. cm.
    ISBN 0–87628–800–X
    1. School libraries—Activity programs. 2. High schoollibraries—
Activity programs. 3. School children—Library orientation.
4. High school students—Library orientation. 5. Research—
Methodology—Study and teaching (Elementary) 6. Research—
Methodology—Study and teaching (Secondary) I. Morris, Patricia
S. II. Title.
Z675.S3B473 1990   89–29997
                                                     CIP

ISBN 0-87628-800-X

The authors wish to acknowledge the following companies for graciously permitting replication of their items:

National Geographic Society for *National Geographic Index* ©1984; H. W. Wilson Company for *Current Biography* and *Abridged Readers' Guide to Periodical Literature**; American Heritage for *American Heritage Cumulative Index* and *A Chronological Subject Guide to American Heritage;* Ebsco Subscription Services for *Magazine Article Summaries;* The World Almanac and Book of Facts for *The World Almanac and Book of Facts;* World Book, Inc. for *The World Book Encyclopedia;* Grolier, Inc. for *Academic American Encyclopedia;* Macmillan Publishing Company for *Collier's Encyclopedia;* St. Martin's Press for *The Statesman's Yearbook;* George Philip Limited for *Prentice Hall American World Atlas;*

Catalog cards and catalog format from Catalog Card Corporation of American, Creative Education, Specialized Service and Supply Company, Demco, Inc.;

MicroMaps Software for the map graphics

*Pages 458 and 556 from the 1987 annual volume of *Abridged Readers' Guide to Periodical Literature* copyright ©1987, 1988 by The H. W. Wilson Company, New York. Reproduced by permission of the publisher.

*Page 56 from the March 1989 issue of *Abridged Readers' Guide to Periodical Literature* copyright ©1989 by The H. W. Wilson Company. Reproduced by permission of the publisher.

*Page 656 from *Current Biography Yearbook* 1986 copyright ©1986, 1987 by The H. W. Wilson Company, New York. Reproduced by permission of the publisher.

THE WORLD ALMANAC AND BOOK OF FACTS, 1989 EDITION, ©Newspaper Enterprise Association, Inc. 1988, New York, NY 10166.

ABOUT THE AUTHORS

Peg Berry, M. Ed. in Reading, is a study skills and reading teacher for the East Hanover, New Jersey, school district. Her experience includes twenty years of teaching the middle school level, grades six, seven, and eight. She has participated in program and curriculum development on both the school and district level. Most recently, she has presented workshops at local colleges and Educational Media Association of New Jersey conventions on the role of study skills and the reading teacher in fostering a readiness for research in students.

Pat Morris, M. L. S., is a library media specialist for the East Hanover, New Jersey, school district. Her experience includes teaching self-contained classes at the elementary level, as well as high school English instruction plus twenty years of library media experience on the elementary, middle, and high school levels. She participates regularly in program and curriculum development on both school and district levels, and is currently a member of the Curriculum Research and Review Committee for her district. A member of the Executive Board of the Educational Media Association of New Jersey, she has been a presenter and a panelist at their conventions.

ABOUT THE BOOK

The purpose of *Stepping Into Research! A Complete Research Skills Activities Program for Grades 5-12* is to develop a readiness for research in each student before he or she begins to meet the written content demands of a research assignment. The book, as a whole, can be used as a course of study or each individual topic might be infused into an existing program. The book focuses on those steps which precede the written process with the intention that with a thorough knowledge of each skill, the student will develop a proficiency in library usage. It is hoped that the core of known materials from which the students might choose will enlarge and that skills and materials not necessarily used at an elementary school level will become commonplace. Through a thorough understanding of the use of the card catalog, the catalog card, the library organizational systems, the varied book and periodical indices, as well as a development of an awareness of library computer opportunities, it is expected that skill development will provide a base that will foster student success in middle school and junior high school and in the eventual high school experience.

The book's objectives are broad and its skill components are many. Its purpose is to provide a continuum of skills necessary to achieve proficiency in the area of research. All lessons contain interrelated student notes reinforced through a variety of over two hundred skill sheets and extended activities. It presents the teacher or librarian with an overview of the book through lesson goals and objectives, a skill checklist and teacher background information. It offers a thorough accountability of knowledge on the part of the student through a variety of testing experiences.

It contains a management system in the form of a skills' checklist which corresponds each lesson to the representative skills covered. The checklist also includes the skills covered in the hands-on simulation experiences found in the book that deal with the card catalog, the retrieval process and the varied nonfiction indices. Through manipulative activities of the Retrieval Game, The Card Catalog Simulation, and the use of indices in the area of multiple sources in the lesson titled, "Did You Know?," students are presented with various problems and exceptions to which they will be confronted during the research experiences. Both the written and simulated activities and experiences provide the perfect transition into the library setting giving the teacher or librarian the assurance that all of the skills necessary to correctly use the library have been covered and that the exceptions that might eventually pose problems in a library setting have been explained in detail.

The program, itself, can be used in either a classroom or a library setting by a library media specialist, a reading teacher, a study skills teacher, or a classroom content area teacher. It is structured to foster open communication between the librarian and the content area teacher to achieve the goal of increased student research ability among the student population.

The book is easy to use. Although the media specialist has no need for concept development, the study skills teacher, reading teacher, and content area teacher are not required to research further than the program goals, objectives, student notes, teacher background information to feel concept proficient to teach the lessons.

In all the book is comprehensive and proven. It is one that is guaranteed to enhance the research program of any school system.

STEPPING INTO RESEARCH !

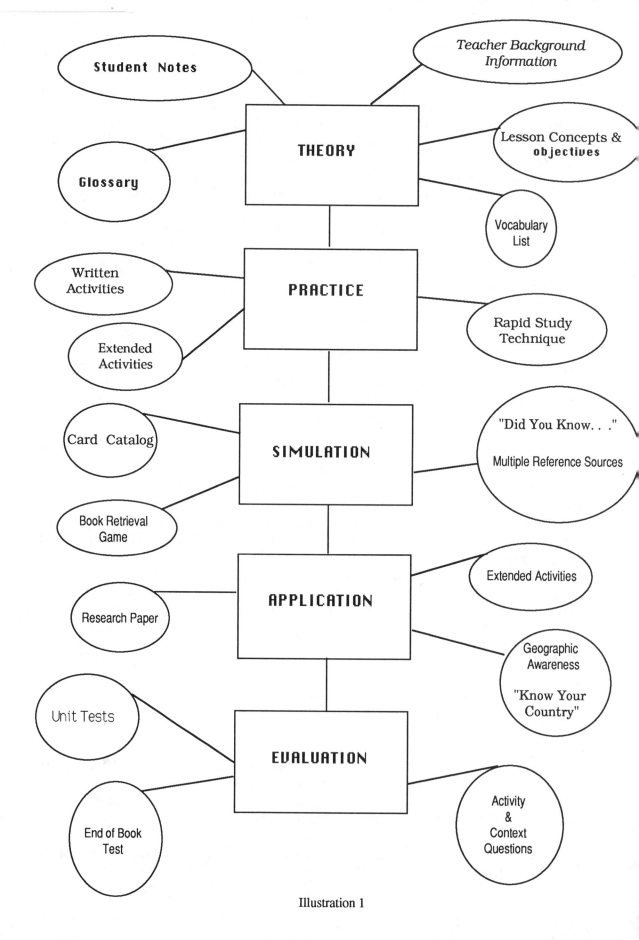

Illustration 1

HOW TO USE THE BOOK

As indicated in illustration 2, the seven basic units of *Stepping into Research!* are:

A.   The Media Center
B.   The Card Catalog
C.   The Four Organizational Systems
D.   Book and Information Retrieval

E.   The Utilization of Sources
F.   The Library Future
G.   The Aspects of Writing

The seven units are also divided into a total of thirty lessons. Both the skills checklist and the table of contents illustrate the interrelationship of all the lessons in terms of theory, practice, simulation, application and evaluation. [See illustration #1] Also shown in the table of contents are the locations of the unit and final tests, all answer keys, the rapid study technique, the glossary, the catalog simulation and index.

Each of the thirty lessons are comprised of the same basic format and each includes: lesson focus, teacher preparation and background information, lesson concepts, objectives, vocabulary development, materials list, student paper activities, extended activities, student notes with context questions. [See illustration #2]

Before beginning to use the book, it is important to understand the usefulness of the checklist, student notes, activity types, simulation, rapid study technique and geographic awareness.

Checklist: The checklist of skills itemizes the skill areas covered in the program and is in lesson sequence. It can be used as a means of monitoring class or individual student progress.

Student Notes: Each lesson provides a detailed explanation of concepts covered and is written in simple language for the student. Its purpose is to provide background information.

Activity Types: Each lesson provides suggested written extended activities for enrichment as well as specific pencil/paper activities for concept reinforcement.

Simulation: The simulation activities are meant to help the student to transition into library skillfulness. The student is exposed to simulated library experiences which contain a variety of problems and exceptions which he/she might be find during his or her years of schooling. There are three areas of simulation included:

     The Card Catalog   (Card Catalog Simulation)
     Book Retrieval   (Retrieval Game)
     Multiple Source Information Retrieval   (Did You Know?)

Geographic Awareness: At the end of each unit, a unit activity sheet will detail application questions which will combine both the unit concepts taught and information about the specific land region of the United States. The purpose of the activities is two-fold: to practice the unit concepts and to reinforce a geographic awareness of the United States and its territories and possessions.

Rapid Study Technique: The RST section of the book is in Appendix A. Over one hundred specific "bits" of information are listed in a format that can be translated easily into a study aid or a game situation. By isolating many of the individual, literal statements and allowing direct study, a frame of reference or foundation can be structured against which many more complex activities might be advanced.

In using *Stepping into Research!*, it is suggested that the teacher or library media specialist follow a sequence:

1. Identify your group according to grade level and ability. (There is a range of activities for each unit.)
2. Identify the teaching time frame in terms of how often the group will be seen and if you will see them the following cycle or the following year(s).
3. Review the book's table of contents and skills checklist for an overview of the concepts presented in the book.
4. Outline your intended program keeping in mind that the book can be used as a sequential whole or in part as skills can easily be infused into an existing program.
5. After completing a skills assessment, review one lesson to ascertain an understanding of the regular lesson format contained in the book.

Stepping into Research

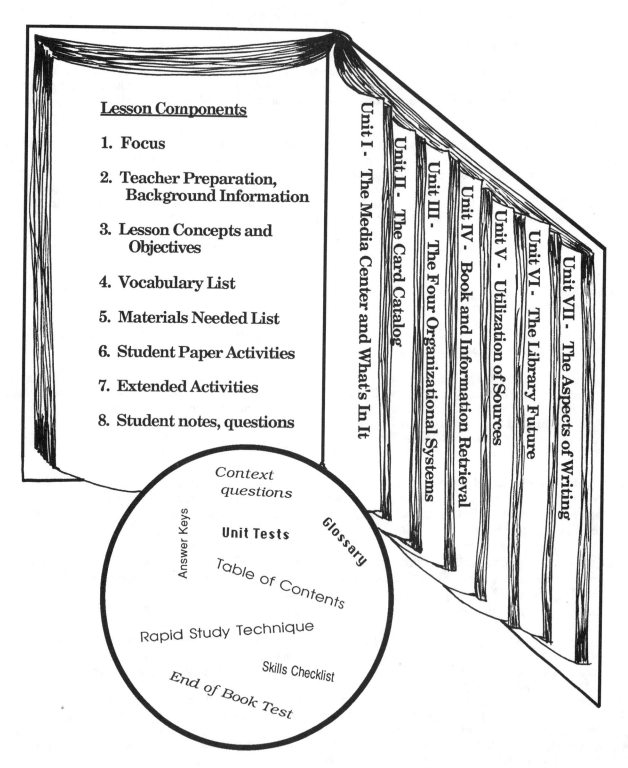

Lesson Components

1. Focus

2. Teacher Preparation, Background Information

3. Lesson Concepts and Objectives

4. Vocabulary List

5. Materials Needed List

6. Student Paper Activities

7. Extended Activities

8. Student notes, questions

Unit I - The Media Center and What's In It

Unit II - The Card Catalog

Unit III - The Four Organizational Systems

Unit IV - Book and Information Retrieval

Unit V - Utilization of Sources

Unit VI - The Library Future

Unit VII - The Aspects of Writing

Context questions

Answer Keys

Unit Tests

Glossary

Table of Contents

Rapid Study Technique

Skills Checklist

End of Book Test

Illustration 2

Checklist of Skills by Lesson Number

1 Recognizes library areas
1 Recognizes library materials
1 Understands classifications
1 Understands divisions of literature

2 Classifies, defines fiction types
2 Recognizes common fiction examples
2 Understands definition, placement of legends, fables, folktales

3 Understands nonfiction areas
3 Recognizes expertise
3 Recognizes importance of accuracy
3 Understands bias

4 Understands purpose of nonfiction, reference
4 Recognizes multiple formats in reference collection
4 Understands relationship of library to researcher

5 Understands purpose of card catalog
5 Understands difference of authorized, unauthorized biography
5 Identifies four library classifications

6 Recognizes purpose of card catalog
6 Understands use of card catalog
6 Differentiates basic card types

7 Recognizes and uses added entry card types
7 Recognizes and uses cross reference cards

8 Understands alphabetical organization in card catalog
8 Understands chronological organization of card catalog

9 Differentiates among card types
9 Recognizes parts in card types
9 Understands correspondence of card types to research

10 Understands, differentiates four organizational systems
10 Understands relationship chronological order to country's history

11 Recognizes, understands catalog card rule exceptions
11 Understands rules of subject retrieval in card catalog

12 Understands multiple subject cards for one book
12 Understands process, book selection in beginning research
12 Understands process of generating keywords
12 Understands book placement on individual shelving unit
12 Understands Dewey Decimal System
12 Understands catalog card information in book retrieval

13 Understands Dewey Decimal System
13 Recognizes item placement in four library classifications
13 Recognizes call number and book placement

14 Understands book placement of individual classification
14 Understands rules of retrieval process

15 Recognizes similarities, differences in card type
15 Applies understandings of library classifications
15 Applies understandings of parts of catalog cards
15 Applies concepts of book retrieval process

16 Recognizes parts of a book for research process
16 Understands cross reference: see, see also
16 Understands punctuation in index

17 Understands encyclopedia set format
17 Understands encyclopedia volume format
17 Understands encyclopedia article format
17 Understands encyclopedia spine information
17 Understands encyclopedia organizations

18 Understands use of encyclopedia index
18 Understands relationship of index to article
18 Understands use of cross reference
18 Understands difference of see, see also
18 Understands article format, print size
18 Understands, identifies use of visual aids
18 Understands use of bibliography
18 Understands relationship encyclopedia to research

19 Understands purpose of almanac
19 Understands format of multiple indices
19 Understands use of index
19 Understands relationship of index to articles
19 Understands purpose of visual aids

20 Understands, utilizes format of atlas index
20 Understands, utilizes format of atlas legend, map key
20 Understands, utilizes coordinates
20 Understands, utilizes map title as main idea or focus
20 Understands importance of atlas to comparative studies

21 Recognizes use, purpose of Readers' Guide
21 Understands format Readers' Guide Index
21 Understands format of index entry
21 Understands use, purpose of cross reference
21 Differentiates: see, see also
21 Understands relationship index entry to magazine article

22 Understands use, purpose of American Heritage Magazine
22 Understands use of multiple indices
22 Understands various formats of indices
22 Understands relationship index entry to magazine article

Checklist of Skills by Lesson Number

CONTENTS

Unit VI The Library Future

Unit VII The Aspects of Writing

Unit I   The Media Center and What's In It

The Media Center and What's In It

FOCUS

In this lesson, the students will understand the areas of his/her own library and that these areas generalize to all libraries.

TEACHER PREPARATION

1. Review the following information:
    a. General overview of the entire course; see Skill Checklist.
    b. Use of the optional student activity workbook.
    c. Classroom-based activities and Media Center activities.
2. Before working on this lesson, a tour of the library is necessary along with a definition of research. Be sure to explain the information explosion and its implication for the student.
3. Review current placement of materials in your library and physical location.
4. Each year reacquaint the students with the library---don't take for granted that they know.
5. Have students walk to areas as located: reference, fiction, nonfiction, biography, periodicals, etc. Explain why an IMC is so important in a school.
6. Student notebooks can be made in full by duplicating all activity sheets for all applicable lessons. Students may therefore take notes on lessons involved.
7. Read through the student activities in Lesson 1 to organize your discussion of what the students need to know.
8. Complete the activity sheets; check your answers, develop all variables and all possible answers according to your school and local library; keep them handy for class reference.
9. If students do not have their own workbook, prepare copies of the activity sheets so that students can work in groups or individually. Have answer keys prepared, if you want them to check their own work.
10. It is important for the student to know the four library classifications. Have ready examples of each classification. In-depth coverage of each will be in the following lessons.

BACKGROUND INFORMATION

1. The need for thorough preparation cannot be overemphasized especially for areas of your media center which might be different than what is described in the text.

2. We use the word *literature* to mean all works that are written. Since we are a "literate" society, we can break down that large grouping of all written works into those writings which are true: nonfiction, and those that are not true: fiction. When you elicit from the students what broad categories are in the library, they will usually give you answers like "information" and "stories."

Examples:
Fiction: *Dragonwings; Watership Down*
Nonfiction: *Grasslands and Tundra; The Viking World*
Reference: *World Book Encyclopedia; Dictionary of American Biography*
Biography: *Brian's Song; Benjamin Franklin*

3. The areas of the library include: the nonfiction section, the reference section, the biography section, the fiction section, the vertical file, the picture file, Reader's Guide, American Heritage, card catalog, periodical room, record bin, microform, newspapers, magazine rack, encyclopedias, atlases, dictionaries, study carrels, check-out desk or circulation desk, and the library media specialist.

4. The various media include: books, records, films, filmstrips, sound filmstrips, slides, film loops, transparencies, picture files, kits, tapes, newspapers, periodicals, vertical file, video tapes, video discs, compact discs, computer software.

5. *CRITERIA* is a good word for students to know, understand and use. After making sure that they know "criteria" is plural and "criterion" is singular, give them the definition that it is a rule, or standard, for making a judgment, test.

CONCEPTS
- **Recognition of the various areas and materials in the media center or library.**
- **Recognition and use of the various media located in the media center.**
- **Recognition of the divisions of literature.**
- **Recognition of the library classifications.**

VOCABULARY
proficient concept technique enhance retrieval confronted familiarize criteria

OBJECTIVES
The student will:
1. Understand the areas of his/her own library and that these areas generalize to all libraries.
2. Be able to locate the many and varied areas of the media center.
3. Identify the various media found in the media center.
4. Understand that literature is divided into two main headings of fiction and nonfiction.
5. Understand that fiction is fabricated either as a whole or in part and that nonfiction is based totally on fact.

MATERIALS NEEDED
Activity Sheets 1-a through 1-d and 1-b through 1-d in optional student workbook.

ACTIVITIES
1. Read through and briefly discuss the material in the first two activity sheets.

2. Indicate the items in the library tour before guiding the students on an actual tour. Discussion of each item is best done in the library.

3. You may use the context questions indicated by the Stop sign as overt active participation in class or as homework assignments.

EXTENDED ACTIVITY
Let students find one-paragraph excerpts from common examples of fiction and nonfiction to share or to quiz classmates on whether it sounds like fiction or nonfiction. Start them with their social studies text for nonfiction and some really descriptive fiction, perhaps fantasy, for the fiction, perhaps *Charlotte's Web*. Real contrast is needed to make this work.

The Media Center and What's In It

The main purpose of *Stepping into Research!* is for you to acquire the necessary skills to become proficient in the area of information retrieval. It is hoped that this skill development will, in turn, support a lifetime of continuous learning in a world experiencing an information explosion. The building of a thorough understanding of the concepts directly related to research in terms of the card catalog, information retrieval, the catalog card, and the organizational shelving systems as used in most libraries is the basis of this program.

The library or I. M. C. (Instructional Media Center) is the heart or hub of every school. It is the place to which you go to find answers to questions or to locate specific information on a variety of subjects. To obtain the most from any library, it is very important that you possess a general understanding of the basic organizational patterns which can be found in any library.

The Classifications

Upon entering any IMC, you are confronted with thousands of books. At first, finding a specific book may seem to be an almost impossible task. But, if you are knowledgeable in the simple, general organizational techniques or patterns used by the librarian in the placement of books, retrieval of a specific item can be accomplished easily.

Let's start at the very basis of library understanding. Together, all of the books in the library can be grouped as LITERATURE: *WRITTEN WORKS*. Each book of the grouping, literature, has been written by an author to either fulfill a general purpose of entertainment known as fiction, or for a purpose of supplying factual information known as nonfiction.

LITERATURE

Fiction   Nonfiction

By recognizing the purpose for which each book has been written, the librarian, or library media specialist, is able to classify the books in the library into four basic sections. This is done by following the generally accepted criteria which describes each classification:

1.) Fiction

2.) Nonfiction

3.) Reference

4.) Biography

Types of Media

It is important that you familiarize yourself with not only the four general classifications of fiction, nonfiction, reference, and biography, but also the location of the variety of media and instructional aids offered to enhance information retrieval. A listing of some of the instructional aids would include: nonfiction records, films, filmstrips, sound filmstrips, slides, film loops, transparencies, picture files, kits, tapes, newspaper, periodicals, vertical files, video discs, CD'S and computer software.

Tour the Library

It is equally important that you be able to locate all the general sections in the IMC. Listed below are those areas found in all libraries. Knowledge of the use of these is important to you as a student researcher.

Locate in the IMC:
1. Sections:
    a. Nonfiction
    b. Reference
    c. Biography
    d. Fiction
2. Vertical file

3. Picture file

4. Dictionaries

5. Atlases

6. Study carrels

7. Check out Desk or Circulation Desk

8. Readers' Guide

9. Encyclopedias

10. American Heritage

11. Card catalog

12. Magazine rack

13. Newspapers

14. Periodical room

15. Microfilm

16. Record bin

17. Library Media Specialist

1. List the four library classifications.

2. List some of the instructional media that might be found in the IMC other than book format.

3. List the two main divisions of literature and define each.

4. Why is it important to be familiar with the areas and materials in the IMC?

The Library Tour Checklist

DIRECTIONS:

Indicate your basic understanding of the various areas of the library by completing the chart.

DO YOU KNOW THE LOCATION OF THE FOLLOWING AREAS OR MATERIALS?

AREA/MATERIAL LOCATION	YES		NO	
1. Nonfiction section				
2. Fiction section				
3. Reference section				
4. Biography section				
5. Vertical file				
6. Picture file				
7. Dictionaries				
8. Atlases				
9. Study carrels				
10. Circulation desk				
11. Readers' Guide				
12. Encyclopedias				
13. American Heritage				
14. Card catalog				
15. Magazine rack				
16. Newspapers				
17. Periodical room				
18. Microfilm				
19. Record Bin				
20. Electronic Encyclopedia				
21. Electronic Catalog				
22. On-line computer terminal				
23. Library Media Specialist				

THE LIBRARY TOUR

DIRECTIONS:

Change the drawing to represent the shape of your library. Indicate the entry door, any windows and the circulation desk. Then, place the corresponding numbers of the general areas until you have completely mapped the library. Include the following and add others that are special to your library.

1. Nonfiction section
2. Fiction section
3. Reference section
4. Biography section
5. Vertical file
6. Picture file
7. Dictionaries
8. Atlases
9. Study carrels
10. Circulation Desk

11. Readers' Guide
12. Encyclopedias
13. American Heritage
14. Card catalog
15. Magazine rack
16. Newspapers
17. Periodical room
18. Microfilm
19. Record bin
20. Library Media Specialist

INFORMATIONAL SOURCES

DIRECTIONS:

    Briefly describe each format as a source of information. Explain how each might enhance the research process.

SOURCE	DESCRIPTION AND	LIBRARY LOCATION
1. book		
2. cassette		
3. computer software		
4. film loops		
5. filmstrips		
6. globes		
7. kits		
8. magazines		
9. map collections		
10. microfilm		
11. models		
12. newspapers		
13. pamphlets		
14. picture file/study print		
15. record		
16. slides		
17. transparencies		
18. vertical file		
19. videotapes		

Criteria of Different Types of Literature
Fiction

FOCUS

This lesson will focus on the types of fiction, examples of the different types, and shelf placement for legends, folktales, and fables.

TEACHER PREPARATION

1. Review the various titles as presented in the background information and the student activity sheets.
2. Read through the student activities. Complete the activity sheets. Check your answers and keep the sheets for reference during class.
3. Check your school and local library for placement of legends, fables, and folktales. It is possible that some will be shelved in the Easy section, or possibly, in the jFic section. Be sure to inform your students where the various items are.

BACKGROUND INFORMATION

1. <u>Historical fiction</u> can be used quite well in the social studies area for giving the flavor of a time period. *Social Education, The Journal for the National Council of Social Studies,* occasionally has teaching lessons on using historical fiction. The Random House/Miller-Brody sound filmstrip: *James Lincoln Collier and Christopher Collier,* a part of the Meet the Newbery author series, does a credible job not only of describing the collaboration process but of showing the research that goes into writing historical fiction. More examples: *Roll of Thunder, Hear My Cry; The Slave Dancer; Sing Down the Moon; The Candle and the Mirror; Cave of Moving Shadows.*

2. <u>Modern Realistic Fiction</u>, like *The Outsiders* and *Summer of the Swans*, is unusually well accepted by students. American Guidance Service, Inc., Circle Pines, Minnesota 55014, publishes *The Bookfinder*, which is a guide to children's literature about the needs and problems of youth aged 2-15. It contains many examples of modern realistic fiction grouped under subject headings applicable to kids and their lives: self esteem, siblings, loyalty. More examples: *With Westie and the Tin Man; A Taste of Blackberries; Deathwatch; Just Dial a Number; Keeping It Secret; The Late Great Me; One Fat Summer; Revenge of the Nerd; Cracker Jackson; The Solitary.*

3. <u>Science Fiction,</u> unfortunately, is not well-liked by some students. Others border on being obsessive about it. Science fiction can stretch the imagination. *The White Mountains* and *A Wrinkle in Time*, both of which begin trilogies, are usually accepted. *The Encyclopedia of Science Fiction and Fantasy* is one example of a reference book in science fiction that you might be able to use with your students. Borrow it from another library if yours doesn't have it. More examples: *Missing Persons League; The Star Beast; Fantastic Voyage; Z is for Zachariah; 2010; Stranger in a Strange Land; Star Wars.*

4. <u>Fantasy</u> requires the willing suspension of disbelief. Share with the students some really good examples: *Konrad; Dogsong; The Ice Bear; The Search for Delicious; Greenwitch; Silver on the Tree; Dragonsong; Tuck Everlasting; The Dark is Rising; The Gammage Cup.*

5. You can ask students if any have ever read any of the titles. You could see if the IMC has any in audiovisual format, and show them to the students or let the students view them in the IMC. The IMC might also have a sound filmstrip series by Guidance Associates, White Plains, NY, that is called *Getting Hooked On . . .* Specific titles include *Getting Hooked on Historical Fiction, Getting Hooked on Science Fiction,* plus others.

6. If an interest is shown, you might permit students to make one list of other examples that they had read and couldn't categorize and let them check with the library media specialist and report back to class.

7. Probably by this point your students will have told you that fiction is shelved separately with F or FIC and apart from the nonfiction which has a number on it. They will also probably know that the number is called the Dewey Decimal System. Their question will be, "How can there be fiction in the nonfiction?" Although there is an in-depth discussion of the Dewey System, let your students know that Melvil Dewey classified everything within his ten category system, fiction and biography included. We, the library community, have taken things out. Folklore (398) and folk literature (398.2) are in the social sciences class which is about all the ways that people interact: culturally, economically, legally, and illegally. Folklore is not that far, Dewey speaking, from cannibalism (394), or games (394), just another social custom.

8. If you want to pursue the topic of fables, legends, and fairy tales with your students, two books should be of interest: Bruno Bettelheim's *The Uses of Enchantment* and Francelia Butler's *Sharing Literature with Children* which has many examples of myths, folktales, folksongs, and fables grouped around themes.

9. Mythology (292, Greek or Roman) or Viking gods and heroes (293.13) would be in the Dewey classification for "other religions and comparative religions." The 800 section, Literature, was, for Dewey, to be classified according to the language of composition with English fiction in 823 and German fiction in 833 and French in 843, and so on. But most libraries will classify all fiction in F or FIC separately and put foreign language works in the 800's. Study texts of novels and critical appraisals of literary works and retrospective compilations of single authors are all in the 800's. Your students can check the 800's in the IMC to see what they find.

CONCEPTS
  • **Recognition of the types of fiction.**
  • **Recognition of popular examples of the different types.**
  • **Recognition of the shelf placement of legends, folktales, and fables.**

VOCABULARY
sequence   partial   plot   plausible   technological advances

OBJECTIVES
The student will understand:
1. That the areas of fiction are historical, modern realistic, science, and fantasy.
2. That historical fiction has a time and place setting based in the past.
3. That modern realistic fiction has a time and place setting in the present.
4. That science fiction is based on current technological advances as projected into the future.
5. That fantasy goes beyond the laws of nature as currently accepted.
6. And recognize popular examples of historical fiction, modern realistic fiction, science fiction, and fantasy.
7. That legends, fables, and folktales are not shelved as fiction but according to the content part of each type as it supported the thinking of the time in which each story was originally communicated.

MATERIALS NEEDED
Activity Sheets 2-a through 2-e and 2-b through 2-e in the optional student workbook.

ACTIVITIES
1. Read through and discuss the material in the first activity sheet using the Background Information.
2. You may use the context questions indicated by the Stop Sign as in-class activity or homework.
3. You may use any of the filmstrips indicated in Background Information.

EXTENDED ACTIVITIES

1.   To recognize and differentiate four types of fiction by taking one set of characters and one basic plot, wrap them around in different ways to make examples of all four types of fiction.

Examples: *Samantha, 12 years old; Samuel, 13 years old*
Typical behavior at meal time.

   A. <u>Historical Fiction</u>:   Samantha and Samuel are at supper with family outside of Conestoga wagon on trail west. Father keeping watch while mother feeds family.

   B. <u>Modern realistic</u>:   Sami is setting the table and Sammy has started to prepare the meal for their divorced mother, who has not yet come home from work.

   C. <u>Science Fiction</u>: SAM $_A$ AND SAM $_U$ are overage robotic kitchen servants. SAM $_A$ is setting dining furniture into multiphased room. SAM $_U$ is programmed to move food from freezer to microwave.

   D. <u>Fantasy</u>: Sam^1 and Sam ^{2} are two statues in the IMC that come alive after the librarian goes home. Tonight they are dining from the *Encyclopedia of Cooking*.

2. Have the students draw scenes from the science fiction.

3. Use the following Venn Diagram to explain the intersecting set of legends, fables, folktales, and myths:

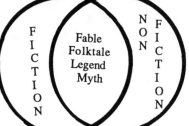

4. Underneath the Venn Diagram, chart the titles of legends, myths, etc., that the students have read. Be sure to include the ones from the basal reader or literature book that the students are using in class.

5. For a class representation of Activity 2-b, use the following for a bulletin board that is updated weekly:

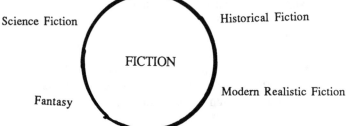

6. Teaching theme development is not always easy. Use the following chart on a bulletin board or on a transparency with an on-going listing of themes. Take five minutes at the beginning of every class to add to the chart. Make sure you add themes.

THEMES

Survival	Friendship	Death	Spiritual Triumph	Sibling Bonds	Courage	Quest

Fiction

Fiction is written for entertainment value. It provides information or plot sequence that is either totally or partially make-believe. Under this classification, there are at least four different types of books. It is easy to tell them apart by recognizing the time setting and determining believability, that is to say that the plot could actually have happened. If this is the case and the time/place setting is in the past, the type is 1.) historical fiction. If the time setting is in the present, the type is 2.) modern realistic fiction. If the focus concerns the future and is based on knowledge of current technological advances and the plot is plausible, the type is 3.) science fiction. When a writer breaks through the basic laws of nature as currently accepted, the type is 4.) fantasy.

Popular examples of each are as follows:
1.) Historical fiction: *Johnny Tremain, Ivanhoe, Ghost Fox, The Master Puppeteer, My Brother Sam is Dead.*
2.) Modern Realistic Fiction: *Ramona, Homecoming, Dicey's Song, The Great Gilly Hopkins, Friends Till the End, The Bumblebee Flies Anyway.*
3.) Science Fiction: *Children of the Dust, Star Trek, Dune, Stranger in a Strange Land, The White Mountains.*
4.) Fantasy: *Wizard of Earth-Sea, Star Ka'at, The Dog Days of Arthur Cane, Below the Root, The Hobbit, The Blue Sword.*

The library also houses other types of literature known as legends, fables, and folktales which are placed by the library media specialist in the nonfiction 300 section rather than as a part of fiction. This is because the contents of the books support a basic understanding of the thinking of the people living at the time in which they were written or were popular. The myths, another area covered in literature, are placed in the library in the non-fiction 200's section because to the ancient people of Greece, Rome, and other countries, mythology served as a religion. The 800's section will also contain works of fiction.

1. Explain the differences and similarities among historical fiction, modern realistic fiction, and science fiction.
2. What is fantasy?
3. Give at least two examples of each of the fiction types.
4. Why would legends, fables, and folktales be placed in the 300's section rather than the fiction section of the IMC?
5. Why are myths placed in the 200's section?

Four Basic Types of Fiction

DIRECTIONS:

Your teacher has a listing of examples of the four basic types of fiction. Select one from each area of fantasy, science fiction, historical fiction, and modern realistic fiction. Write your choices under the appropriate heading below. Then recopy those same choices onto the "contract" at the bottom of the page. Turn the bottom portion of the sheet into the librarian, and keep the rest in the assignment section of your notebook.

Modern realistic fiction:

Science fiction:

Historical fiction:

Fantasy:

_____

_____

Modern realistic fiction:

Science fiction:

Historical fiction:

Fantasy:

Your name_____
I promise to read all four books as listed above during the current school year.

_____   _____   _____
(signature of student)   (signature of teacher)   (signature of librarian)

FICTION TYPES IN SHORT PARAGRAPHS

DIRECTIONS:

Select one theme/topic/idea/concept/item and use this as the title or main idea of four short compositions. Each composition will consist of between two to four paragraphs. Each composition will depict one type of fiction: modern realistic, science, historical, fantasy. Through this written experience, show knowledge of the differences among the four basic types of fiction. **TOPIC:** _____

MODERN REALISTIC FICTION:

SCIENCE FICTION:

HISTORICAL FICTION:

FANTASY:

TIME LINE FOR HISTORICAL FICTION

DIRECTIONS:

At the top of the vertical line, put the beginning date in your story; at the bottom, place the ending date. Divide the rest of the line in even increments. Place the significant happenings in the right order at the appropriate place on the line. On the left side of the line, place all fictional occurrences. On the right side of the line, place all factual occurrences.

FICTION   Beginning Date   FACT

Ending Date

Name_____   **Activity 2-e**
Date_____
FICTION SHELVED WITH NONFICTION

DIRECTIONS:

    Listed below are four areas of fiction that are not shelved with the other fiction books, but are shelved in the nonfiction area. Fill in the chart below by giving the reasons for the change in shelving and common examples of each. Be sure to use the card catalog to help locate the examples.

Fiction Types	Reasons for Shelf Placement	Common Examples
1. Legends		
2. Fables		
3. Folktales		
4. Myths		

Criteria of Different Types of Literature
Nonfiction: Expertise/Bias

FOCUS

This lesson focuses on nonfiction and its companions: expertise and bias.

TEACHER PREPARATION

1. Review the activity sheets.

2. Since no specific nonfiction titles are listed, you may pull some books on the same social studies topic on which the students are working and discuss expertise and bias with your selections.

3. Check with the media specialist in your school and the reference librarian at the local public library and the local college library to see if they have a policy for determining expertise.

BACKGROUND INFORMATION

1. Looking for bias and understanding bias must be taught. Visually, a see-saw with fulcrum in the middle shows balance. Let the students fill in two columns of good and bad about subjects near and dear to them: teen music, candy, ice cream, teen fashion, etc. Then show by transferring one column, either the good or the bad, to one side of the see-saw that the result is unbalanced. It weighs the see-saw to one side. The second visual is a square of material. By pulling on opposing corners you can concretely demonstrate bias and distortion. By indulging in bias, the writer distorts the whole. Bias is sometimes expected: *China Reconstructs*, a magazine published by the Republic of China. Or take writings from both the English and American points of view on the American Revolution. The teaching of persuasion and propaganda is handled admirably in some basal reading series and even better in some kits devoted to just that. You can reinforce by explaining how some magazine advertisements use endorsements and repetition. Show students the handbook on *Stereotypes, Distortions and Omissions in U. S. History Textbooks*, published 1977, by The Council on Interracial Books for Children, 1841 Broadway, NY, NY 10023. Draw out the fact that bias is subtle. Portraying one group of people in subservient, passive roles will lead to negative assumptions about that group. The portrayal might be in words, or in pictures, or in both.

2. <u>Nonfiction</u> so often becomes the stepchild in reading. Share some nonfiction with the students that doesn't relate at all to any current assignment; or share some brand new nonfiction and discuss <u>why</u> the author wrote it, <u>why</u> it was published, and <u>why</u> it was purchased. You might need to get some help from the selector of the material before this discussion takes place.

3. Determining expertise can sometimes be thoroughly intimidating to an adult, let alone a young person, but since this is the age to question adults, examining an author's credentials provides a legitimate outlet.

4. You can share with students any material that uses footnotes or endnotes and bibliographies: their own texts, college texts, journal articles, or even papers or theses that you have written.

5. You can show them, using books on the same topic, that sometimes the same author is quoted or cited in several books. You, no doubt, found this out when you started writing your own research papers.

6. Encyclopedia articles are usually written by people with some expertise in the field and bibliographies are usually included. Check the same topic in several encyclopedias, taking care to limit your topic. See if the students can find the same source cited more than once. Check the references of the authors of the articles. The library media specialist or the selector of reference material might have a professional selection tool that you could share with students to show that expertise is considered valuable: *Recommended Reference Books*, published by Libraries Unlimited; or *RQ, Reference Quarterly*.

CONCEPTS
- **Recognition of nonfiction as a section in the IMC.**
- **Recognition of the importance of understanding expertise.**
- **Recognition that some nonfiction writings will present a bias.**

VOCABULARY
footnote   sway   consumer views   issue   subtle   propaganda technique

OBJECTIVES
The student will understand:
1. That nonfiction is based totally on fact.
2. That it is important to determine a process to check author expertise to ensure accuracy of information when researching.
3. Using an index of experts to develop a list of sources or to determine the credibility of an author's sources.
4. That information as presented in print form is not automatically accurate and that author bias might be present.
5. That an author might show bias for or against a subject in very subtle ways.

MATERIALS NEEDED
Activity Sheets 3-a through 3-c and 3-b through 3-c in the optional student workbook.

ACTIVITIES
1. Read through and briefly discuss the material in the activity sheets.
2. Discuss the items in the Background Information.

EXTENDED ACTIVITIES
1. Bias: Introduce propaganda techniques: band wagon, loaded words, testimonial, name-calling, glittering generalities, transfer, plain folks, card-stacking, repetition. After some preliminary work with these, assign students to underline words that affected their thinking in any article in a current newspaper, paying attention to descriptions of persons involved, actions taken, and/or corporate or government entities involved. Permit the student to find the same current topic in two different newspapers plus two different news magazines. See if bias for or against can be detected.
2. Students can make booklets with visual representations of bias. Remember, sometimes it is subtle.
3. If there are any old textbooks in the school or district, let the students examine them for bias, misrepresentation, subtle forms of discrimination, under-representation of minorities or women, not only in illustrations but also in the text. Lead discussions on the consequences of the continuing use of such materials.
4. Lead a discussion on what makes an expert an expert.

Nonfiction: Expertise/Bias

Nonfiction involves totally factually based information concerning many subjects. It offers an in-depth factual study of general and specific topics by authors who are considered experts in the field in which they are writing.

Expertise

It is important to check an author's credentials or expertise in his/her field when using his/her books as a basis of a report to determine the accuracy of the information. You might accomplish this by possibly examining those people the author used as sources through his footnotes or his bibliography. In some libraries, there might be a reference book that would provide the names of persons considered to be expert in the specific fields. A book with information of this sort can be used by the researcher in two ways.

The first way of use would be to list the names of experts in a field and then go to the card catalog to see if the library has any books by these authors. But, cards for these authors might not be found because many experts write on a reading level that would be too difficult for most middle school students.

Instead, another writer might have reexplained the ideas of the experts in language that is easier to understand and in so doing referenced their names and books as sources in footnotes and bibliographies. This suggests the second use of the list that you created and that would be to check out a writer's original sources and see if they are considered experts in the field.

Bias

Bias, prejudice for or against a subject, should also be your concern when researching for a report. Not every book automatically presents both sides to a question. Many authors write books to present a point of view and that becomes their theme. It is important to have a balanced presentation in a report. It is correct to use books presenting opposing views on a subject as long as both sides of the issue are revealed.

Sometimes, though, you do not readily recognize an author's bias because it is not clearly stated. It is just as important to be a good consumer of ideas in book form as it is to be an educated consumer at the supermarket or the clothes store. It is important to keep in mind that just because something is in print or is stated, it isn't automatically true. Students are taught at an early age to recognize the propaganda techniques used in commercials or advertisements and not to be swayed to buy a product on the basis of

Nonfiction, continued

them. It is equally important to recognize the emotional words or techniques that are used by some authors to sway you as a reader. If you, after having finished reading a book, realize a change in your own original attitude toward a subject, an idea, or a person, it might mean that the author's point of view has entered into your awareness. It would prove helpful at this point for you to take the time and try to sort out the possible mode or method by which the author effected this change. In other words, did the author use emotional words to cause inner anger in you or sorrow for the subject? Was there an unbalanced presentation of negative or positive aspects of a subject? Did the author repeat his point of view so often that you began to accept it due to sheer repetition? Did the author cause you to feel you were alone in your acceptance or rejection of an idea, that you held the only opposing view? Did the author namedrop, in that by idea association with a well-known person infers a correct position in the author's thinking? Bias is often subtle. Good consumers of ideas learn to sort the propaganda techniques from the facts.

6. Why is it important to check the credentials of the authors (or possibly their sources) who are writing in the nonfiction, reference, or biography section of the IMC?
7. In what way might a student check an author's expertise in a field?
8. What is bias?
9. How might a student detect bias in an author's writings?

FICTION/NONFICTION

DIRECTIONS:

    Show the difference between fiction and nonfiction through the writing of two separate stories (approximately 2-3 paragraphs each). Select a topic/title such as <u>The Chair</u>. Through the use of language, show your knowledge of the difference between fiction and nonfiction.

FICTION: The Chair

NONFICTION: The Chair

WRITING COMMERCIALS

DIRECTIONS:

   Write a commercial for a favorite or a fictional product or service. Underline words of persuasion. Create an illustration to accompany your commercial.

Criteria of Different Types of Literature
Reference

FOCUS
The student will learn all about the reference collection and why a book would be considered reference.

TEACHER PREPARATION
1. Review the information in the student activities.
2. Review the titles in the Background Information.
3. From your school library, pull some of those titles and/or other reference books in order to discuss with the class why those particular books are in reference.
4. It is important for students to understand why a limited circulation on reference books is imposed.
5. If CD-ROM and on-line accessing of reference material is available, demonstrate it and compare the currency of information in each medium.

BACKGROUND INFORMATION
1.   Common examples of books that are strictly reference would be a general encyclopedia such as *World Book* or the *Academic American Encyclopedia* and an atlas such as the *National Geographic Atlas of the World* or *The Rand McNally Great Geographical Atlas*. Both the encyclopedias and the atlases cover broad areas of information. Those and specific topical encyclopedias such as *Van Nostrand's Scientific Encyclopedia* are usually overwhelming physically and prohibitively taxing to carry around for five minutes reading in the park or ten on the bus.
2.   Some examples of books that might be found either in the reference section or in the nonfiction section are collections of poetry or specific science books.
3.   More complex reference materials that are either on a higher reading level or contain broader information or are more highly specialized need to be introduced so that students will know that they exist and could be used at a later date. Examples: *Encyclopedia Britannica, Oxford English Dictionary, Unabridged Reader's Guide*, specialized indices such as *Library Literature, Social Sciences, Education Index, ERIC*, plus *The New York Times* on microfilm, *Grove's Dictionary of Music and Musicians, Contemporary Authors, Great Books of the Western World*.

4.   Local histories of town, county and state might be a special collection in either or both school and public libraries. A field trip to the public library, local or county, will show how information needs of all sectors can be met. While there, show the students some specialized reference aids such as *Moody's, Ulrich's*, or a local union list of periodicals. Explain their function and use.

CONCEPTS
 • **Recognition of the different purposes for nonfiction and reference.**
 • **Recognition of the various materials contained in the reference collection.**
 • **Recognition of value of the public library as a source for the researcher.**

VOCABULARY
collection confronted interfiled exposed discretion extensive

OBJECTIVES
The student will understand:

1. That the library reference collection may be housed separately or as part of the nonfiction collection at the discretion of the library media specialist.

2. That the selection of the reference collection is based on curriculum demands and student/patron needs.

3. That a topic as covered in a book in the reference collection will most likely be less detailed than as covered in a book in the nonfiction section, which, in turn, would present a more in-depth study.

4. That the public library offers information which is useful to the student in research.

MATERIALS NEEDED
Activity Sheets 4-a through 4-c and 4-b through 4-c in the optional student workbook.

ACTIVITIES

1. Read through and discuss the material focusing on the purposes of the reference section as compared to the nonfiction section.

2. Discuss any special collections that you know to exist either in your library or in libraries in surrounding areas.

3. Tour the reference area in your library, in the public library, and in the county and/or college library.

4. Ascertain if the students need cards to use the libraries and if they have them.

5. You may use the context questions indicated by the Stop Sign as class participation or for homework.

EXTENDED ACTIVITIES

1. Reference: Using a transparency of any index page, show how to find volume and page number. Go from very easy (volumes numbered and pages numbered) to those with parts of the page indicated by a letter to those where the volume is an abbreviation with a key given separately.

2. Assign topics or use topics that the students are developing in other subject areas and let students generate lists of pages and subtopics from several encyclopedia indexes.

3. Use the New York Times School Collection on microfilm if available.

4. Use CD-ROM and on-line searching if available.

Reference

The third classification is reference. Even though you automatically think encyclopedia, the reference collection includes more than that. In some libraries, the reference collection is interfiled among the nonfiction books, although many libraries do have a reference collection which is separated from the nonfiction area. There are also some libraries which have the reference in a separate room. The decision to place a book in nonfiction or in reference is at the discretion of the library media specialist. Usually, the librarian makes the decision based on a survey of the curriculum research needs of the students in a school. If it is a selection or book that will be used continuously or a collection of information housed in one book, such as an encyclopedia, quotation collection, etc., it will usually be found in the reference section. Usually books found in the reference section are overnight books while those found in the nonfiction area can be check out for a week or more. The reason is that topics as developed in the nonfiction section usually contain a more in-depth study and will therefore require a longer time to read.

While it is true that most nonfiction and reference collections are selected in response to current school curriculum, the next level of education to follow is also taken into consideration. In other words, it is important that the basic reference materials to which you will be exposed at the high school level be made available to you at the junior high. This is to develop a readiness in you to meet the demands of information retrieval with which you will be confronted at the high school level.

In town, county, and state libraries, public use also has a bearing on the selection of the nonfiction and reference collections. This is true not only in terms of local clients but very often the employees of industries in the surrounding communities are library patrons. So, the needs of many groups must be met. One public library might specialize in a business reference collection while another might have an extensive collection on one topic. You as a student researcher should become familiar with the offerings of your local public libraries and utilize them effectively.

10. What is the general purpose of the reference collection?
11. How does the general purpose of the reference section differ from the purpose of the nonfiction section?
12. If you are presently in Junior High or Middle School, why would it be important to learn to use many of the reference sources that you will be required to use when researching at the High School level?

Reference

DIRECTIONS:
   Select five topics that might be used as research topics. Then through the use of the catalog, generate three book titles from the reference collection and three from the nonfiction collection that might be used in researching the individual topics.

TOPIC	REFERENCE COLLECTION	NONFICTION COLLECTION
1.		
2.		
3.		
4.		
5.		

Reference

DIRECTIONS:
   With a classmate, fill in the chart below with the titles from some selected reference materials.

GENERAL ENCYCLOPEDIAS   ATLASES

1.   1.

2.   2.

3.   3.

REFERENCE MATERIALS

1.   1.

2.   2.

3.   3.

 SCIENCE   SOCIAL STUDIES

Criteria of Different Types of Literature
Biography

FOCUS

The students will concentrate on biography and will review the four general classifications of the library.

TEACHER PREPARATION

1. Review the material to be presented, including shelving procedures.
2. Pull some biographies and some autobiographies from the school library.
3. Pull some 920's, collected biographies, from the library.
4. Know the areas in your library where these are to be found.
5. Find any reference material that is 920.
6. Complete the activity sheets.

BACKGROUND INFORMATION

1. Remind students that initially Melvil Dewey had all biography within his ten classifications. We, in the library profession, have pulled it out and filed it differently for efficiency. We have B for individual biography and autobiography and 920 for collective biography which is a book with biographical information on three or more people who are grouped by a topic: queens of Egypt, presidents of a country, astronauts, kings of England, comedians, scientists. B, individual biography, is shelved alphabetically by the name of the person about whom the book is written. 920 is shelved alphabetically by the author's name.

920   Haskins, James
       Revolutionaries: agents of change.
Lippincott [©1971]
224p
 	
Biographical sketches of revolution-
ary leaders, from George Washington
to Mao Tse-Tung describe their lives
and philosophies. Glossary
Bibliog
 	
1. Revolutions   I. T   II. T: Agents
of Change   o
	B Haskins, James, 1941 -
	Wonder The story of Stevie Wonder/ James
	       Haskins. -- New York: Lothrop, Lee &
	       Shepard Co., ©1976.
	        126 p. : ill. : 22 cm.
	
	Discography: p. 121-123.
	A biography of the blind composer, pianist,
	and singer who was a child prodigy and went
	on to win nine Grammy awards.
	Includes index.
	ISBN 0-688-41440-X. 0-688-51740-4
	lib bdg. (Cont. next card) o

The same author wrote these biographical books. The first is shelved alphabetically by his last name in the 920 section; the second is alphabetical by W-O-N-D-E-R for the biographee's last name, and it is in the Biography section. If you wish, you can share these two cards with students by making transparencies of them.

2. You can cite lawsuits by famous people against biographers who wrote unauthorized biographies.

CONCEPTS
- Recognition of the differences between biography and autobiography.
- Recognition of the purposes of an authorized and an unauthorized biography.
- Recognition of the four general classifications of the IMC.

VOCABULARY
accounts   unauthorized   credentials   current

OBJECTIVES
The student will:

1. Understand that biography and autobiography are interfiled among the shelves of biography.
2. Understand that biography and autobiography deal with the factual accounts of the lives of people.
3. Understand that a biography is a factual account of a person written by another person.
4. Understand that an autobiography is a factual account of a person written by that same person.
5. Understand that unless all the information in a biography or autobiography can be verified as true, the book can not be classified as nonfiction.
6. Identify the four general classifications of the library as fiction, nonfiction, reference and biography.

MATERIALS NEEDED
Activity Sheets 5-a through 5-c and 5-b through 5-c in the optional student workbook.

ACTIVITIES
1. Read through and discuss the material.
2. Discuss shelving procedures somewhat. It will be discussed later.
3. You may use the context questions indicated by the Stop Sign for oral classroom evaluation or for homework.
4. The last set of activity sheets are Know Your Country Questions having to do with all the information presented in Lessons 1 through 5 and with the geographical areas indicated on the Know Your Country activity sheets.

EXTENDED ACTIVITIES

1. You might initiate an opposing viewpoint discussion on the advantages of autobiography as opposed to biography or authorized as opposed to unauthorized.

2. To recognize and differentiate four general classifications of written work, give the students "Plain Jane" titles, and from each, let students add enough "meaty" details in the subtitles to form examples of all four classifications.

Example: Grasslands   NF =Grasslands and Tundra
      B =Grasslands: The Story of the Governor of Kansas
    FIC =Grasslands, A Prairie Diary
   REF =Grasslands, A Compendium of Lawn Seeds

Example: Soul Music   NF =Soul Music; The Instruments and Tempos
      B =Soul Music, The Life of Ray Charles
    FIC =Soul Music and Marmalade
   REF =Soul Music, An Annotated Chronology

3. Using the chart in Activity 5-a, have students cut circles in size of categories. Label them. Place the appropriate circles inside one another.

4. Make a mobile of the parts of literature.

5. Make a mobile of biographical subjects.

6. Do a class timeline, possibly separated geographically, of biographies that were read. Key the timeline to major historical events, or to scientific events, or to any facet of the social studies which they are currently studying.

7. If the map activity in Activity 5-b proves too difficult, you might wish to have them map the journeys of their subjects. Recreate their activity sheets on a bulletin board map and see if any of their paths crossed.

8. You might wish to extend the Activity 5-c. After each one has written his/her own autobiography, pair them off and let each one of the pair interview the other for a biography using the same questions and the same directions.

Biography

The fourth and last classification under study is that of biography which is the factual account of a person's life. An autobiography is a book written by a person about his or her own life. Autobiography is usually interfiled on the shelves among the volumes of biography. Again, it is important that the credentials of the person writing a biography be checked in that current biographies written by unauthorized individuals may be more properly classified as fiction than nonfiction. Without the proper research or cooperation of the subject of the book, it is almost impossible for an author to fashion a totally truthful and factual book. If this is the case, it can never be classified as nonfiction biography.

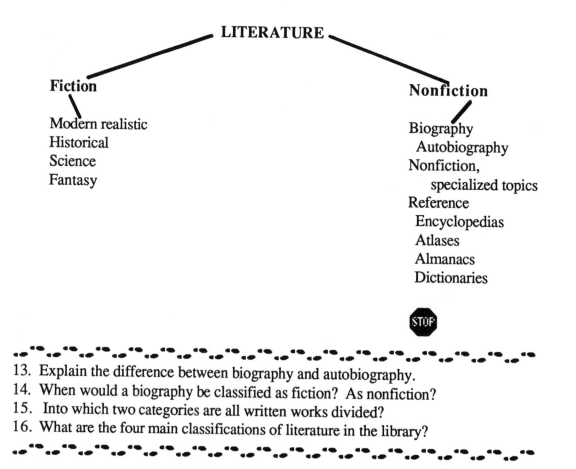

LITERATURE

Fiction

Modern realistic
Historical
Science
Fantasy

Nonfiction

Biography
  Autobiography
Nonfiction,
      specialized topics
Reference
  Encyclopedias
  Atlases
  Almanacs
  Dictionaries

13. Explain the difference between biography and autobiography.
14. When would a biography be classified as fiction? As nonfiction?
15. Into which two categories are all written works divided?
16. What are the four main classifications of literature in the library?

Biography Map

DIRECTIONS:

Choose and read a biography. Draw a map of the general geographic area in which the subject lived. Place an X on each locality in which the subject lived. Now number the X-marked places in the order in which the subject lived in them. Key the numbers to any major events or happenings which occurred in the life of the person while living in that particular place. Select a setting that was a factor in the happening of the event. Explain how the specific history of your subject might have been changed had another setting been involved.

Biography/Autobiography

DIRECTIONS:

Answer the following questions about yourself. Write an autobiography only from your answers remembering that you do not have to use every answer, but must include information from the starred questions.

*SUBJECT_____AUTHOR_____

*Date of birth

*Where were you born?

*Family?

Relatives?

*What neighborhood do you live in?

*Schools attended?

Favorite subject?

Least favorite subject?

Hobbies?

Pets?

Favorite time of year?

Best friend?

Vacations?

Favorite color?

Favorite book?

Favorite TV show?

Favorite music?

Play instruments?

Favorite foods?

Favorite place to visit?

Favorite pastime?

Name_____

Date_____ **Know Your Country:**
The Northeastern Region of the U. S.

The northeastern region of the United States is formed by 9 of the original 13 states.

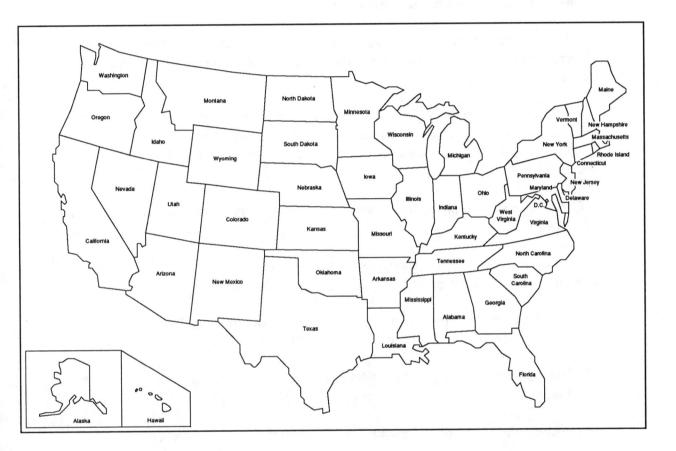

The Northeastern Region of the United States

Maine = ME   NY = New York
New Hampshire = NH   VT = Vermont
Massachusetts = MA   CT = Connecticut
Rhode Island = RI   NJ = New Jersey
Pennsylvania = PA   DE = Delaware
Maryland = MD

1. Choose one of the states indicated in this unit from the Northeast section of the United States and make a list of general questions concerning the state that you'd like answered.

2. Collect information from newspapers, magazine articles, pamphlets, brochures on
   the Northeastern section of the United States and on each of the individual states in that section.

Unit I Activity   The Northeastern Region of the U. S.

3. In groups, develop a listing of the topics covered in the articles that you have collected and place the list in the folder with the articles for delivery to the media center vertical file.

4. Anytime during the year that you see an article about the region or any of the states, cut and place in vertical file box in media center.

5. Take one article or an aspect of the article and develop it into a one or two paragraph rendering of historical fiction, science fiction, or fantasy, keeping the geographical locale.

6. Choose one state in the region. Based on your readings in the regional area, write a letter to a friend to convince your friend to move into that state. Underline what you consider to be the bias. Read the letter to a buddy in class or to the class to see if they can perceive the bias.

7. Choose one state in the region. Construct a diorama representing recreation in your chosen state.

8. Survey your class to see if anyone has visited the region. Interview those people who have. Chart the percentages of students in your class who have visited the states.

9. Consult a map of the region and list the states you would cross if you were to drive to any state in the Northeast section from your house.

10. List the modes of transportation which are available to go from your state to a state in the region.

11. Evaluate the practicality of each mode of transportation for different seasons.

12. Based on the facts you unearthed in your readings, compose a television slogan enticing visitors to your state.

13. Use the card catalog for a Dewey location in the media center and list nonfiction and reference materials that you might consult concerning your state.

14. Using a telephone book research the available libraries in your area. Chart them listing addresses, phone numbers, hours, distances to travel, and methods of transportation.

15. On a county map provided by your teacher or library media specialist, indicate the neighboring library facilities by highlighting and placing flags.

Unit II The Card Catalog

Understanding Organization
The Card Catalog

FOCUS
In this lesson the student will recognize that the catalog is an index to all materials located in a library setting and that there are differences among the card types.

TEACHER PREPARATION
1. Read and review the material in this lesson and in the two lessons following. All three are about the card catalog and its component cards.
2. If your library has adopted an electronic catalog, either a CD-based catalog or an on-line one, your students will still need to differentiate among title, subject, and author listings. On-screen information will be basically that which is on a catalog card. The material that is presented here about the card catalog will still be valid if there is a card catalog for pre-electronic items, and if there are card catalogs in other libraries to which they go.
3. Complete all activity sheets and keep for handy class reference. You might use the actual drawers in the media center for the inside guides.

BACKGROUND INFORMATION
1. The outside guides will probably not be just one letter. The guides might be three or four letters or even whole words. Examples:

INC -   INS
INCA - INSE
INCAS - INSECTS

2. The inside guides can also be used just as guide words on a dictionary page, allowing the student to zero in on a finer location. Within certain subject areas, the inside guides will be chronologically arranged in accordance with the subject headings on those cards. A thorough explanation of this is given in the text under "Chronological Order of Some Cards."
3. In some libraries, two separate catalogs are used. All subject cards are in one and author, title cards are usually grouped together in the other.
4. From the card examples in Activity 6-a, students will see that all are about the same book and that the only thing different is the very top line.
5. The subject headings are obtained from a standardized list of such headings. *Sears List of Subject Headings* or *The Library of Congress Subject Headings* is used to bring cohesion.

CONCEPTS
    • **Recognition that the catalog is an index of all materials located in a library setting.**
    • **Recognition of the differences among card types.**

VOCABULARY
index   basic catalog cards   facsimiles   base card

OBJECTIVES
The student will:
1. Understand that the card catalog contains many drawers in which cards are alphabetically organized aided by a system of outside, then inside, alphabetical guides.

2. List the types of cards located in the card catalog as subject, author, title.

3. The student will understand that in some libraries the subject cards are filed in another card catalog separate from the other types of cards.

MATERIALS
Activity Sheets 6-a through 6-c and Sheets 6-b through 6-c in the optional student workbook.

ACTIVITIES
1. Read and discuss the material.
2. Prepare transparencies of the cards listed in the activity sheets to aid in understanding.
3. Use the context questions indicated by the Stop Sign to check student understanding.
4. If necessary, give bibliographic information for one book for Activity 6-b.

EXTENDED ACTIVITY
Students can generate subject bibliographies and can be given extra credit by that subject teacher.

The Card Catalog

The card catalog is an index of all the items in the library. It consists of many drawers, all of which house hundreds of cards. It is easy to use because the general organization of the card catalog is alphabetical. Each drawer has an outside guide on the front and has many inside guides separating the cards within each drawer. In effect, in terms of information retrieval, the outside guides alphabetically place you at the correct drawer. The inside guides allow you to locate alphabetically the correct card according to subject, author, or book title. That means you spend less time looking for the card.

1. What is the purpose of the card catalog?
2. What is the basic organization of the card catalog?
3. Of what importance are the outside and inside guides?

As stated, in each drawer, you will find basic catalog cards filed in alphabetical order according to subject, title, and author. In certain libraries, though, the subject cards are separated from the title and author cards and two separate card catalogs are used. But even so, all the subject cards have the subject in capital letters on the top line.

<u>AUTHOR CARD</u>

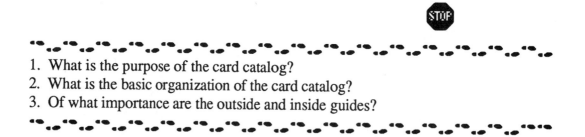

Fic   Clarke, Mary Stetson
Cla   The glass phoenix. Viking 1969
            [256p]
            Ben's father and grandfather oppose the glassworks in Sandwich,
            Massachusetts; many glass blowers are irate about its
            mechanization. But Ben, fascinated by the new process, struggles
            for its acceptance.

            1. Glass manufacture - Fiction   2. Sandwich, Massachusetts
            - History - Fiction   I. Title

<u>TITLE CARD</u>

	The glass phoenix
Fic	Clarke, Mary Stetson
Cla	The glass phoenix. Viking 1969
	[256p]

Ben's father and grandfather oppose the glassworks in Sandwich, Massachusetts; many glass blowers are irate about its mechanization. But Ben, fascinated by the new process, struggles for its acceptance.

1. Glass manufacture - Fiction 2. Sandwich, Massachusetts - History - Fiction   I. Title

<u>SUBJECT CARD</u>

	GLASS MANUFACTURE--FICTION
Fic	Clarke, Mary Stetson
Cla	The glass phoenix. Viking 1969
	[256p]

Ben's father and grandfather oppose the glassworks in Sandwich, Massachusetts; many glass blowers are irate about its mechanization. But Ben, fascinated by the new process, struggles for its acceptance.

1. Glass manufacture - Fiction 2. Sandwich, Massachusetts -History - Fiction   I. Title

<u>SUBJECT CARD</u>

	SANDWICH, MASSACHUSETTS-HISTORY-FICTION
Fic	Clarke, Mary Stetson
Cla	The glass phoenix. Viking 1969
	[256p]

Ben's father and grandfather oppose the glassworks in Sandwich, Massachusetts; many glass blowers are irate about its mechanization. But Ben, fascinated by the new process, struggles for its acceptance.

1. Glass manufacture - Fiction 2. Sandwich, Massachusetts - History - Fiction   I. Title

For every book in the library there will be a minimum of three cards. Some items will have more cards because of the variety of key words that might be used to describe a topic (e.g., garbage, refuse, waste, pollution, etc.). It is up to the library media specialist to define the number of cards necessary to support the research needs of the students in his/her school. This is usually in answer to the ability range of the students in terms of vocabulary usage.

4.   What three basic types of cards for each book are found in the card catalog?

5.   Why might one book have many corresponding subject cards located in the card catalog?

Use the following cards for class practice:

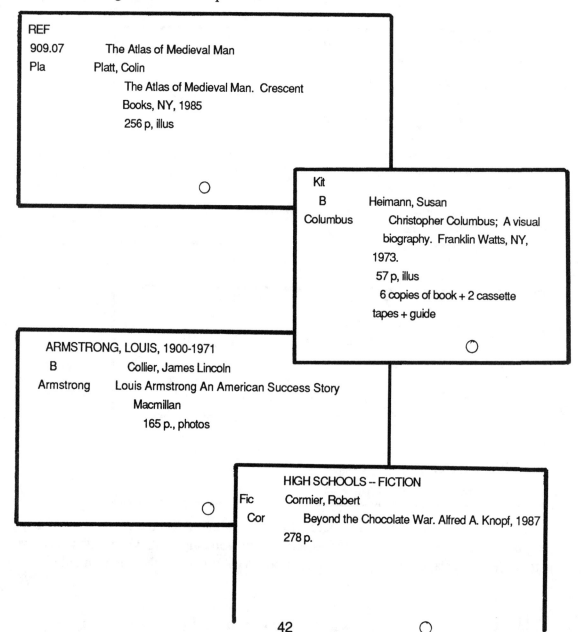

REF
909.07   The Atlas of Medieval Man
Pla   Platt, Colin

                        The Atlas of Medieval Man. Crescent
                        Books, NY, 1985
                        256 p, illus

Kit
B   Heimann, Susan
Columbus   Christopher Columbus; A visual
                        biography. Franklin Watts, NY,
                    1973.
                    57 p, illus
                    6 copies of book + 2 cassette
                tapes + guide

ARMSTRONG, LOUIS, 1900-1971
B   Collier, James Lincoln
Armstrong   Louis Armstrong An American Success Story
                        Macmillan
                        165 p., photos

HIGH SCHOOLS -- FICTION
Fic   Cormier, Robert
Cor   Beyond the Chocolate War. Alfred A. Knopf, 1987
        278 p.

Basic Card Types

DIRECTIONS:
    Using the card facsimiles as provided, create examples of an author card, title card, and a subject card. Do two of each.

Author Card

Author Card

Title Card

Title Card

Subject Card

Subject Card

Alphabetical Order: The Inside and Outside Guides

DIRECTIONS: Fill in the outside guide. Then using
the outside guide as the basis, alphabetically fill in
the inside guides with appropriate terms. Use C-D
as the outside guide.

Understanding Organization
The Card Catalog

FOCUS

This is a continuation of the card catalog focusing on the added entry cards and the cross reference cards.

TEACHER PREPARATION

1. Review all material in this lesson and the preceding one and the following one.
2. Complete the activity sheets; check your answers and keep for handy reference.

BACKGROUND INFORMATION

1. Cross reference cards do the same job that cross references do in indexes: point the way toward more information. A tidbit of data: the entry word on the *see card* sometimes might have been the only choice for retrieval. Example: Russia was a perfectly acceptable heading until it was changed to Soviet Union. So for some research, especially older volumes of *Reader's Guide*, "Russia" would be the only word used. Students should be taught that alternative key words will produce more information for them.
2. Added entry cards contain the same information that a title or an author card would have. The very top line would have the additional information. It is worth reiterating to students that the alphabetical order of the card catalog is taken from the very first line of the cards.

CONCEPTS

- **Recognition of the differences among catalog cards.**
- **Understanding of *see* and *see also* cards.**

VOCABULARY

added entry   joint author   series   flexible   illustrator   discretion

OBJECTIVES

The student will understand:
1. That the cross reference cards will be indicated by *see* or *see also* and must be used to obtain optimum information retrieval.
2. That in *see* cards, the "see" indicates that no information will be found under that key word and that the student must look under the other suggested key words instead.
3. That the *see also* cards indicated that some information will be found under the entry keyword, but still more will be found under the other suggested keywords.
4. That added entry cards, which include illustrator, series, and joint author, are additional means of retrieving information.

MATERIALS NEEDED

Activity sheets 7-a through 7-b and Sheet 7-b in optional student workbook.

ACTIVITIES

1. Read and discuss material. Use copies of 6-b, change the headings to added entries and complete.
2. Prepare transparencies on cards listed to aid understanding.
3. Prepare transparencies on added entry cards and cross reference cards from your catalog.

EXTENDED ACTIVITIES

1. Make added entry cards. The library media specialist can show how to make analytics.
2. Let students make bulletin board charts for all cards, showing the interrelationships.

The Card Catalog

<u>Added Entries</u>

In addition to the three basic catalog cards of title, author, and subject, the card catalog also offers added entry cards. The added entry cards provide additional means of retrieving information because they are indexed according to book illustrator, name of book series, or by joint author. The added entry cards are known as an illustrator card, series card, or joint author card. Again, the process is most flexible in that keywords can be added or deleted according to the discretion of the librarian.

<u>JOINT AUTHOR CARD</u>:

```
        Tomlinson, Richard H.
Fic       Fries, Chloe.
Fri     Full of the moon, by Chloe Fries and Richard H.
        Tomlinson.Illustrated by E. J. Abrams Associates.
        Creative Ed., 1978
          56p. illus.
          Juan and his father have differing opinions on science until
        a  disaster at sea changes both their opinions.
        1. Sea stories  2. Fathers and sons-Fiction I.  Tomlinson,
        Richard  H. II. Abrams (E.J.) Associates III. Title
```

<u>ILLUSTRATOR CARD</u>:

```
        Abrams (E.J.) Associates
Fic       Fries, Chloe.
Fri     Full of the moon, by Chloe Fries and Richard H.
        Tomlinson.  Illustrated by E. J. Abrams Associates.
        Creative Ed., 1978
          56p. illus.
         Juan and his father have differing opinions on science until a
        disaster at sea changes both their opinions.
        1. Sea stories  2. Fathers and sons-Fiction
        I.  Tomlinson, Richard H. II. Abrams (E.J.)Associates III.
        Title
```

SERIES CARD:

```
           Tomorrow's World Series
621.36 Bender, Lionel
Ben      Lasers in action.  The Bookwright Press, New York,
           ©1985.
           48 p. illus., (Tomorrow's World)


           What will tomorrow's world be like?


           1. Lasers.  I. Title.  II. Tomorrow's World Series.
```

Along with the subject, author, and title card, the card catalog also houses cross reference cards indicated by the topic (key word) at the top of the card and the word(s) *see, see also*. The *see* cards mean that no books are referenced under that particular key word. The card will then supply more appropriate words with which you will be able to continue to research. The *see also* cards, in turn, indicate that although some references may be found under the given key word, alternate key words are also provided to allow a more comprehensive research.

SEE CARD:	SEE ALSO CARD:
Russia see Soviet Union	Mineralogy see also Gems

6. In addition to the three basic types of cards, list other cards that might be found in the card catalog.

7. Of what importance are the added entry cards?

8. Explain the use of the *see* card.

9. Explain the use of the *see also* card.

10. What is meant by the term cross reference?

The Card Catalog
Cross References

DIRECTIONS:

Make cross reference cards for the following:

Needlework   see also Embroidery; Lace and Lace making.

Near East   see Middle East   Floods   see also Natural Disasters

Holland   see Netherlands   National songs   see also Folk songs

Understanding Organization
The Card Catalog

FOCUS
The focus on this last part of the card catalog will be on the chronological organization of the US-HISTORY drawer.

TEACHER PREPARATION
1. Review the material.

2. Evaluate student understanding of the previous two lessons.

3. Complete the activity sheets; check answers and keep handy for class reference.

BACKGROUND INFORMATION
1. Chronological order: Make sure first that your students understand that chronological means time order, earliest to latest. The cards involved will be subject cards with the topic UNITED STATES and the subtopic HISTORY. Other countries' histories can also be organized in this manner.

2. The graphic of the catalog drawer will show how the chronology is arranged from earliest to latest. Within each chronological period, the breakdown will be alphabetically by the next line which is usually author or by a further delineation of the subject heading.

3. For instance, there might be four books that have the subject heading: UNITED STATES - HISTORY - COLONIAL PERIOD - COSTUMES. The cards will be grouped together and alphabetized by main entry which will probably be author's name.

4. The four step sequence should be practiced.

5. You can show the *Sears List of Subject Headings* to students to ascertain how UNITED STATES - HISTORY is set up and how other countries' histories can be set up. Be aware that Dewey Decimal numbers for the history of most countries can be classified in the same chronological manner. You can share a Dewey classification book with the students (the 930-990 section).

CONCEPTS
• **Understand the chronological organizational system as used in the card catalog.**

VOCABULARY
chronological   alphabetical   cluster   time period   time era   topic   subtopic

OBJECTIVES
The student will:
1. Understand that the topic/subtopic of UNITED STATES - HISTORY will be alphabetically placed according to the topic, UNITED STATES, but then the cluster of cards dealing with UNITED STATES - HISTORY will be chronologically organized by time period as indicated by the inside guides.

2. Realize that although the cards are separated chronologically by the inside guides, the cards between the inside guides revert back to an alphabetical organization by detail.

3. Understand that only subject or topic cards can be found in the cluster of UNITED STATES - HISTORY and that all other corresponding cards dealing with each individual book such as author, title, or added entry will be alphabetically filed respective to their individual card entry spellings and will be found throughout the card catalog.

MATERIALS NEEDED
Activity Sheets 8-a through 8-b and Sheets 8-a through 8-b in optional student workbook.

ACTIVITIES
1. Read and discuss the activity sheet.

2. Use the context questions as indicated for class discussion, for homework, or to evaluate student understanding.

3. Complete the activity sheet, which has a representation of a US-HISTORY drawer. See if the students can figure out where in that drawer the practice card which appears on page 52 might belong.

EXTENDED ACTIVITIES
1. Pull all books on one subject (Russia or England), recategorize chronologically. Using the Dewey number, add all biographies, magazines, videotapes, audiovisual material. Final bibliography product retained permanently in the school library or IMC.

2. Students can program bibliographies. Credit given by computer teacher.

3. Construct a time line from inside guides for country.

The Card Catalog

Chronological Order of Some Cards

Although the general organization of the card catalog is alphabetical, there is at least one cluster of cards that will have a chronological order. Usually, that cluster is topic/subtopic: UNITED STATES - HISTORY. Cards found in this cluster will be organized by time period/time era. This is indicated by the inside guides which will also indicate the corresponding years.

But once the cards are separated by the inside guides, the cards in between the guides revert back to an alphabetical listing by topic, subtopic, and detail.

Topic: UNITED STATES
Subtopic: HISTORY
Detail: COLONIAL PERIOD
Subdetail: COSTUMES

UNITED STATES - HISTORY - COLONIAL PERIOD - COSTUMES

591   Copeland, Peter F.

Cop   Everyday dress of the American Colonial Period. (Coloring Book)
        Dover Publications, NY ©1975.
        46p illus

        Summary: 46 drawings reproduce the everyday dress of
              numerous American colonists of the 1770's.

        1. Costumes - History 2. U.S.- History-Colonial Period-Costumes
        I.Title.   O

This area of the card catalog is more confusing to explain than to use. Follow the sequence and problems will be avoided:
1.) Using the outside guides, find the drawer marked *United States*.
2.) Using the inside guides, find UNITED STATES - HISTORY.
3.) Behind U.S. - HISTORY will be a series of inside guides chronologically marked in sequence with the time periods of American history.
4.) Once you've selected the appropriate inside guide representing the correct era or period of time to correspond to the topic being researched, alphabetically find the card by subtopic and detail within the cluster.

Since the cards in this area will be topic/subject cards, you must be aware that all the corresponding title and author cards will be interfiled alphabetically appropriately throughout the rest of the card catalog.

As mentioned, at least one area in every card catalog will have a chronological organization and that probably will be UNITED STATES-HISTORY. But, any country's history can be organized this way if there are enough books located in the library to warrant this approach. Once again, curriculum demands and librarian discretion will dictate.

11. Name and explain the organization of the cluster or group of cards marked or labeled UNITED STATES-HISTORY.

12. Explain a sequence to follow when working in the area of UNITED STATES - HISTORY.

13. Draw a card and develop a corresponding outline to show the relationship of the topic to subtopic to detail as it appears on the subject card in the area: UNITED STATES - HISTORY.

14. If all the cards in the chronological cluster of UNITED STATES - HISTORY are subject cards, where would you find the corresponding title and author cards?

15. Might any area other than the history of the United States be organized chronologically? Explain.

Use this card for class practice:

	UNITED STATES - HISTORY - 1865-1898
973.8	Buckmaster, Henrietta
Buc	Freedom Bound. Macmillan, [©1965]
	185 p.

A detailed and authoritative account of the social, political and economic reforms which took place during the Reconstruction era, directly following the Civil War.

Bibliography: p. 183-184.

1. Reconstruction 2. US - History- 1865-1898. I. Title

CHRONOLOGICAL ORDER - UNITED STATES HISTORY

DIRECTIONS:
1. Use the two cards that are in
Activity 8-a.
2. Decide where in the
drawer they will go.
3. Put cards in
 drawer order.
4. Make a key,
and color code
the order.

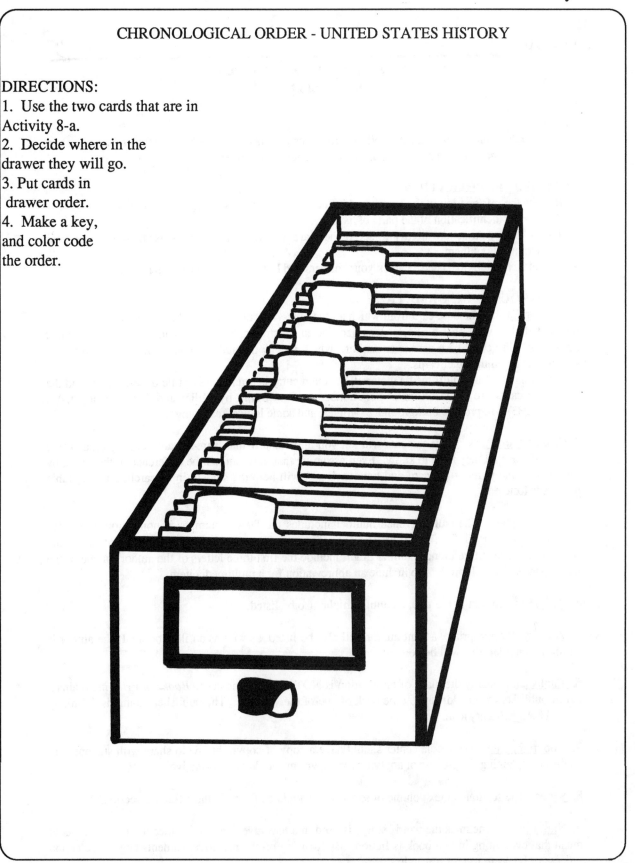

UNDERSTANDING ORGANIZATION, The Card Catalog

Understanding Organization
The Catalog Card

FOCUS

The student will not only understand the difference among card types but also understand each part of an individual card and its purpose as it supports the research process.

TEACHER PREPARATION

1. Review the information in the lesson and in the student activities.
2. Review the identification of the parts of a card.
3. Check with your school library to see if there are any different symbols used. Make sure your students know about them.
4. Complete the activity sheets. Check your answers and keep for handy class reference.

BACKGROUND INFORMATION

1. Catalog Card: The base card from which all the others are made is called the main entry card. The line added above is either a title, or a subject, or an illustrator, or series, or joint author. For most books, the main entry base card is an author, which is why the author's name will always be on the second line on all the other cards.

With much of the multi-media material, the main entry is usually either title or series title, and the additional cards are based on that. *Commonsense Cataloging* by Miller and Terwillegar (H. W. Wilson, 1983) will provide background, examples, and some logical reasoning.

2. Catalog Card Parts: Your students will tell you immediately that there are author, subject, and title cards and that's all they need to know. Even assuming that they can tell the difference in the cards, by focusing on the parts of the card and how each part will help the student in research, a more viable process is fostered.

3. Call Number: The call reference number includes the Dewey number if nonfiction, the B for biography, or F or Fic for fiction, or REF for reference. Those indications will pinpoint the media center area. The call reference number might include the first three letters of the author's name or the biographee's name. It might also include an abbreviation for a multimedia item.

4. Title: In addition to the title, a subtitle might also be listed.

5. Author: If appropriate, a joint author will also be listed, as well as an illustrator. If the author is editor or compiler, that will be noted.

6. Publisher: Usually the place of publication is NOT noted on the card. *Books in Print* maintains a list of publishers with addresses at the back of one of the volumes. The publisher's name is definitely needed for interlibrary loan.

7. Copyright date: The media center should have a copy of copyright law to share with students. In addition, explaining the process of applying for copyright should be informative.

8. Series: The separate index volume of some series might be found in the reference section.

9. Narrative: Sometimes the word "story" is used in a narrative and is misunderstood by students to mean that everything in that book is fiction. By focusing on the narrative, students begin a selection process of books to use for research.

10. <u>Tracings</u>: The tracings are the additional cards that have been made. The subject headings are the ones that will provide the most assistance to the student.

11. In addition to Visual Aids and Page numbers, bibliographies and glossaries are sometimes indicated.

12. In the first activity, a practice title card for student use is available. Not every card has every kind of information on it.

13. The number that follows the narrative on this card is the ISBN (International Standard Book Number), a unique number for each book published. But beware of pitfalls: it has been noted that after several years' lapse, an ISBN might be reissued to a completely different book.

14. The abbreviations listed usually head the call reference number.

CONCEPTS
- **Recognition of the difference in card types.**
- **Recognition of each part of an individual card and its purpose.**

VOCABULARY
except differentiate copyright narrative corresponding visual aids tracings
parenthesis parentheses setting reliability media

OBJECTIVES
The student will:
1. Understand that in the card catalog, all catalog cards for one book are exactly alike except for the first line which will indicate the type of card and will differentiate one card from among others.
2. Understand that all subject/topic cards will have first lines in capital letters.
3. Understand that the individual parts of a catalog card provide a great deal of information for the student in terms of furthering research.
4. List the parts of the catalog card to include the call number, title, author, publisher, copyright date, series, narrative, tracings, visual aids, page numbers, bibliography, illustrator. (See text for explanation of research use.)
5. Recognize many of the commonly used abbreviations found on the various types of catalog cards.

MATERIALS NEEDED
Activity Sheets 9-a through 9-e and 9-b through 9-e in optional student workbook.
You may make transparencies of cards in text of activity sheets so that students may follow your explanations.

ACTIVITIES
1. Read through and discuss the material focusing on the individual parts of the cards, how they relate to each other and how they would be used by the student in research.
2. Discuss any specific *see* and *see also* examples that they would come across pertaining to any of their curriculum.
3. Complete the activity sheets; check your answers and keep for handy class reference.
4. You can use the context questions indicated by the Stop Sign for in-class evaluation.

EXTENDED ACTIVITIES
1. Let students make bulletin board charts for all cards.
2. Students can make a game out of parts of the bulletin board charts and test each other.

The Basic Catalog Cards

There are three types of cards that can be found for each book in the library and they are subject, author, and title. Note that except for the first line, all the cards are exactly alike. The first line indicates the type of card. An author card will introduce the author's name first. The title card will offer the title first, and the subject/topic card will have the subject first which will always be in capital letters. It is important to note that sometimes the title of the book will have the same phrasing as the subject, but the capital letters will immediately differentiate the subject card from the title card.

AUTHOR CARD

Fic	Clarke, Mary Stetson
Cla	The glass phoenix. Viking 1969
	[256p]

Ben's father and grandfather oppose the glassworks in Sandwich, Massachusetts; many glass blowers are irate about its mechanization. But Ben, fascinated by the new process, struggles for its acceptance.

1. Glass manufacture - Fiction   2. Sandwich, Massachusetts - History - Fiction   I. Title

TITLE CARD

The glass phoenix

Fic	Clarke, Mary Stetson
Cla	The glass phoenix. Viking 1969
	[256p]

Ben's father and grandfather oppose the glassworks in Sandwich, Massachusetts; many glass blowers are irate about its mechanization. But Ben, fascinated by the new process, struggles for its acceptance.

1. Glass manufacture - Fiction 2. Sandwich, Massachusetts - History - Fiction   I. Title

SUBJECT CARD

GLASS MANUFACTURE--FICTION

Fic	Clarke, Mary Stetson
Cla	The glass phoenix. Viking 1969
	[256p]

Ben's father and grandfather oppose the glassworks in Sandwich, Massachusetts; many glass blowers are irate about its mechanization. But Ben, fascinated by the new process, struggles for its acceptance.

1. Glass manufacture - Fiction 2. Sandwich, Massachusetts -History - Fiction   I. Title

O

Cross Reference and Added Entry Cards

Along with the subject, author, and title card, the card catalog also houses cross reference cards and added entry cards. See examples:

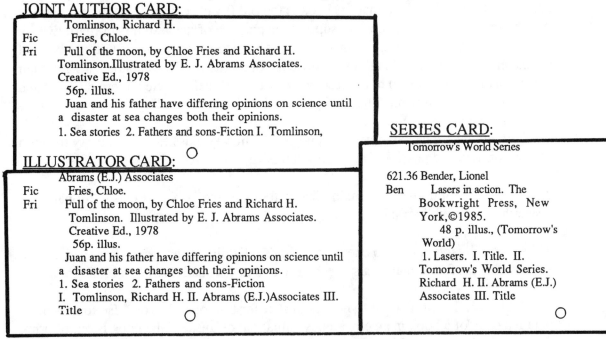

JOINT AUTHOR CARD:

	Tomlinson, Richard H.
Fic	Fries, Chloe.
Fri	Full of the moon, by Chloe Fries and Richard H. Tomlinson.Illustrated by E. J. Abrams Associates. Creative Ed., 1978
	56p. illus.
	Juan and his father have differing opinions on science until a disaster at sea changes both their opinions.
	1. Sea stories 2. Fathers and sons-Fiction I. Tomlinson,

ILLUSTRATOR CARD:

	Abrams (E.J.) Associates
Fic	Fries, Chloe.
Fri	Full of the moon, by Chloe Fries and Richard H. Tomlinson. Illustrated by E. J. Abrams Associates. Creative Ed., 1978
	56p. illus.
	Juan and his father have differing opinions on science until a disaster at sea changes both their opinions.
	1. Sea stories 2. Fathers and sons-Fiction
	I. Tomlinson, Richard H. II. Abrams (E.J.)Associates III. Title

SERIES CARD:

Tomorrow's World Series

621.36	Bender, Lionel
Ben	Lasers in action. The Bookwright Press, New York,©1985.
	48 p. illus., (Tomorrow's World)
	1. Lasers. I. Title. II. Tomorrow's World Series. Richard H. II. Abrams (E.J.) Associates III. Title

SEE CARD:

Russia

see

Soviet Union

SEE ALSO CARD:

Mineralogy

see also

Gems

1. Name the different types of catalog cards that can be found in the card catalog.
2. Explain the similarities and differences of the three basic cards as found in the card catalog.

The Catalog Card Parts

The catalog card, itself, provides a multitude of information in the hopes that you will take the time to make a determination about books before you leave the card catalog drawers. It might be found that the book is too old (by checking the copyright date) or that the focus of the book does not support the purpose of the assignment (narrative) or that the book is classified as fiction even though the topic corresponds to the subject of the paper (call number). In all, the knowledge of the parts of the catalog card and their corresponding relationship to the research process will help create a more efficient and effective research student. The card parts and their corresponding definitions as they apply to research are as follows:

1.) Call number: The call number identifies the library classification, library location of book or item and possibly, an expression of media type.

2.) Title: The title gives the main idea or focus of the book. It is usually part of a research paper's bibliography.

3.) Author: It is important to check an author's reliability as an expert in a field as well as possible bias for or against a subject. The author is usually part of a bibliography.

4.) Publisher: It is important to note publisher for bibliography, but also to be able to obtain a copy of a book in an emergency situation, or to see if the book is out of print, or if the publisher is thinking about reprinting.

5.) Copyright date: It is important to note the copyright date of a book for research. Make sure that the book does not have outdated information.

6.) Series: It is important to identify a book as part of a series ( ) in that there may be a separate volume index. Series are indicated on the card within parentheses. If one book in a series is valuable to the student in research, then another book for another topic might prove just as fine.

7.) Narrative: The narrative gives a short summary or the focus of the book. It often identifies the main character, the time/place setting, or the scope of the book.

8.) Tracings: The tracings provide alternate keywords with which to expand information retrieval by way of the card catalog. Tracings include authors, joint authors, illustrators, other related subject headings, book subjects, key words.

9.) Visual aids: Visual aids help break down the author's message by visually supporting what the author has stated in printed form. Visual aids include: maps, graphs, charts, pictures, illustrations, tables, diagrams.

10.) Page numbers: Indicate the length of written discussion on the topic.

IDENTIFICATION OF THE PARTS OF A CARD

A. Copyright date

B. The title

C. Call Reference (Nonfiction)

D. Indication of pages

E. Author

    (Bibliography not indicated)

F. Narrative

G. Tracings

H. Series Indication

I. Visual Aids

J. Publisher

Type of Card: Subject
(Note tracings=G)

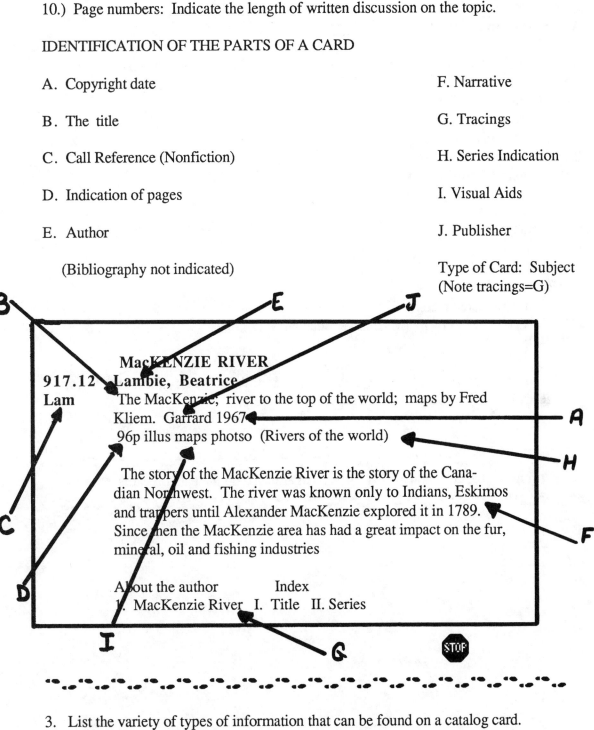

3. List the variety of types of information that can be found on a catalog card.
4. Explain the importance of each part to the research process.

Abbreviations

Many abbreviations are used on the catalog card and should be recognized on sight.

Fic - Fiction
Ref - Reference
B   - Biography
Rec - Record
SFS - Sound Filmstrip
Map - Map collection
MPL - Film Loop
Tra - Transparencies
Prof - Professional
PS/PA - Picture File
Vertical - Vertical File
Kit - Kit with mixed media
MRDF - Computer software [Machine Readable Data File]
VT - Video tape

Some media are not kept in the stacks and therefore must be found in their proper storage areas. See the librarian/media specialist for help.

5. List some of the common abbreviations that are used on the catalog cards.

Date_____
Understanding Catalog Card Parts

DIRECTIONS: Using this card, indicate the following:

```
920        Aaseng, Nathan
Aas            Winners never quit.  Lerner Publications,
           Minneapolis,  c1980.
               80p illus (Sports heroes library)

           Summary:  Brief biographies of 10 athletes
           who achieved greatness while overcoming a
           handicap or misfortune.  Includes Bobby
           Clarke, Wes Unseld, Rocky Bleier, John
           Miller, Kitty O'Neill, Lee Trevino, Tom Dempsey,
           Larry Brown, Ron LeFlore, and Tommy John.

           1. Athletes - Biography   2. Physically
           handicapped        I. Title
```

1. Card Classification

2. Card Type

3. Tracings

4. Narrative

5. Book Title

6. Illustrator

7. Publisher

8. Copyright Date

9. Author

10. Bibliography (if given)

11. Pages

12. Visual Aids

13. Call Number

14. Basic Book Focus

15. Series

The Catalog Card Parts

DIRECTIONS: Identify the card parts.

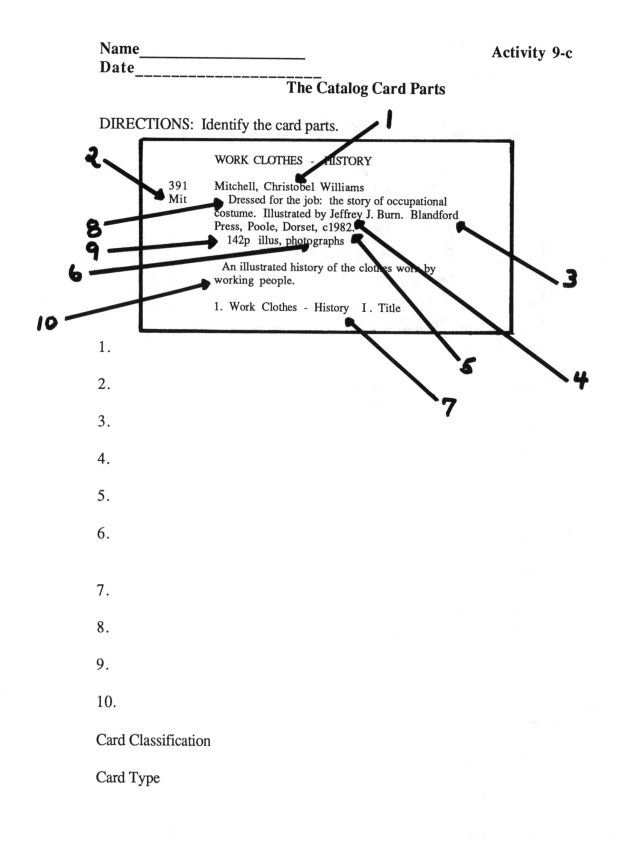

WORK CLOTHES - HISTORY

391   Mitchell, Christobel Williams
Mit   Dressed for the job: the story of occupational
         costume. Illustrated by Jeffrey J. Burn. Blandford
         Press, Poole, Dorset, c1982.
         142p illus, photographs

         An illustrated history of the clothes worn by
         working people.

         1. Work Clothes - History   I. Title

1.

2.

3.

4.

5.

6.

7.

8.

9.

10.

Card Classification

Card Type

Name_____

Date_____

DIRECTIONS:

Through an examination of each call number
and first line, identify the type of each card. (Subject, Title, Author, Series, Joint Author,
Illustrator)

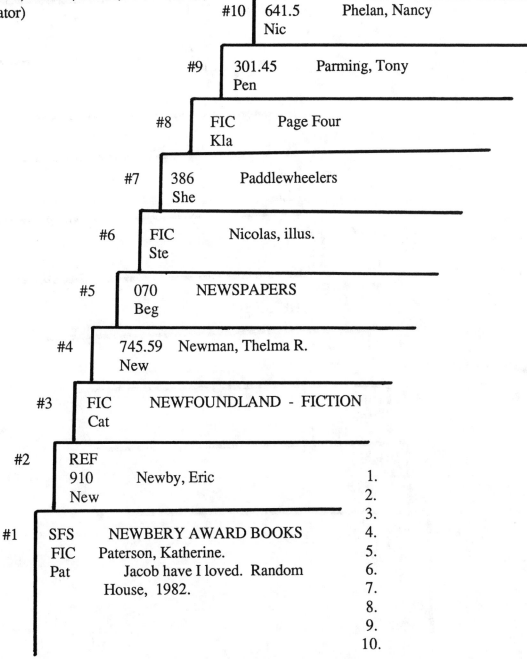

#10   641.5   Phelan, Nancy
Nic

#9   301.45   Parming, Tony
Pen

#8   FIC   Page Four
Kla

#7   386   Paddlewheelers
She

#6   FIC   Nicolas, illus.
Ste

#5   070   NEWSPAPERS
Beg

#4   745.59   Newman, Thelma R.
New

#3   FIC   NEWFOUNDLAND - FICTION
Cat

#2   REF
910   Newby, Eric
New

#1   SFS   NEWBERY AWARD BOOKS
FIC   Paterson, Katherine.
Pat   Jacob have I loved. Random
House, 1982.

1.
2.
3.
4.
5.
6.
7.
8.
9.
10.

Name_____
Date_____

DIRECTIONS:

Through an examination of each call number, identify the classification of each card. (Biography, Reference, Fiction, Nonfiction)

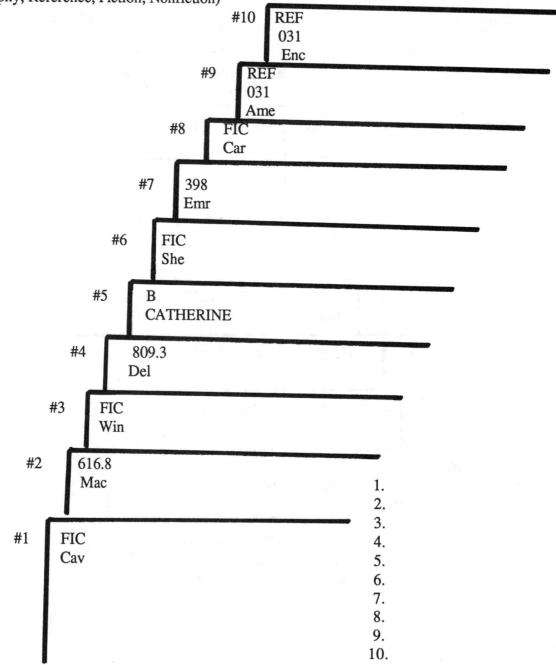

#10 REF 031 Enc

#9 REF 031 Ame

#8 FIC Car

#7 398 Emr

#6 FIC She

#5 B CATHERINE

#4 809.3 Del

#3 FIC Win

#2 616.8 Mac

#1 FIC Cav

1.
2.
3.
4.
5.
6.
7.
8.
9.
10.

The Southeastern part of the United States is bounded on two sides by major bodies of water. Major river systems and bays form other borders. Can you name them? What generalizations can you make about early exploration and settlement? Which state is like a peninsula?

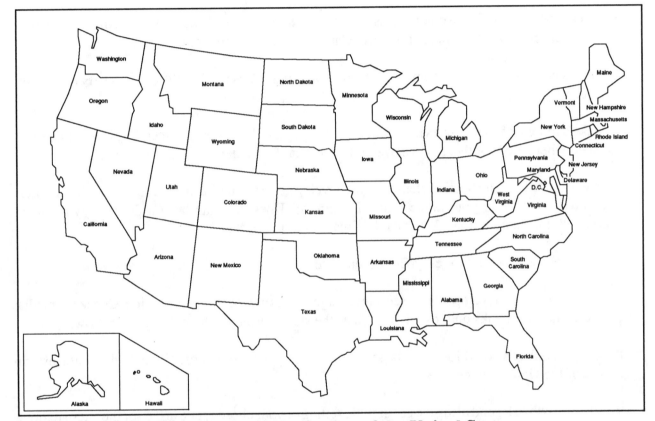

The Southeastern Region of the United States

West Virginia = WV   VA = Virginia

South Carolina = SC   NC = North Carolina

Tennesseee = TN   FL = Florida

Mississippi = MS   GA = Georgia

Kentucky = KY   AL = Alabama

1. Work in ten groups and have each group choose a state. Locate your state by subject heading in

the catalog. Go through the cards or references and chart the information according to classification: Nonfiction, Fiction, Biography, Reference. Do another chart for media type.

2. List all the tracings found on the cards under your state's subject heading in two columns: fiction and nonfiction. Do not duplicate tracings. Can you make any generalizations?

3. Draw a cartoon depicting a comic character explaining the use and/or differences between inside and outside guides.

4. Make a mobile of all the states in the Southeastern region. Indicate by descending a yes or no from the state whether or not there is material in the vertical file under the state's own name.

5. Select a state from the Southeastern region. Develop a questionnaire to include specific facts which you could compare to your home state. Examples: Does the state have a problem with water pollution? Beach pollution? What wild animals exist in the state?

6. Develop a commercial to sell your chosen state.

7. Check atlases or encyclopedias to see which major rivers are located in the region. Check the media center catalog for books on those rivers. Chart the states through which these rivers flow.

8. Design a bulletin board for your classroom on the importance of those rivers to the southeastern region of the United States.

9. Write a myth or legend using the geographic setting of your chosen state in the southeastern region.

10. Construct a puzzle using photocopies of the states in the southeastern region which you have attached to a contact adhesive paper. Cut and make a puzzle.

11. Look up the section in the media center catalog on U. S. History. Try to find books that include your state. Hint: Find historical events that took place in your state and then, by the date and the event, look it up chronologically.

12. Develop a bulletin board of the southeastern region with state capitals, state flowers and/or state birds.

Understanding Organization
Organizational Systems

FOCUS

The student is introduced to four organizational systems: alphabetical, numerical, chronological, and topical. The student will realize that, in addition to rules for each system, there are two systems for alphabetizing.

TEACHER PREPARATION

1. Review all material especially word-by-word and letter-by-letter.

2. Check your school library catalog to see which alphabetical system is used.

3. Complete all activity sheets; check your answers and keep for handy classroom reference.

BACKGROUND INFORMATION

1. Two ways of alphabetizing are discussed in lengthy detail in the student text. For an in-depth look at cataloging practices, see *Commonsense Cataloging* by Miller and Terwillegar. The Library of Congress employs an alpha-numeric ordering.

2. Topically arranged encyclopedias are: *Childcraft; Our Wonderful World; The Encyclopedia of Visual Art; The Book of Popular Science; The Realm of Science.* To use these, students <u>must</u> use an index.

3. A paperback collection is sometimes arranged by topic.

CONCEPTS

• **Recognition of the four organizational systems, each with its own rules.**
• **Recognition that the only exception to the alphabetical nature of the card catalog is the chronological aspect of a country's history, particularly U. S. - HISTORY.**

VOCABULARY

media   sequence   era   retrieval   classification

OBJECTIVES

The student will:

1. Realize that all materials shelved in a library are housed by a well-developed organization system and that all libraries use some type of organization system.

2. List the four organizational systems to include:
   a. the alphabetical
   b. the numerical
   c. the chronological
   d. the topical.

3. Define alphabetical order as simple A-B-C order and list its uses as in the card catalog, shelving of fiction books, and most indexes.

4. Define numerical order as simple number sequence and list its uses to include the Dewey Decimal

System, the Library of Congress System as found in the nonfiction and reference sections.

5. Define chronological organization as sequence by year, time period or time era and list its uses as in the chronological section of the card catalog, i.e., UNITED STATES - HISTORY.

6. Define topical order as placement by subject or topic and list uses as in most tables of contents located in nonfiction books such as content area books.

7. Realize that alphabetical listings can be arranged by two different systems, known as word-by-word or letter-by-letter.

MATERIALS NEEDED
Activity Sheets 10-a through 10-g and 10-b through 10-g in the optional student workbook.

ACTIVITIES
1. Read through material focusing on the different aspects of the four systems.

2. Complete the activity sheets and keep handy for ready classroom reference.

3. Use the context questions indicated by the Stop Sign as an in-class evaluation or homework assignment.

EXTENDED ACTIVITIES
1. Take one organizational system and superimpose it on another: categorize biographies by chronology, by theme, by area, by subject. Product can be a computer printout; can be retained permanently in IMC.

2. Pull all books on one subject (China, Middle Ages), recategorize chronologically. Using the Dewey number, add all biographies, magazines, videotapes, audiovisual material. Final bibliography product retained permanently in IMC.

3. Categorize all periodicals in IMC by Dewey number.

THE FOUR ORGANIZATIONAL SYSTEMS

To find a specific item, it must be remembered that all books, types of media or instructional aids that are housed in the library have a specific area of placement, or perhaps, "address." Each item has <u>not</u> been housed by chance, but by a well-developed organizational system. All libraries have some type of organizational system.

There are four simple, basic organizational systems used for item placement. If you are able to understand each, information retrieval will be quite easy. The four systems are:

1.) Alphabetical Order: Simple A, B, C order; used in the card catalog, shelving of fiction books and most indexes.

2.) Numerical: Simple number sequence as used in the Dewey Decimal System and Library of Congress classification system.

3.) Chronological: Placement by year, by time period, or time era. It is used in the U.S.--HISTORY section of the card catalog.

4.) Topical: Also known as subject. Used in most tables of content in nonfiction books such as content area books. It is also the basis of shelf placement of the biography section of the library in that the topics are the lives of people.

As indicated, the card catalog, book indexes, and many nonfiction books such as encyclopedias are alphabetically organized. Interestingly, alphabetical listings can be arranged by two different systems. The systems are *word-by-word* and *letter-by-letter*. Once the system is put into use in a card catalog or index, it remains constant throughout. There will never be a mixture of the two systems. Most of the time, you will not even be aware of the alphabetical system that is in use because the use of the system becomes automatic.

The main, or most important, reason for having an awareness of the existence of the two systems is that if you do not immediately locate a specific entry, you might be using the wrong system (word-by-word) and should then switch to the other (letter-by-letter). Above all else, don't assume that the entry isn't there. Keep looking.

One instance comes to mind in the locational confusion that the alphabetical systems do sometimes create. One student needed information on the topic, "Newark," but when he looked in a very commonly used encyclopedia and couldn't find the entry, he became confused. Through an explanation of the simple workings of both alphabetizing methods, the student found the "Newark" entry 137 pages away from where he expected to find it originally.

An explanation of both systems is very easy to understand. In a letter-by-letter system, the spaces are ignored and the letters of all words are pushed together as

though only one word exists.
    Example: New Jersey = newjersey

In a word-by-word system, all of the same first words are clustered together and are alphabetically organized by the spelling of the second word.
    Example: New Jersey
               New York
An example of both systems follows. The letters that regulate the organization of the list according to both systems will be underline to help you understand.

Letter-by-letter (Ignore spaces.)	Word-by-word (Same first words are clustered.)
New Amsterdam	New York
Newark	New Yorker
New Bedford	Newark
New Bern	Newars
Newbold	Newberry
New Britain	Newbold
Newburgh	Newburgh

STOP

1. Why is it important to have organization within a library setting?

2. Explain the alphabetical organizational system as used in the library. Give examples of where it might be found within this setting.

3. Explain the chronological organizational system as used in the library. Give an example as to where it might be found in this setting.

4. Explain the numerical organizational system as used in the library. Give examples as to where it might be found in this setting.

5. Explain the topical organizational system as used in the library. Give an example as to where it might be found in this setting.

6. What is the difference of the word-by-word and the letter-by-letter alphabetical systems?

DIRECTIONS: Insert each card into the correct alphabetical placement by matching number to arrow.

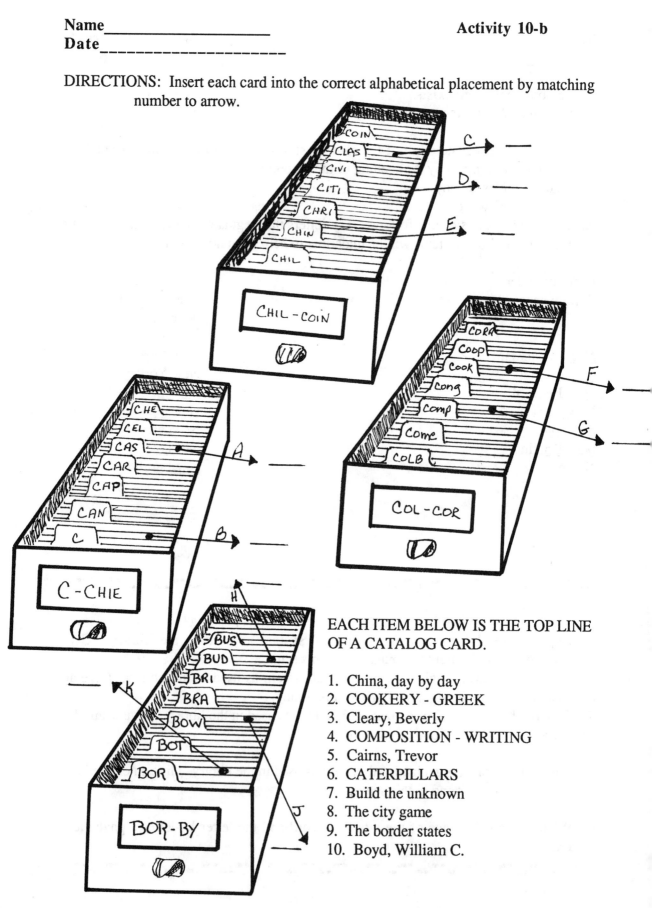

EACH ITEM BELOW IS THE TOP LINE OF A CATALOG CARD.

1. China, day by day
2. COOKERY - GREEK
3. Cleary, Beverly
4. COMPOSITION - WRITING
5. Cairns, Trevor
6. CATERPILLARS
7. Build the unknown
8. The city game
9. The border states
10. Boyd, William C.

DIRECTIONS: Insert each card into the correct alphabetical placement by matching number to arrow.

EACH ITEM BELOW IS THE TOP LINE OF A CATALOG CARD.

1. SPORTS CARS
2. The secret garden
3. The snow goose
4. SCAVENGERS
5. SEEING EYE DOGS - STORIES
6. SANTA FE TRAIL
7. SOCCER
8. Sleator, William
9. Spier, Peter
10. STATISTICS

DIRECTIONS: Listed below are four organizational systems. Also listed are a multitude of sources that can be found in the library to further research. Analyze each according to the type/types of organization/organizations that can be found in each source.

ORGANIZATIONAL SYSTEMS:

A. Chronological
B. Numerical
C. Alphabetical
D. Topical

_____1. Dictionary

_____2. Card Catalog (as a whole)

_____3. Table of contents

_____4. Encyclopedias' format

_____5. U. S. History section of the card catalog

_____6. Fiction section of the library

_____7. Thesaurus

_____8. Nonfiction section of the library

_____9.**National Geographic Index

_____10. Atlas

_____11. Book Index

_____12.**Readers' Guide

_____13. Reference section of the library

_____14.**Current Biography

_____15. Biography section of the library

_____16.**American Heritage   [**Answers based on your use of
                                            index as a first step.]

DIRECTIONS: Insert each card into the correct alphabetical placement by matching number to arrow.

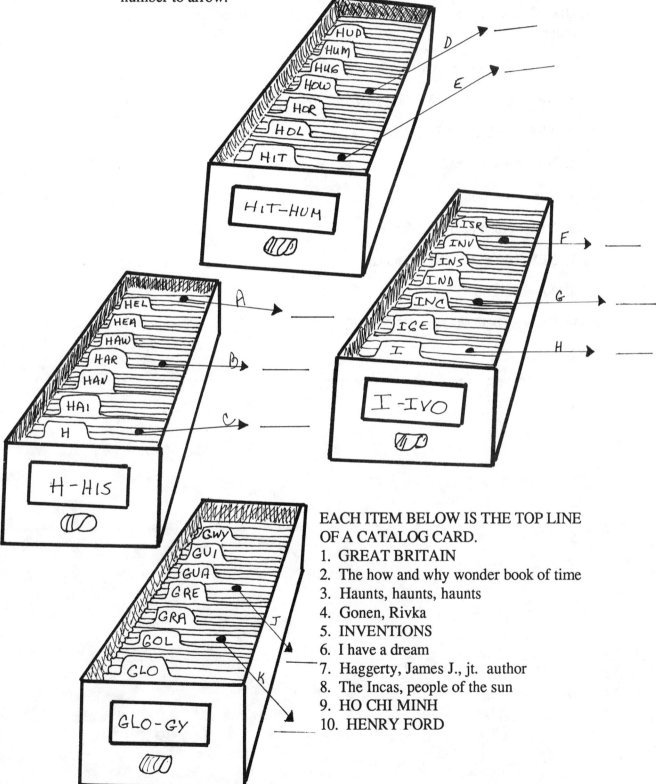

EACH ITEM BELOW IS THE TOP LINE OF A CATALOG CARD.

1. GREAT BRITAIN
2. The how and why wonder book of time
3. Haunts, haunts, haunts
4. Gonen, Rivka
5. INVENTIONS
6. I have a dream
7. Haggerty, James J., jt. author
8. The Incas, people of the sun
9. HO CHI MINH
10. HENRY FORD

Alphabetizing: Letter by Letter

DIRECTIONS: Using the letter by letter method of alphabetizing, put the following in order.

1. New women in media

2. NEW JERSEY - REVOLUTIONARY WAR

3. NEW JERSEY - CIVIL WAR

4. New worlds ahead

5. The new world

6. New women in art and dance

7. NEWBERY AWARD BOOKS

8. Newark, Tim

9. NEW YORK STOCK EXCHANGE

10. New year

_____

1.

2.

3.

4.

5.

6.

7.

8.

9.

10.

Alphabetizing: Word by Word

DIRECTIONS: Using the word by word method of alphabetizing, put the following in order.

1. The New Family Cookbook

2. Nesbit, E.

3. Nervous System

4. New Jersey

5. The New Jersey Almanac and Travel Guide

6. The New Jersey Almanac

7. The New Guide to The Planets

8. The New Golden Book of Astronomy

9. New Hampshire Beautiful

10. Neuberger, Richard

11. Ness, Loch

12. Nesbitt, Rosemary

1.

2.

3.

4.

5.

6.

7.

8.

9.

10.

11.

12.

Understanding Organization
Organizational Exceptions

FOCUS

This lesson will be focusing on the many and varied exceptions to the rule.

TEACHER PREPARATION

1. Review the material to be presented.
2. Pull any or all of the books listed in any of the rules to illustrate.
3. Complete the activity sheets and keep for handy classroom reference.

BACKGROUND INFORMATION

Exceptions: Some examples, corresponding to the rules in the student activity:

Rule 1:   All of these would be alphabetized by the second word.
   The Long Escape
   The Slavery Ghost
   The Box Car Children
   The Blue Sword
   The Girl Who Owned a City
   A Book of Directions
   A Wrinkle in Time
   An Enemy at Green Knowe
All of these would be alphabetized starting with the first word, "And . . ."
   And I Alone Survived
   And Everything Nice
   And Forever Free
   And Now Miguel

Rule 2.   *Louis Armstrong* by James Lincoln Collier
   Samuel J. Tilden by Bill Severn
   Lillian Wald by Beatrice Siegel

Rule 3:   *Dr. Christiaan N. Barnard*
   Dr. George Washington Carver
   Dr. Ralphe Bunche
   The St. Lawrence
   Mr. President
   Mr. Wizard's Science Secrets
   Mrs. Abercorn and the Bunce Boys
   Mrs. Frisby and the Rats of NIMH

Rule 4:   *101 Dalmations*
   1001 Questions Answered About Flowers
   101 Soft Toys
   100 Plus American Poems
   100 Quotable Poems

Rule 5:   Check out your media center card catalog to see if there are any local variations before teaching this unit. Then check with the phone book. The directory is usually strictly letter-by-letter with admonishments on alternative spellings. Check different encyclopedia indexes to see the variations.

Rule 6: Sometimes the author will include a middle initial on some books and not others. Sometimes, the author's name will be two initials and a last name; other times all three names will be fully spelled. If one is reasonably certain that the author is the same person, those author cards will be interfiled.

Rule 7: Subject cards are alphabetically arranged. If the subject is CHINA, the subtopic is HISTORY, the detail is a chronological period, there might be a subdetail.

All cards with just CHINA on them would be alphabetized first. All cards with CHINA-HISTORY would be alphabetized after, and so on. It's important for the students to realize that each word or group of words between the dashes are separate entities.

CONCEPTS
  • **Recognition and understanding of the many catalog card rule exceptions.**
  • **Recognition that the topics are grouped alphabetically in the card catalog by subject card and within the cluster of subject cards, the subtopic and details of the topic are also alphabetically grouped in turn.**

VOCABULARY
    exception differentiate conjunction abbreviated corresponding article cluster

OBJECTIVES
    The student will understand:
1. That although the general rules of alphabetizing apply to the use of the card catalog, there are some exceptions to be noted.

2. That the articles a, an, the, are dropped when they appear at the beginning of a title but are kept when they are located within the title. (It is important not to confuse the article "an" with the conjunction "and.")

3. That in the card catalog, a person's name as a subject or as an author will be filed alphabetically by the last name and not by the first EXCEPT if the name represents the title of a book, then the title card for the book will be filed by the first name of the person.

4. That even though the title of a book may be abbreviated and also appears that way on the corresponding catalog card, the catalog card will be filed alphabetically as though the abbreviated part of the title were completely spelled out.

5. That even when written numerically in a title, to locate a book title in the card catalog, a numerically written number must be respelled in letters and then alphabetically located.

6. That Mc and Mac are alphabetically filed as though they are spelled the same and that within the Mc/Mac cluster the names are alphabetized by the spelling of the second syllable.

7. That when more than one book is written by an author, the author cards will be filed, first by the author's last name, then by the first name, and then each book will be filed alphabetically by the individual title within the author name cluster.

8. That topics are grouped alphabetically in the card catalog by topics card and within the cluster of topic cards the subtopics and details of the topic are also alphabetically grouped in turn.

MATERIAL NEEDED

Activity Sheets 11-a through 11-e and 11-b through 11-e in optional student workbooks.

ACTIVITIES

1. Read through and discuss material.
2. Use actual examples of cards on transparencies to illustrate.
3. Use context questions for homework or class evaluation.

EXTENDED ACTIVITIES

1. Let each student take one drawer from the card catalog and list examples of every exception found in that drawer.

2. Permit student to examine school media center card catalog to ascertain exact sequences. Compare to local public library. Compare to county or regional library.

3. Let the library media specialist share with the students the convention of filing for authors with pseudonyms.

Organizational Exceptions

With the exception of the chronological organization of the cluster for U. S. -- HISTORY, one would have to think long and hard to find an easier index to use than the alphabetically ordered card catalog. Although, a few extra rules should be remembered when using the card catalog.

<u>RULE 1</u>:   The articles *a, an, the* are dropped when they appear at the beginning of a title. Keep them when they are located within the title, though. The student should be sure to differentiate between the article *an* and the conjunction *and*. *And* would definitely be used in alphabetizing while *an* would be dropped at the beginning. This has been noted to be a common student mistake.

<u>RULE 2</u>:   A person's name as a subject or as an author will be alphabetized by the last name, not the first. But, if the name represents the title of a book then the book title will be filed by the first name of the person.

Example: (Book) *Thomas Edison* by Sylvia Archer

Alphabetized: Author card = <u>A</u> for Archer, Sylvia
      Subject card = <u>E</u> for Edison, Thomas
      Title   = <u>T</u> for *Thomas Edison*

<u>RULE 3</u>:   Even though the title of a book may be abbreviated and also on the corresponding catalog card, the catalog card will be filed alphabetically as though the title were completely spelled out.

Example: Mr. = Mister

    Dr. = Doctor

    Lt. = Lieutenant

<u>RULE 4 :</u> Even though written numerically in the title, to locate the book's title in the card catalog, the number must be respelled in letters.

Example: 20th = twentieth
    as in *20th Century Genius (Twentieth Century Genius)*

<u>RULE 5</u>:   Mc and Mac are alphabetically filed as though they are spelled the same. Within the Mc/Mac cluster the names are alphabetized by the second syllable.

Examples: McEnroe
MacGrath
McHenery
MacMillan

The Mc/Mac's come before the Ma's in the drawer. This is different from the way they would be indexed in a telephone directory. In some libraries, one might find all the Mc/Mac's filed between the Ma's and the Mad's. To check, just look for the word MACHINERY. If "machinery" comes after MacMillan, then one will find all the Mc's and Mac's together. Check to see how it is in your library.

RULE 6: When more than one book is written by an author, the author cards will be first filed by the author's last name, then first. Then each book will be alphabetically filed by the individual title of each book in the author name cluster.

RULE 7: Topics are also grouped alphabetically in the card catalog. Within this cluster the subtopic and details are also alphabetically grouped.

Example: {POLAND--ECONOMICS} will be followed by
{POLAND--GOVERNMENT}
{POLAND--HOUSING}

1. Explain the rule regarding the articles *a, an, the,* when each word begins a title when looking for a title card in the card catalog. What is the rule when the articles *a, an, the,* are found in the middle of the title?
2. Why is it important not to confuse the article "an" and the conjunction "and" when both begin a title on a title card?
3. In using the card catalog, when would you look for the last name of a person? When would you look for the first name of a person?
4. How do you handle abbreviations in a book title when looking up a corresponding title card in the card catalog?
5. If a number is numerically written in the title of a book, how would you find the corresponding title card in the card catalog?
6. If you wanted to find a complete list of the books in the library written by an author, how would you proceed?
7. How are names whose first syllables are Mc or Mac organized in the card catalog?
8. How would subtopics of a topic be clustered in the card catalog? How would you locate a corresponding detail?

Name_____

Date_____

Directions:

Read through the rules regarding the catalog card exceptions. Listed below are a series of first lines taken from catalog cards. Carefully read them to determine by which rule the library media specialist would file each card in the card catalog.

A. Drop *a, an, the* when it appears at the beginning of a title but keep when it is within the title.
B. Abbreviations are filed as though they are fully respelled.
C. Numbers are respelled in letters.
D. Mc's and Mac's are interfiled as though they are spelled the same.
E. Alphabetically without exception.
F. Chronologically in the U. S.- HISTORY section.

_____

1._____ 4 - H CLUBS - FICTION

2._____ Mr. Jefferson's Washington

3._____ The acts of King Arthur and his noble knights

4._____ McAlister, James

5._____ Dr. George Washington Carver

6._____ 20,000 years of world painting

7._____ U. S. HISTORY - FRENCH AND INDIAN WAR

8._____ Mr. Lincoln's proclamation

9._____ U. S. HISTORY - COLONIAL PERIOD

10._____ Mr. President

11._____ 2201 fascinating facts

12._____ AFRICA

13._____ The Aeneid for boys and girls

14._____ U. S. HISTORY - WAR OF 1812

15._____ Mr. Mysterious and company

ALPHABETICAL ORDER BY TOPIC/SUBTOPIC/DETAIL

DIRECTIONS:

The following is a listing of topics, subtopics, and details. Alphabetize them as they would be found in a card catalog.

---

1. INDIANS - FICTION
2. INDIANS
3. INDIANS OF MEXICO - FICTION
4. INDIANS - LEGENDS
5. INDIANS OF ANTIQUITIES
6. INDIANS OF NORTH AMERICA - BIOGRAPHY
7. INDIANS OF NEW JERSEY
8. INDIANS OF NORTH AMERICA - ANTIQUITIES - COLLECTIONS
9. INDIANS OF NORTH AMERICA - CAPTIVITIES - FICTION
10. INDIANS OF NORTH AMERICA - EDUCATION
11. INDIANS OF NORTH AMERICA - FICTION - CANADA
12. INDIANS OF NORTH AMERICA - DICTIONARIES
13. INDIANS OF MEXICO - ANTIQUITIES
14. INDIANS OF NORTH AMERICA - ART
15. INDIANS OF NORTH AMERICA

Use the space below to put them into order.

INFORMATION RETRIEVAL: FIRST OR LAST NAME?

Directions:
    Listed below are a series of names. Each might be found as the first line on a catalog card. Next to the name is an indication as to whether the name represents a book title, a subject , or an author's name.
    Circle that part of the name that you would use to retrieve the books represented by the names as they appear below.

_____

1. GEORGE WASHINGTON CARVER (Subject)
2. George Washington Carver (Title)
3. Sam Epstein (Author)
4. COCHISE (Subject)
5. Edgar Wyatt (Author)
6. JEFFERSON DAVIS (Subject)
7. Margaret Green (Author)
8. Charles Dickens (Title)
9. Charles Dickens (Author)
10. CHARLES DICKENS (Subject)
11. Wolf Mankowitz (Author)
12. WALTER DISNEY (Subject)
13. Walter Disney (Title)
14. Walter Disney (Author)
15. EDGAR ALLAN POE (Subject)

DIRECTIONS: Insert each card into the correct alphabetical placement by matching number to arrow. (Remember: Numerically written numbers must be respelled in letters. e.g. 20 = twenty)

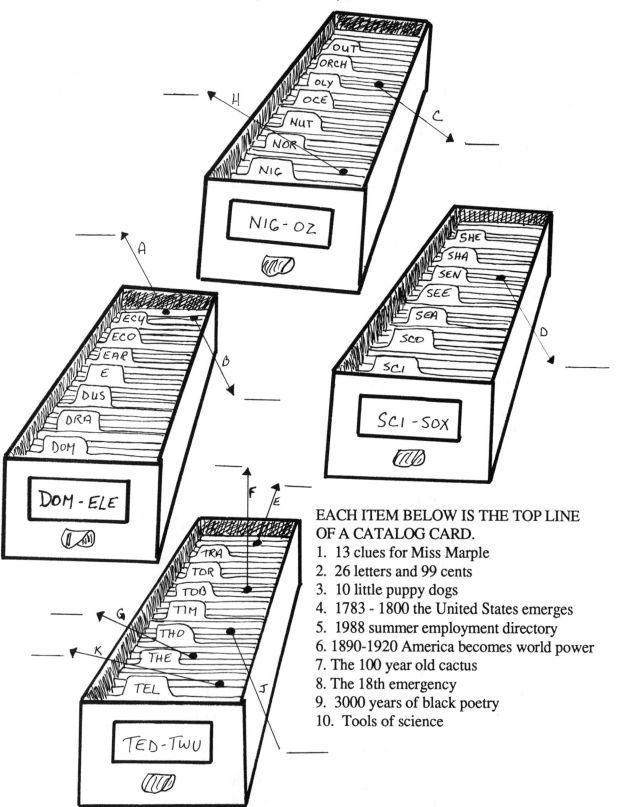

EACH ITEM BELOW IS THE TOP LINE OF A CATALOG CARD.
1. 13 clues for Miss Marple
2. 26 letters and 99 cents
3. 10 little puppy dogs
4. 1783 - 1800 the United States emerges
5. 1988 summer employment directory
6. 1890-1920 America becomes world power
7. The 100 year old cactus
8. The 18th emergency
9. 3000 years of black poetry
10. Tools of science

Date_____   **Know Your Country:**
The South Central Region of the U. S.

Draw in the countries which border the United States. Check with an atlas to correct your border. Which state borders another country? What are some of the water boundaries? What is the largest of the four? Which state shares a border with all three other states in the section?

The South Central Region of the United States

Texas = TX   OK = Oklahoma

Arkansas = AS   LA = Louisiana

1. Find the zip codes of three major cities in each state. Put in numerical order.

2. Find the area codes for all parts of all four states. Put in numerical order along with the cities they represent.

3. Topically arrange the four states in the South Central region and categorize

Unit III Activity   The South Central Region of the U. S.

information for six subtopics. Examples: Produce, Population by years, Common Historical Event

4. Compare and contrast the exploration and settlement of the four states in the South Central Region.

5. Construct a recipe booklet of popular foods of the South Central area.

6. Alphabetically arrange the names of wildlife common to the South Central area.

7. Chronologically arrange events in the South Central area that took place before entry into the Union. Construct with state time lines.

8. Topically arrange battle sites from the South Central Region of the United States.

9. Construct a bar graph comparing the area in square miles of the four states in the South Central Region of the United States.

10. After having read about all four states, choose one about which to write a poem.

11. Using the national section of your local newspaper or a newspaper to which your media center subscribes, find four articles about one of the states in the South Central region. Analyze and summarize for an oral class presentation.

Unit IV Book and Information Retrieval

Information Retrieval

FOCUS
The focus of this lesson is on "how" to begin research: physically, at a catalog; mentally, through the use of multiple keywords. In addition, the physical placement of books on a shelf in a stack is reinforced.

TEACHER PREPARATION
1. Read and review the material as presented.
2. Complete the activity sheets and keep for handy reference.
3. Customize Activity Sheet 12-b to conform to one area in your library. Draw in the number of units in a stack, the number of shelves in each unit. Identify it locationally for the students.
4. Ascertain what topics the students are working on in other classes and develop an example or two on a transparency of multiple key words, or do it in a brainstorming session in class.
    Example: Slavery in Afro-American History, *Amistad*, Blacks in America, manumission, triangular trade.
    Example: Russia, Soviet Union, USSR, Union of Soviet Socialists Republics, Moscow and other cities, Kazakhstan and other republics, communism, socialism, *glasnost*.

BACKGROUND INFORMATION
1. We have seen students starting research become very frustrated when a topic they have chosen, or were assigned, is not easily transposable to subject heading phrases or entry word phrases. If it's not down in black and white in exactly the same terms, they can't handle it. Therefore, brainstorming as many key words as possible is the best route. No rights or wrongs, just possibles.
2. This lesson is <u>NOT</u> on narrowing a topic. It is on how to gather as much information about a broad topic: that critical first step before choosing a viewpoint and narrowing a topic.
3. Many students do not know that when they reach the end of one shelf, they should go to the next shelf below it. Many students continue to the next shelf adjacent on the right. The drawing of the stacks in this lesson is very important. It leads into the Retrieval Game in Lesson 14.
4. Part of the answer in making students good researchers is in making them intellectually comfortable in library surroundings.
5. Interlibrary loan is an easy way of obtaining needed information. In New Jersey, the State Library correlates the OCLC Loan Program which is the nationwide Online Computer Library Center library network. All of New Jersey's libraries --public, school, college, special libraries-- are eligible to be in geographic regional networks. Networking is one way of extending the parameters of a collection. Your school library media specialist can telephone the bibliographic information in and a search will be made. Or if your library is online, you can search many collections yourself. If you have a facsimile machine, it is possible that information can be faxed to you.

6. Where should the student begin! Generate key words and many of them. In addition to alternate names for a topic, historical names and people and places can be used. Reading a brief encyclopedia article on the topic will focus the reader. Using keywords from that article and from the tracings on the catalog cards and from a dictionary or thesaurus will generally give enough avenues to begin research. Have the student list the key words and methodically go through them.

7. The drawing is a visualization of the directionality involved in perusing the stacks. Sometimes the students need to be shown exactly how the books are physically arranged.   Often the physical limitations of a library media center mean a detour in the normal flow of shelving. Explore the idiosyncrasies.

CONCEPTS
  • **Recognition of the rationale and use of the multiple subject cards located in the card catalog for an individual book.**
  • **Recognition that initial preparation in the card catalog and not "in the**

stacks" is the correct way to begin research.
- Recognition of the need to generate multiple key words for a topic when beginning research.
- Recognition of the track or route to follow in terms of the physical set of books on the multiple shelves in the library.
- Recognition that the Dewey Decimal System and the Library of Congress System structure a numerical organization for the shelving of books corresponding to the topic, subtopic, and detail of a book.
- Recognition that the call number of the book gives the specific place location of a book in the library and that it is necessary that the student access the author's name and book title from the card for the most efficient method of book retrieval.

VOCABULARY
retrieval   network resource generate utilize access precise pertinent
specialized   technical barrier traditional   designate   categorize
correspondence   sequence

OBJECTIVES
The student will understand:

1. That each book in the library can have multiple subject headings according to the variety of the areas of the book's content; therefore, it will have multiple corresponding subject cards in the card catalog devised at the library media specialist's discretion.

2. That the most efficient and effective way to begin a search for book selection for research is through the appropriate use of the card catalog and not "at the stacks" randomly in the general area of the topic.

3. That when beginning research, it is necessary to generate multiple keywords to obtain the optimum amount of information on the subject.

4. The appropriate track or route to follow in terms of the physical set of books on the multiple shelves in the library. (See diagram on Activity 12-b.)

MATERIAL NEEDED
Activity Sheets 12-a through 12-c and 12-b through 12-c in the optional student workbook.

ACTIVITIES
1. Read and discuss 12-a.
2. You can use context questions indicated by the Stop Sign as in-class activity.
3. On the customized Activity Sheet 12-b, let the students work in pairs and fill in the beginning and ending call numbers on each shelf or each unit. (As stated in the Teacher Preparation, you may wish to customize one activity sheet yourself to correspond to an area in your library. Then, you can assign 12-b to be done by individuals or groups of students.)
4. On Activity Sheet 12-c, assign as many of the topics as you wish to individual students letting them circle their assigned topics at the top of the paper. They can generate some key words and/or information needed in order to progress. List the words, then go to the catalog to list four sources by call number, author and title.

EXTENDED ACTIVITIES
1. Students can map the surrounding libraries highlighting special collections or sections, such as local histories, college information, foreign language books, government documents.

2. Use students who have become proficient in beginning a search to help other students work through similar problems.

Information Retrieval

Successful information retrieval or the location of specific information involves the understanding of an entire network of library-related skills. The focus of the previous chapters has been to develop understanding of those skills that include the correct use of the card catalog, the catalog card, and the four major organizational systems. It is also intended that through a tour of the IMC, you will develop an appreciation of the vast array of resources available and of the multiple ways (media) by which information is presented. In other words, the main concepts presented in a nonfiction book might also be found in a sound filmstrip, a record, on transparencies, on a video tape, on a film loop, in computer software, in a kit or possibly as part of a picture or vertical file.

Successful information retrieval begins at the card catalog and/or at the screen and keyboard. You start by identifying your topic through the help of content area teacher instruction. With the topic key word selected, the next step is to generate other multiple key words associated with the original key word. You should realize that in generating new key words, you are actually listing a variety of synonyms (words that mean the same) for your topic. This can be achieved through the use of your own knowledge of vocabulary of the field under study. But if more words are needed, you might utilize a dictionary, thesaurus, or the tracings on the catalog cards located in the cluster represented by the original topic word. Another good source for the key words would be the index cross reference words, located through retrieving the topic as the entry word, as found in an encyclopedia, the *Readers' Guide* or the *National Geographic Index*.

In terms of good research, the more key words to which you have access, the better your chances of collecting the precise information necessary for writing a good report. The library media specialist has also aided you to this end in that the librarian will often develop many subject/topic cards for a specific book based on the vocabulary needs of the students in a school. Another purpose in the use of multiple subject cards is that the librarian recognizes the fact that when you are in the early stages of researching a topic, you might not possess the field vocabulary necessary to retrieve the specific, pertinent information desired. This is especially true in science reports where a very specialized, technical vocabulary is often employed.

If you choose to omit the card catalog, catalog card, key word steps of the research process and instead goes directly "to the stacks," you will more than likely encounter a great deal of difficulty. In fact, you might miss the most important books dealing with the topic because you might be in the reference section when, in fact, the book has been shelved in the nonfiction section. A fast review of the call number of the catalog card through the use of the card catalog would have avoided this waste of time.

Another problem that you might encounter starting at the stacks rather than at the card catalog is that few, if any, books might be on the shelves that cover that topic.

You might walk away from a topic thinking that there is not enough information to support research when in reality the best books are out in circulation. If this is the case and you have done your "preparation" at the catalog and realize these books exist, you can then ask the librarian to place a reserve on these particular books. You will then receive them as soon as they are available. Knowing the existence of these books also gives you the option of an interlibrary loan if you find that the town, county, or state library has a copy that is not in circulation. In this way, the books can be in your possession in a short while and research can be started. In the meantime, you might begin to organize an outline and collect other appropriate materials that will support the research topic. The interlibrary loan is also important when working from a bibliography (listing of books on a specific topic) given by a content area teacher. The library might not own all the books on the list and you will have to search elsewhere. Only by checking the catalog will you be able to make a determination.

Once an understanding of the importance of the use of the card catalog and catalog card information is developed, the next area of concentration should be to develop an understanding of the organization of the books on the library shelves. Below is a drawing of a typical shelving unit and is a reminder that books are not placed on the shelves wall to wall. The shelves are in units on which books are placed in numerical or alphabetical order (dependent upon library area and classification). When the top shelf of one unit is filled then the next lower shelf of the same unit is filled. When the entire unit is filled, the top shelf of the next is filled and so on until all the books are appropriately placed. Sometimes the shelves are filled so completely, and the barriers between the units so indistinct that you, if not careful, can get lost either numerically or alphabetically in the stacks if you are not knowledgeable of the traditional placement of library books on shelving units.

1. How would you go about generating key words for a topic?
2. What types of problems might you have in developing a topic if you started at the stacks rather than the catalog?
3. What is an interlibrary loan?
4. Draw a likeness of a shelving system and through the use of arrows indicate the pattern of placement of books on the shelves.

Shelf Location of Books

DIRECTIONS:
  The sample stacks that you see below are very similar to those in your library.

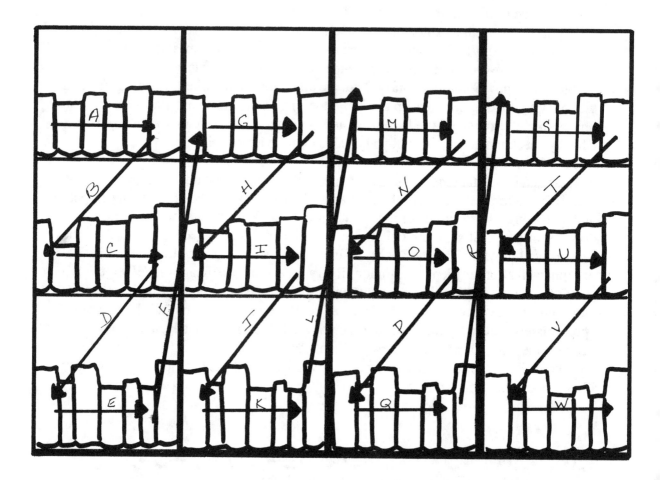

Choose any nonfiction area in your library. Count the number of shelving units and shelves. Make a drawing of an empty stack and divide it into the same number of shelving units and shelves, so that it is a representation of your chosen area. Then place at the beginning and ending of each shelf and each shelving unit the call numbers that are on that shelf and that unit.

Date_____

Topics and Possible Sources of Information

DIRECTIONS:

Below is a listing of topics. Circle the ones that your teacher assigns to you. In the space below the topic, generate some key words or list some information that's necessary. Then go to the catalog to find four possible sources of information for that topic. List those four sources by call number, author and title.

TOPICS: horses, kites, moon landings, bacteria, flu, pine trees, snakes, ink, lasers, publishing, magazines, sculpture, vision, architecture, shoes, cars, motorcycles, locks, money, banks, mythology, rivers, elephants, whales, television, elevators, churches

TOPIC   Source: Call Number, Author, Title

1. _____   a._____

                         b._____

                         c._____

                         d._____

2. _____   a._____

                         b._____

                         c._____

                         d._____

3. _____   a._____

                         b._____

                         c._____

                         d._____

4. _____   a._____

                         b._____

                         c._____

                         d._____

Dewey Decimal System

FOCUS

The focus of this activity is to have the student understand the Dewey Decimal System as an organizational pattern, to understand the organizational pattern of fiction and biography and to understand the organizational pattern of the book shelves in order to retrieve material.

TEACHER PREPARATION

1. Read and review material, understanding that the Dewey numbers in Activities 13-b are completely fictitious.
2. Understand the basic concept that Melvil Dewey had concerning dividing all knowledge into ten categories.

BACKGROUND INFORMATION

1.   The student should become familiar with the three basic organizations, as delineated in the biography, fiction, nonfiction/reference sections. As an aside, the Library of Congress system, an alpha-numerical system, allows for 26 main classes. Each class can be subdivided by use of a second alphabet: AA-AZ. Each subclass can then be divided numerically, 1-9999. After a period or point comes the Cutter author number which is the first letter of the author's name plus two or three numbers from a specially devised table, correlating those digits to the part of the author's last name following the first letter.

2.   Going through the ten Dewey categories can be enlightening to students. Show them that items of which Melvil Dewey was never aware do indeed have a number in the library. Examples: Hair dryers, dishwashers, satellites, lunar landing modules, etc. Get a Dewey classification book and share with students the Second and Third summaries.

3.   Share with the students the fact that there is a group of people who have the responsibility for updating the classifications of Dewey. There are abridged Dewey classification books for small libraries.

4.   Melvil Dewey was an interesting, if eccentric, person. His eccentricities extended to some of the categories.   Biographical information could be shared.

5.   A specific sequence of steps is listed. Although we focus on the call reference number to locate the physical area of the library media center, the student will have to know the full title and the author's full name to retrieve the item.

CONCEPTS

   •   **Recognition that the Dewey Decimal System is a numerical organization for classification of information.**
   •   **Recognition of the organization of the other library classifications: biography and fiction.**
   •   **Recognition that the call number indicates the library location.**

VOCABULARY

Dewey Decimal System   Library of Congress System   numerical   topic   subtopic   detail designated   categorized   categorization   classification   sequence   procedure   interfiled   simulated retrieval

OBJECTIVES

The student will understand that:
1. Although the Dewey Decimal System and the Library of Congress System structure a numerical organization for the shelving of books, those same numbers, in fact, represent topic, subtopic, and a detail approach to classification.

2. A breakdown of a specific Dewey or Library of Congress number would reveal topic, subtopic, and lesser details of any corresponding book.

3. The call number of a book indicates the library location of the item and that by following each line of information as contained in the call number, one will be led to the physical place location of the book.

MATERIAL NEEDED
   Activity Sheets 13-a through 13-b and 13-b from the optional student workbook.

ACTIVITIES
1. Read through 13-a and tour the IMC pointing out various Dewey categories and the fiction, biography, nonfiction and reference sections.

2. The context questions indicated by the Stop Sign may be done orally in class.

3. This lesson leads right into the Retrieval Game (Lesson 14).

EXTENDED ACTIVITIES
1. Let the students develop a bulletin board of the ten Dewey categories. A possibility would be to divide the ten categories vertically. Then using a horizontal line, divide all ten in half. The top half would have words or pictures representing those items that were in existence during Melvil Dewey's lifetime; the bottom half would contain those items that have been created, invented, or discovered since Dewey. The obvious implication is that the Dewey System is elastic enough to expand.

2. Let students bring in titles of books to place in the categories on the Dewey bulletin board. Or they could make dust jacket book reports that would be hung in the category.

3. A book report contract for one book from each Dewey category.

4. Recategorize some individual biographies into a Dewey number.

Dewey Decimal System

You, as a student researcher, should realize that the Dewey Decimal and the Library of Congress Systems structure a numerical system for the shelving of books. Those same numbers, in turn, represent a topic, subtopic and detail approach to classification. All of the books written on the same topic, subtopic and detail will be shelved together in one area of one unit in the nonfiction and reference section of the library by a designated Dewey number classification (and placed by the librarian).

The Dewey Decimal system is a numerical coding by topic and subtopic of the factual information found in nonfiction and reference books. Dewey organized ten basic, general topics and assigned each topic a specific number. His numerical system of topics is in multiples of 10.

Numerical Coding	Topic
000	Generalities
100	Philosophy and related disciplines
200	Religion
300	The Social Sciences
400	Language
500	Pure Sciences
600	Technology (Applied sciences)
700	The arts
800	Literature
900	General geography and history

Dewey then categorized each topic into a subtopic and each subtopic into details. This was done so that each book could be categorized and numerically coded with a three place whole number which sometimes included a single or multiple place decimal number.

Example: 796.332

The general to specific categorization or each book allows the library media specialist to better organize by topic the factual information of the books in the library. The librarian is able to cluster books of the same specific content together on the shelves, thereby making information retrieval easier for you, the researcher. If you would envision the numerical breakdown of a Dewey Decimal number on a continuum as general to specific in terms of broadness of information, it might appear this way:

General topic < _ _ _ _ _ _ _ _ _ _ _ _ _ >specific detail

In turn, a breakdown of a specific number would reveal topic, subtopic, and lesser details:

700	=	The Arts
790	=	Recreational and Performing Arts
796	=	Athletic and Outdoor sport & games
796.3	=	Ball Games
796.33	=	Inflated ball driven by foot
796.332	=	American football

Although it is necessary that you have a basic understanding of the Dewey Decimal System, it is not necessary to commit any part to memory. The books are already placed on the shelves according to a number=topic correspondence.

All of the information to which you have been exposed to this point has been provided to support the act of book retrieval. The call number on the catalog card, in turn, indicates by the first line the book classification and therefore the general area where the book will be shelved. The remaining lines of the call number indicate specific shelf and specific book location.

There is a sequence of steps to follow when leaving the card catalog to locate a specific book on the shelf. This procedure will be discussed in detail according to the four basic book classifications.

Steps To Follow:

I. Catalog Card: FICTION

FIC   #1   #1= Fiction location in IMC

SMI   #2   #2=Author's Last name

Sequence:
A. Go to fiction section.
B. Alphabetically locate the last name of the author.
C. Within the book cluster, find author's first name.
D. Within the cluster of books written by that person, alphabetically locate the title of the book.

II. Catalog Card: REFERENCE

REF   #1   #1=Reference location in IMC
973.2 #2   #2=Dewey Decimal number
ARN   #3   #3=First three letters of author's last name.

Sequence:

A. Go to the Reference Section.

B. Numerically locate the 900's; then within the cluster locate 973's; within this cluster, locate the 973.7's.

C. Within the cluster of books marked 973.7, find the author's last name, then first name.

D. Find the title of the book.

III. Catalog Card: NONFICTION:

974.974	#1	#1=Dewey Decimal number
Per	#2	#2=First three letters of author's last name

Sequence:

A. Go to the nonfiction section.

B. Numerically locate the 900's. Then within this group, locate the 974's.

C. Within the cluster of 974.974, find the author's last name, then first.

D. Within this cluster, find the title.

IV. Catalog Card: BIOGRAPHY:

B	#1	#1=Indicates the biography section
EDISON	#2	#2=Name of the person about whom the book is written.

Sequence:

A. Go to the biography section.

B. Alphabetically locate the last name of the person about whom the book is written.

C. Locate the first name.

D. Within this cluster, alphabetically locate the last name of the author.

E. Locate the first name.

F. Alphabetically locate the book.

* Autobiography will be interfiled among the volumes of biography. The same rules apply.

Before beginning actual research, it is important that you practice some the library-related skills involving many of the individual source materials to which you will be confronted while involved in the practical steps of research.

As previously mentioned, all of the library classifications of fiction, nonfiction, reference and biography are located in different areas of the library and as indicated or explained are shelved in different ways. It is important to develop a good understanding of these different organizations so that actual book retrieval by classification (fiction, nonfiction, reference, biography) will be quite automatic.

In addition, some number activities with decimals is good practice. The following list is in number order from smallest to largest; in other words, the way that the books would appear on the shelves:

973
973.1
973.2
973.45
973.6
973.8
973.91
973.94
974

It is impractical for the librarian to supply four stacks of books to each student to practice retrieval. Instead, this unit will provide a series of practical exercises depicting the individual organization of each classification or area that is involved in research: reference, fiction, nonfiction, biography. The game is called "Retrieval." The librarian or teacher will explain the various steps and will provide the assortment of materials needed to complete each facet of the puzzle. In this way, each of you will be provided with a hands-on simulated library experience involving shelf location of books by individual classification.

1. How do the Dewey Decimal system and the Library of Congress System combine a numerical and topical approach to classification?
2. Discuss the basics of the Dewey Decimal System, in terms of what a breakdown of a Dewey number would reveal.
3. Why is it not necessary to commit any part of the Dewey Decimal System to memory?
4. Create one call number for each of the classifications. Explain what each line means in terms of retrieval.
5. List the sequence of steps to follow in retrieving a fiction book when given a fiction call number.
6. List the sequence of steps to follow in retrieving a nonfiction book when given a nonfiction call number.
7. List the sequence of steps to follow in retrieving a reference book when given a reference call number.
8. List the sequence of steps to follow in retrieving a biography book when given a biography call number.

Dewey Decimal System

DIRECTIONS:

Put the following Dewey Decimal numbers in correct sequence as they would be found on the library shelf.

1. 014.63	1._____
2. 001.4	2._____
3. 463.03	3._____
4. 001.43	4._____
5. 123.8	5._____
6. 848.07	6._____
7. 014.6	7._____
8. 848.7	8._____
9. 123.84	9._____
10. 463.3	10._____

_____

1. 124.008	1._____
2. 246.121	2._____
3. 002.6	3._____
4. 359.06	4._____
5. 684.73	5._____
6. 246.12	6._____
7. 684.7	7._____
8. 002.06	8._____
9. 359.6	9._____
10. 134.08	10._____

The Retrieval Game

FOCUS
This lesson game reinforces the rules of book retrieval.

TEACHER PREPARATION
1. This lesson should be used in conjunction with, and immediately after, Lesson 13, The Dewey Decimal System.
2. Read thoroughly through the directions and practice following the steps in the game.
3. The game reinforces the rules of book retrieval and also provides the framework for teacher diagnosis and correction of student misconceptions of the retrieval process.
4. Game can provide practice on an individual, group or class level.
5. Other than copies of materials included in the program, the only other materials needed are a pair of scissors and possibly an envelope or paper clip per student.

BACKGROUND INFORMATION
1. The game provides a simulation of the organizational experience to which the student would be confronted on the library shelf. Devising this game proved to be a boon when it came to evaluating how well the students understood shelf arrangement. The answer sheet represents a shelving unit of a stack and thus reinforces the concept of book placement.
2. Retrieval is a game that can be used to help students increase understanding of the steps involved in book retrieval, by classification.

CONCEPTS
- **Understanding of the rules of book retrieval.**
- **Understanding of book placement on shelves.**

VOCABULARY
simulation   organizational   confronted

OBJECTIVES
The student will:
1. Understand how books are arranged on a shelf.
2. Understand how different classifications are arranged.

MATERIAL NEEDED
1. Gameboard (Activity Sheet #14-b)
2. Activity Sheets containing printed spines (Activity Sheet #14-c through Activity Sheet #14-g)
3. Scissors
4. Envelope/paper clip
5. Activity Sheet #14-g, which is the answer board

ACTIVITIES

1. The following is an explanation of the game steps for RETRIEVAL.

Gameboard Sample:　　　　　"Spine" Sheet Sample:

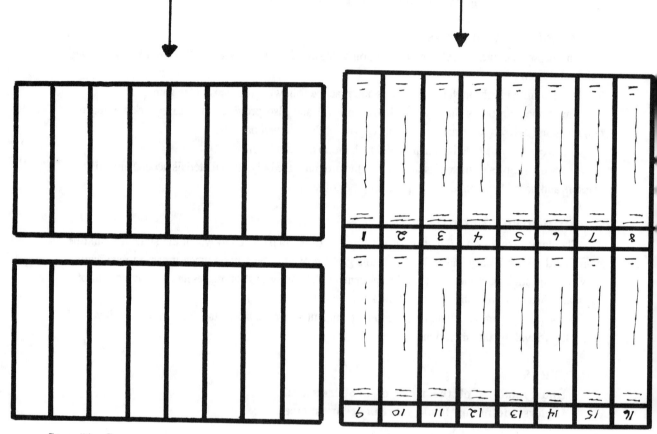

Step #1: Storage

1.) This is one method by which materials (book spine simulations) might be stored. (Paper clips work, also.)

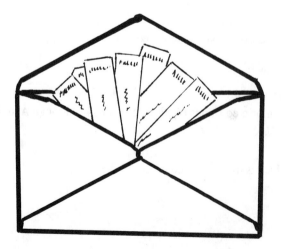

Step #2: Game in Progress

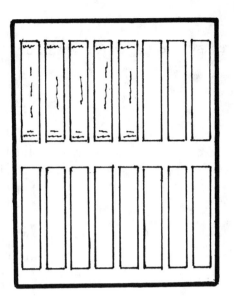

2.) This is another gameboard sample with the game in progress. At this point, as depicted, the students have:

a. Cut the binding sheet into strips realizing that each strip represents a spine of a book.

b. Folded the numbers to the back so that only the spine information appears.

c. Examined the spines to determine classification so to identify appropriate organization for the determined classification. *(See: Classification sequence in the student text under "Steps to Follow", page 9.)

d. Begun to organize "spines" on the gameboard by classification as they would appear on a shelf in the library.

e. Begun to complete the gameboard.

Step #3: Proofing

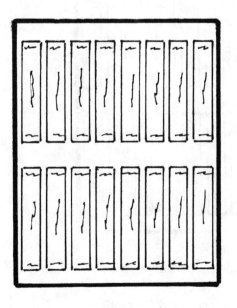

3.) Once all spines are organized, student proofs to correct any mistakes. Once student is satisfied, he/she proceeds to the next step.

Step #4: Creating an Answer Sheet

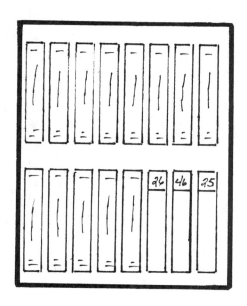

4.) Student turns all "spines" over so that only numbers show, in preparation of preparing an answer sheet.

Step #5: The Answer Sheet

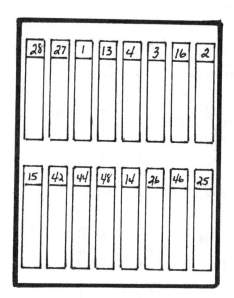 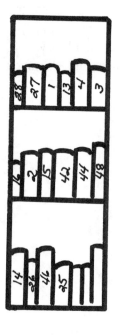

5.) Once all numbers are exposed, student enters numbers on answer sheet.

Step #6: Diagnosis and Correction

6.) Each individual answer sheet is then given to the teacher or librarian for correction.

CORRECTION HINTS:

The numbers are transferred on the answer sheet for a variety of reasons:

a.) If class ends and a student is still in progress, he/she might quickly draft answers in pencil on the answer sheet and will therefore be able to start at the point where he/she left off from the last class. This eliminates wasting time with having to redo.

b.) The answer sheet provides flexibility for the teacher in that gameboards do not have to be corrected while in progress. This frees the teacher to provide support where it is needed during class.

c.) The answer sheet also allows the teacher time to analyze mistakes. If a student incorrectly aligns a portion of the puzzle, the teacher is able to just reach for the numbers, turn to the "spine" side and easily diagnose the problem in preparation for the next class. Possibly, a problem might include misconceptions in: 1) recognition of classification; 2) confusion as to where information appears on the spine; 3) inability to handle decimal sequencing; or 4) alphabetical inability.

d.) The answer sheet allows the librarian the flexibility of setting up corrective lessons for an individual, group or class. It also allows for other students to proceed if it is found that they are concept proficient in the area. This program, as a whole, allows for this type of continuum of skill development.

ADDITIONAL HINTS:

1. Stretching the skill. . . Students may also be given more than one classification with which to work.

2. Cutting preparation time. . .All "spine" sheets can be attached to a sticky-backed paper to provide a firmer substrate with which the student might work. This should be prepared prior to student cutting the spines into strips. All game boards can also be backed in this way and then can be used repeatedly.

3. Gameboards do not have to be used but do provide a structure, especially for the younger student. Use is therefore recommended by the authors.

4. For reality on labels, type the call numbers from the 100 books that follow 327 in the librarian's shelf list. Place the labels on 4" x 6" index cards: (as pictured below); fold on dotted lines. You'll have a simulated book spine with true-to-life call numbers. Have students arrange them on 3-tier shelving units.

EXTENDED ACTIVITIES

1. Mix the activity sheets of two classifications together.

2. Use all the sheets together.

The Retrieval Game

Retrieval is a game that can be used to help you increase understanding of the steps involved in book retrieval, by classification.

The game provides a simulation of the organizational experience to which you would be confronted on the library shelf. The rectangular areas on this activity sheet represent spines of books. You are to cut them apart, fold back on the solid line, arrange them in order on the gameboard(Activity Sheet 14-b), and then transfer the correct answer numbers to the answer sheet.

A facsimile of the answer sheet is seen below. As you can tell, it resembles a section of media center shelving. Above each section is the nature of that section. You are to put your answers from the reference activity in the reference section and so on. On the answer sheet you will see a blank to be filled in after the section. That refers to the activity sheet number: 14-c, 14-d, 14-e,and 14-f, for instance.

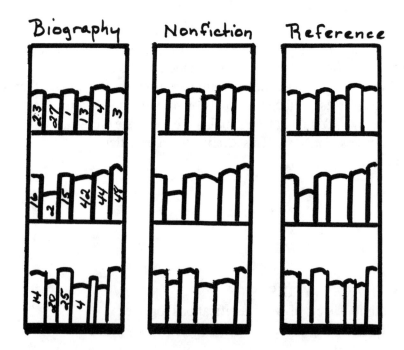

Name_____   Activity 14-b

Date_____

The Retrieval Game Board

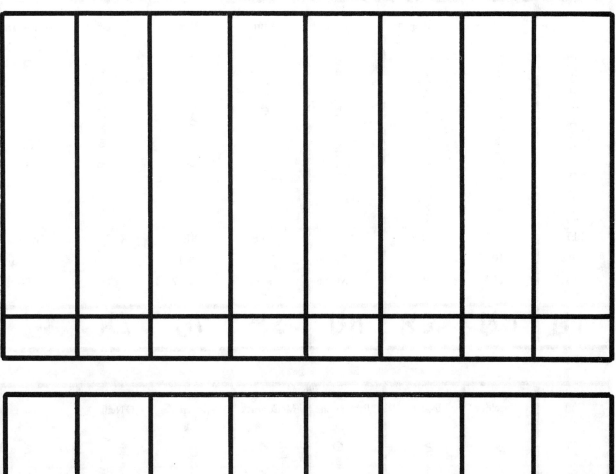

The Retrieval Game
Reference Retrieval

Burnham	Low	Bragonier	Worth	Kurian	Newman	Colligan	Ben-Asher
Dictionary of Misinformation	Encyclopedia of Black America	What's What, A Visual Glossary of the Physical World	The Trivia Encyclopedia	World Data	Girls are People Too	The A+ Guide to Taking Tests	The Junior Jewish Encyclopedia
REF	REF	REF	REF	REF	REF	REF	REF
001.9	310.45	031	310	317.3	011	153.9	296.03
BUR	LOW	BRA	WOR	KUR	NEW	COL	BEN
R1	R2	R3	R4	R5	R6	R7	R8

Cuff	Hazeltine	Douglas	Brownstone	McCormick	Robert	O'Neill	Stuart
United States Energy Atlas	Anniversaries and Holidays	American Book of Days	Complete Career Guide	New York Times Guide to Reference Materials	Robert's Rules of Order	The Women's Book of World Records and Achievements	Who Won What When
REF	REF	REF	REF	REF	REF	REF	REF
333.7	394.2	394.2	371.42	028.7	328	210	001
CUF	HAZ	DOU	BRO	MCC	ROB	O'NE	STU
R9	R10	R11	R12	R13	R14	R15	R16

Name_____ **Activity 14-d**
Date_____

The Retrieval Game
Nonfiction Retrieval

Johnston	Latham	Berger	Markun	Katz	Sims	Frank	Tames
Together in America	Rise and Fall of "Jim Crow" 1865-1964	Religion	Politics	Early America, 1492-1812	Labor Unions in the U.S.	The Pictorial History of the Democratic Party	The Muslim World
301.451	323.4	291	329	302.454	331.8	329	297
JOH	LAT	BER	MAR	KAT	SIM	FRA	TAM
N1	N2	N3	N4	N5	N6	N7	N8

Perowne	Clark	Pinchot	Doty	Papale	Bolles	Faber	Sung
Roman Mythology	Energy for Survival	The Mexicans in America	Money of the World	Banners, Buttons, and Songs	What Color is your Parachute?	The Perfect Life	An Album of Chinese Americans
292	333.7	301.34	332.4	324.5	331	289.8	301.4
PER	CLA	PIN	DOT	PAP	BOL	FAB	SUN
N9	N10	N11	N12	N13	N14	N15	N16

The Retrieval Game
Fiction Retrieval

Avi	Adams	Bellairs	Bellairs	Adler	Bennett	Bethancour	Bellairs
Encounter at Easton	Watership Down	The Revenge of the Wizard's Ghost	The Figure in the Shadows	Roadside Valentine	Deathman, do not follow me	Doris Fein, Superspy	The House with a clock in its Walls
FIC	FIC	FIC	FIC	FIC	FIC	FIC	FIC
AVI	ADA	BEL	BEL	ADL	BEN	BET	BEL
F1	F2	F3	F4	F5	F6	F7	F8

Babbitt	Armstrong	Anderson	Arrick	Bach	Baker	Aiken	Beagle
The Search for Delicious	Sounder	A Midsummer Tempest	Nice Girl from Good Home	Jonathan Livingston Seagull	Dupper	Silent Snow, Secret Snow	The Last Unicorn
FIC	FIC	FIC	FIC	FIC	FIC	FIC	FIC
BAB	ARM	AND	ARR	BAC	BAK	AIK	BEA
F9	F10	F11	F12	F13	F14	F15	F16

The Retrieval Game
Biography Retrieval

Holt	Green	Frost	Bourdon	Knoop	Killingray	Keller	Peck
George Washington Carver	Marie Curie	The Custer Album	Calder: Mobilist, Ringmaster, Innovator	A World Explorer	Constantine	Marie Curie	Something for Joey
B	B	B	B	B	B	B	B
CARVER	CURIE	CUSTER	CALDER	CORONADO	CONSTANTINE	CURIE	CAPPELLETTI
B1	B2	B3	B4	B5	B6	B7	B8

Henry	Sullivan	Costello	Meltzer	Latham	Sims	Axthelm	Dupuy
Marie Curie	Wilt Chamberlain	Lou's on First	Tongue of Flame	Bill Cosby--For Real	Confucius	The Kid	The Military Life of Winston Churchill of Britain
B	B	B	B	B	B	B	B
CURIE	CHAMBERLAIN	COSTELLO	CHILD	COSBY	CONFUCIUS	CAUTHEN	CHURCHILL
B9	B10	B11	B12	B13	B14	B15	B16

The Retrieval Game
Answer Board

DIRECTIONS: Circle the classification with which you are working. Transfer your answer numbers to the "book" on the shelf.

Reference Biography
Nonfiction   Fiction

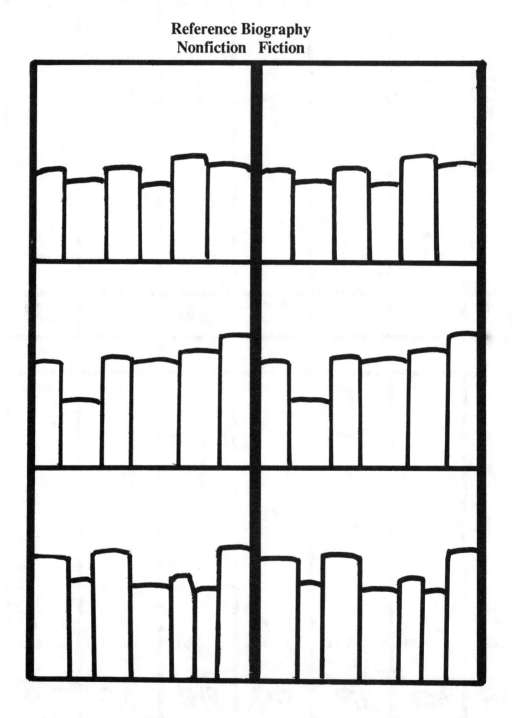

Catalog Card Application

FOCUS
This lesson will focus on retrieving information from the catalog card.

TEACHER PREPARATION
1. Read thoroughly all information.
2. Work through the exercises and keep for handy reference.

BACKGROUND INFORMATION
1. Be sure to review the abbreviations found on cards.

2. Use the sample cards in Activity 15-a to show other information, not just what's listed. In other words: the title location on each card; the visual aid indication on each card; ask what's missing from each partial card(the narrative, the tracings). Key the locations of these items to a map of your school media center.

3. This activity offers an easy transition from skills to catalog use during research. We have chosen to ask the student for information garnered from the cards that is usually ignored by students. The process and the type of information will aid effectiveness in research.

4. Missing from this selection of cards are the guide cards found in drawers, cross reference cards, analytic cards, and the sheer quantity of cards in a drawer.

5. For this reason, we have put a simulated catalog card drawer application in Appendix B. There are pages of groupings of cards, and three lists of questions to use with them: an introductory, a reinforcement, and an evaluative. We suggest that using this simulation will aid the students in gaining confidence and proficiency.

6. After proficiency is gained with the application activities, finding items in the catalog in your school media center would be the next step.

CONCEPTS
• **Identification of the four general classifications of the library as fiction, nonfiction, reference and biography.**
• **Recognition that in the card catalog, all catalog cards for one book are exactly alike except for the first line which will indicate the type of card and will differentiate one card from among others.**
• **Recognition that all subject/topic cards will have first lines in capital letters.**
• **Understanding that the individual parts of a catalog card provide a great deal of information for the student in terms of furthering research.**
• **Recognition of many of the commonly used abbreviations found on the various types of catalog cards.**
• **Understanding that the most efficient and effective way to begin a search for book selection for research is through the appropriate use of the card catalog and not "at the stacks" randomly in the general area of the topic.**

VOCABULARY
access   network   pertinent   retrieve

OBJECTIVES

The student will:

1. Identify the four general classifications of the library as fiction, nonfiction, reference and biography.

2. Understand that in the card catalog, all catalog cards for one book are exactly alike except for the first line which will indicate the type of card and will differentiate one card from among others.

3. Understand that all subject/topic cards will have first lines in capital letters.

4. Understand that the individual parts of a catalog card provide a great deal of information for the student in terms of furthering research.

5. Recognize many of the commonly used abbreviations found on the various types of catalog cards.

6. Understand that the most efficient and effective way to begin a search for book selection for research is through the appropriate use of the card catalog and not "at the stacks" randomly in the general area of the topic.

MATERIAL NEEDED

Activity Sheets 15-a and 15-b and 15-b in optional student workbook. In addition, the pages of cards and the questions from Appendix B.

ACTIVITIES

1. Discuss the sample cards given in the text.

2. Ask for all information: publisher, pages, etc.

3. You might wish to make a transparency of Card Cluster #1 to point out various bits of information.

4. Assign all the activity sheets for homework or to be done in class.

EXTENDED ACTIVITIES

Using the same pages of card clusters from the text, ask these questions:

1. Why is the name John Steptoe in the tracings of the Adoff book?
2. On the card for the sound filmstrip series, what does the "mono" mean? What is the series title?
3. What is the series title for Mike Blanch's book?
4. Make a different subject card for Jim Haskins' book.
5. Try to discover what subject card would be made for James Baker's book?

Answers:

1. An illustrator card could be made just like the Abrams card for the Cebulash book.
2. "Mono" means monaural, not stereo cassette tape. The series title is the main entry: Ancient civilizations of North America.
3. History Eye-Witness is the series title and a card might be made for it although none is indicated in the tracings
4. BLUFORD, GUION would be on the top line instead of ASTRONAUTS-BIOGRAPHY. Otherwise everything else would be the same.
5. MAGIC is one subject heading that more than likely would be used. The *Sears List of Subject Headings* could be used with the students to arbitrate their answers.

116

Catalog Card Application

Accessing information, retrieving it, and using it are integral parts of research. Up to this point, we have focused on the sections of the media center, understanding the organizational systems of the media center, and understanding the catalog card and the card catalog.

A brief review of catalog information is necessary before beginning the catalog application. Pertinent parts of each card are highlighted. Note that the upper left hand corner of each card gives the media, classification, and author indication, thus forming an address of the book in the library, providing, of course, that you already know where the different parts of the library are.

Type of Card: <u>Title</u>

Classification:

Reference	REF
Nonfiction	909.07
Author's Indication	Pla

The Atlas of Medieval Man
Platt, Colin
    The Atlas of Medieval Man. Crescent
Books, NY, 1985
256 p, illus

Type of Card: <u>Author</u>

Classification:

Nonprint media	Kit
Biography	B
Name of subject	Columbus

Heimann, Susan
    Christopher Columbus; A visual
biography. Franklin Watts, NY, 1973.
57 p, illus
    6 copies of book + 2 cassette tapes + guide

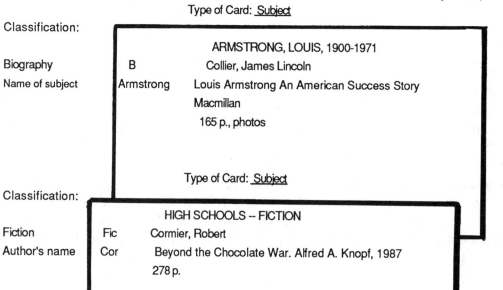

Type of Card: _Subject_

Classification:

ARMSTRONG, LOUIS, 1900-1971

Biography   B   Collier, James Lincoln

Name of subject   Armstrong   Louis Armstrong An American Success Story

Macmillan

165 p., photos

Type of Card: _Subject_

Classification:

HIGH SCHOOLS -- FICTION

Fiction   Fic   Cormier, Robert

Author's name   Cor   Beyond the Chocolate War. Alfred A. Knopf, 1987

278 p.

On the following pages are groupings of catalog cards, several clustered together in the order you would encounter them in a drawer. In applying the skills that have been learned, you will encounter the same type of problems you would face while working directly with the catalog. You will be using all five pages to answer the questions here in the samples and also in the activity sheets.

The numbers of the card groupings correspond to the question numbers which in turn correspond to the answer lines. Question #1 would refer to grouping or cluster #1 and the answer would be placed on line #1.

Try these samples together as a class: (The Card Cluster Grouping Pages referred to follow Activity 15-b.)

Card Cluster #1. How many pages does Nathan Aaseng's book have?

Card Cluster #2. Who is the author of <u>And Everything Nice</u>?

Card Cluster #3. What is the call number of Walter Buehr's book?

1. _____

2. _____

3. _____

Try these samples on your own:

Card Cluster #1. What would be two subject cards that could be made for Barbara Murphy's book?

Card Cluster #2. What is the title of Rebecca Anders' book?

Card Cluster #3. What is a subject heading for M. L'Engle's book?

1. _____ & _____

2. _____ 3. _____

Catalog Card Application

Use the card grouping clusters to answer 15-B, Questions 1-5; to answer 15-C, Questions 1-5; to answer 15-D, Questions 1-5 (Question 1 in each group refers to Cluster 1, Question 2 in each group refers to Cluster 2, and so on):

15-B
1. How many author cards are in this group?
2. Who do all these cards have in common?
3. What are the classifications of the two books on the Spanish Armada, 1588?
4. What is the individual title of the only nonprint media here?
5. What is the subtitle of *Settlers and strangers*?

15-C
1. Who is the publisher of *Ace hits the big time*?
2. Which book would probably tell you about Greek inventions?
3. What is the title of the book which won a Newbery Medal?
4. What is the only reference book in the cluster?
5. What type of fiction is *Seven spells to farewell*?

15-D
1. About whom is the biography written?
2. Who published Anne Millard's book?
3. There is no library classification call number on the Madeleine L'Engle book. You write a correct one.
4. Do you think that Guion Bluford agreed to his biography? State the reason for your answer.
5. Which of these books might be put in the reference section? Write the new call number as your answer.

Cluster #1

811.5
Ado   Adoff, Arnold.
         OUTside/INside Poems/by Arnold Adoff;
illustrated by John Steptoe. New York:
Lothrop, Lee and Shepard, ©1981.
         29p.: ill.

1.   Children's poetry, American [1.
America poetry] I. Steptoe, John II. Title

Ace hits the big time.

F   Murphy, Barbara.
MUR   Ace hits the big time / Barbara
         Beasley Murphy and Judie Wolkoff. -- New
         York: Delacorte. ©1981
            183 p.
            On the day he enters Kennedy High in
         Manhattan wearing a patch over one eye,
         sixteen-year-old Horace Hobart is urged
         to join the toughest gang at school.
            0-440-00299-0

1. Gangs - Fiction 2. New York (N.Y.)-
Fiction   I. Wolkoff, Judie. II. Title

Abrams, Edward

Fic   Cebulash, Mel.
CEB   Champion's jacket. Illus. by
         Edward Abrams. Creative Ed., 1978
            54p. illus.
            A young player examines his schoolyard
         friendships when he is offered a spot on
         an organized basketball team.

1. Basketball - Fiction 2. Friendship -
Fiction I.Abrams, Edward II. Title

B   Aaseng, Nathan
Geldof   Bob Geldof, the man behind Live
         Aid. Lerner Publications Co.,
         Minneapolis, MN, ©1986.
         32p. photographs

         Describes the early life, career,
         and charity work of the Irish
         singer-songwriter.

1. Geldof, Bob, 1952- . 2. Live Aid
(Fund raising enterprise). 3. Rock
musicians. I. Title

Cluster #2

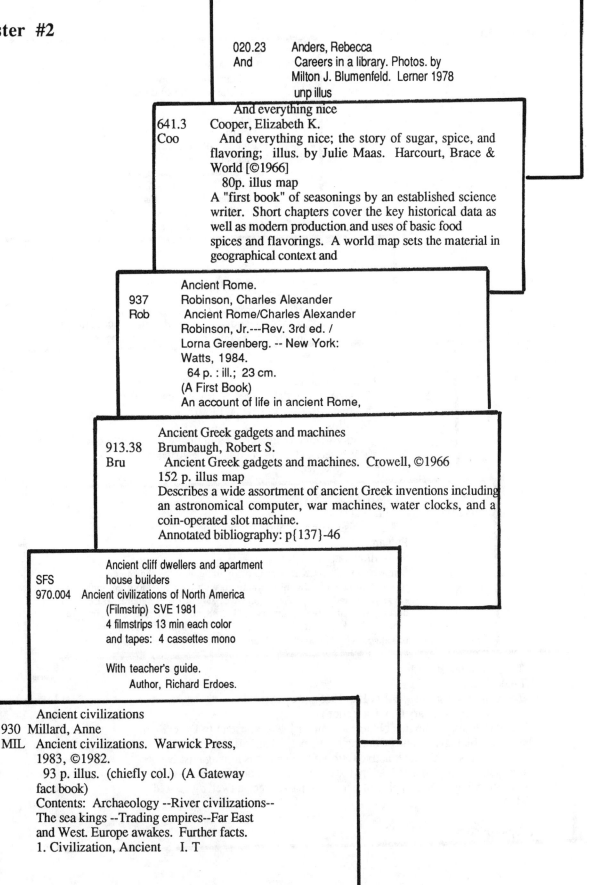

020.23 Anders, Rebecca
And Careers in a library. Photos. by
Milton J. Blumenfeld. Lerner 1978
unp illus

And everything nice
641.3 Cooper, Elizabeth K.
Coo And everything nice; the story of sugar, spice, and
flavoring; illus. by Julie Maas. Harcourt, Brace &
World [©1966]
80p. illus map
A "first book" of seasonings by an established science
writer. Short chapters cover the key historical data as
well as modern production and uses of basic food
spices and flavorings. A world map sets the material in
geographical context and

Ancient Rome.
937 Robinson, Charles Alexander
Rob Ancient Rome/Charles Alexander
Robinson, Jr.---Rev. 3rd ed. /
Lorna Greenberg. -- New York:
Watts, 1984.
64 p. : ill.; 23 cm.
(A First Book)
An account of life in ancient Rome,

Ancient Greek gadgets and machines
913.38 Brumbaugh, Robert S.
Bru Ancient Greek gadgets and machines. Crowell, ©1966
152 p. illus map
Describes a wide assortment of ancient Greek inventions including
an astronomical computer, war machines, water clocks, and a
coin-operated slot machine.
Annotated bibliography: p{137}-46

Ancient cliff dwellers and apartment
SFS house builders
970.004 Ancient civilizations of North America
(Filmstrip) SVE 1981
4 filmstrips 13 min each color
and tapes: 4 cassettes mono

With teacher's guide.
Author, Richard Erdoes.

Ancient civilizations
930 Millard, Anne
MIL Ancient civilizations. Warwick Press,
1983, ©1982.
93 p. illus. (chiefly col.) (A Gateway
fact book)
Contents: Archaeology --River civilizations--
The sea kings --Trading empires--Far East
and West. Europe awakes. Further facts.
1. Civilization, Ancient I. T

Cluster #3

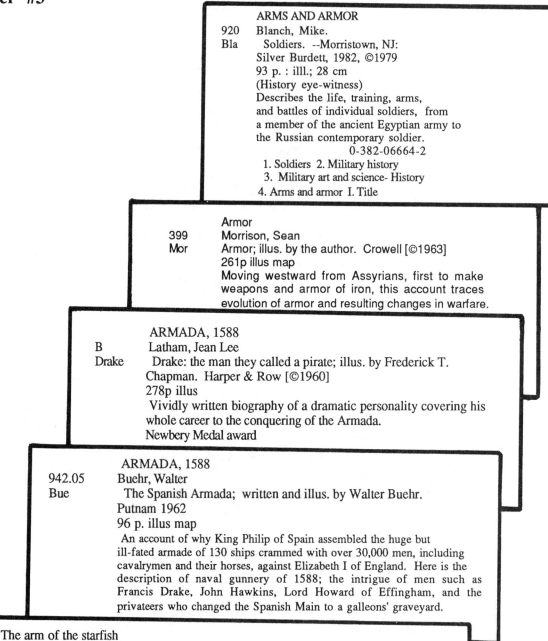

ARMS AND ARMOR
920   Blanch, Mike.
Bla   Soldiers. --Morristown, NJ:
       Silver Burdett, 1982, ©1979
       93 p. : illl.; 28 cm
       (History eye-witness)
       Describes the life, training, arms,
       and battles of individual soldiers, from
       a member of the ancient Egyptian army to
       the Russian contemporary soldier.
                    0-382-06664-2
          1. Soldiers 2. Military history
             3. Military art and science- History
             4. Arms and armor I. Title

           Armor
399   Morrison, Sean
Mor   Armor; illus. by the author. Crowell [©1963]
       261p illus map
       Moving westward from Assyrians, first to make
       weapons and armor of iron, this account traces
       evolution of armor and resulting changes in warfare.

           ARMADA, 1588
B   Latham, Jean Lee
Drake   Drake: the man they called a pirate; illus. by Frederick T.
       Chapman. Harper & Row [©1960]
       278p illus
        Vividly written biography of a dramatic personality covering his
       whole career to the conquering of the Armada.
       Newbery Medal award

           ARMADA, 1588
942.05 Buehr, Walter
Bue   The Spanish Armada; written and illus. by Walter Buehr.
       Putnam 1962
       96 p. illus map
        An account of why King Philip of Spain assembled the huge but
       ill-fated armade of 130 ships crammed with over 30,000 men, including
       cavalrymen and their horses, against Elizabeth I of England. Here is the
       description of naval gunnery of 1588; the intrigue of men such as
       Francis Drake, John Hawkins, Lord Howard of Effingham, and the
       privateers who changed the Spanish Main to a galleons' graveyard.

    The arm of the starfish
  L'Engle, Madeleine
    The arm of the starfish. Ariel Bks 1965
  243 p. (A Junior Literary Guild selection)
    Young Adam Eddington obtains a summer job as assistant to Dr. O'Keefe,
  the marine biologist, who is working on a small island off the coast of
  Portugal. In New York, attractive Carolyn Cutter warns him against two
  passengers on his plane, and before the day has passed ominous events take
  place, including the kidnapping of one of the passengers, a twelve-year-old
  girl.

    1. Spies-Fiction   I. Title

Cluster #4

ASTRONOMERS
REF.
920   The biographical Dictionary of Scientists.
Bio   General Editor: David Abbot, PhD.
        Peter Bedrick Books, NY ©1984.

ASTRONAUTS (CHALLENGER)
629.4 Cohen, Daniel
Coh   Heroes of The Challenger. Archway
          Paperbacks, NY, ©1986
          115p photographs (paperback)

ASTRONAUTS--BIOGRAPHY
B   Haskins, Jim
Bluford   Space challenger; the story of Guion
              Bluford; an authorized biography, by
          Jim Haskins and Kathleen Benson.
          Carolrhoda 1984
          64p illus

ASSASSINATION--LINCOLN, ABRAHAM--
VT   PRESIDENT U.S.
973.7 The Lincoln Conspiracy (Video
Lin   Tape). #R-925 - Starring Bradford
          Dillman; John Dehner & John

ARTISTS' MATERIALS - DICTIONARIES
741.2 Zaidenberg, Arthur
Zai   Dictionary of drawing. Bonanza
          Books, NY, © 1983
          np
          Terms & techniques concisely define

ARTISTS--PORTRAITS
704.94 Lerner, Sharon
Ler   The self-portrait in art; designed by Robert Clark Nel-
          son. Lerner Publications ©1965
          64p ports
          The artist speaks through portraits of the face he knows best--
          his own. The text of this volume is a guide to an understanding
          of style and technique. Biographical material gives an insight into the
          personality of each artist and helps the viewer interpret the self-

ARTILLERY
358 Gander, Terry
Gan Artillery. Illus. by Tony Gibbons,
      Peter Sarson [and] Tony Bryan. Lerner
      1987
      48p illus
        Surveys modern artillery in military
      use, including towed and self-propelled
      guns, rockets, ammunition, and associated
      equipment.
      1. Ordnance 2. Artillery I. Title

Cluster #5

BAKER, JOHN
B Buchanan, William
Baker A shining season.

793.8 Baker, James W
Bak Illusions illustrated; a professional
magic show for young performers.
Drawings by Jeanette Swofford. Photos.
by Carter M. Ayres. Lerner 1983
 120p illus
 A description of ten illusions that
make up a complete magic show with

629.4 Baker, David PhD.
Bak The Rocket. The history and development
of rocket & missile technology. Crown Pub.
NY ©1978.
 276p. illus
Summary: The history and development
of rockets and missiles, includes 350

Fic Baker, Betty.
Bak Seven spells to farewell. Macmillan, ©1982.
 123p
 On a long journey to find the kingdom of Iskany and
become a sorceress, a resourceful girl shares adventures
and magic with a talking raven and a performing pig.

970.4 Baker, Betty
Bak Settlers and strangers; native Americans of the desert
Southwest and history as they saw it. Macmillan, ©1977.
88p. illus., map, photos
 A history of the Indians who have lived in the American
Southwest from the Ice Age to the present day, told from
their point of view.
1. Indians of North American--Southwest, New ---History.
 I. Title

Draw in the Canadian border and the Canadian provinces. Check with an atlas to correct your drawings. Name the provinces. Which states border Lake Michigan? Which states border Lake Erie? Which states border Lake Huron? Which states border Lake Superior? Which state is divided by a Great Lake? Which states border Canada? Which provinces border this region?

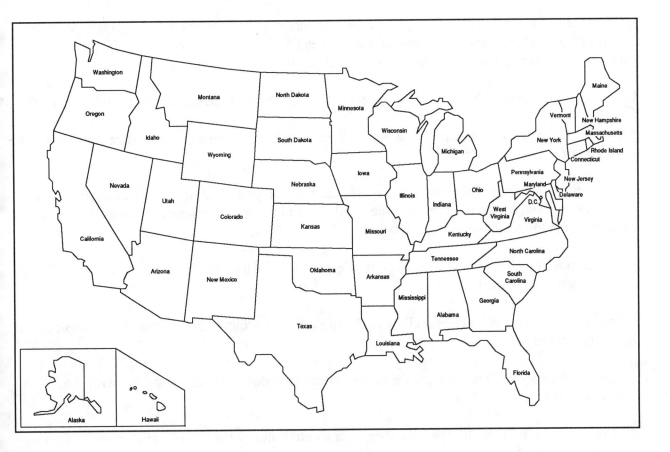

The North Central Region of the United States

Ohio = OH	WI = Wisconsin
Michigan = MI	MN = Minnesota
Iowa = IO	IL = Illinois
Indiana = IN	MO = Missouri
North Dakota = ND	SD = South Dakota
Nebraska = NE	KS = Kansas

Unit IV Activity   **The North Central Region of the U. S.**

1. Make a mobile of the states in the North Central region with state flowers, state birds, and/or state mottos. This can be drawn or written.

2. Construct a chart in grid form with the names of the states in the North Central region across the top and all lakes, rivers, waterways down the side. Develop a key and place symbols where they apply on the chart.

3. Draw the basic configuration map of your media center, placing reference, biography, nonfiction, fiction sections. Using the catalog, find all subject heading references for one state. Place symbols on your library map for all book and media shelf locations that you found.

4. Compare and contrast the daily life of a person in your chosen state in 1820 and another in 1990.

5. Create a magazine with articles and advertisements extolling the virtues of one state from the North Central region.

6. Develop six questions to be used as a class project. Student groups, taking one state each, will answer the questions about a specific state from the North Central region. Compare and contrast the answers for all states in the region on a bulletin board.

7. Chronologically arrange events in the North Central area that took place before entry into the Union. Construct with state time lines.

8. Construct a diorama of an historically significant event that occurred in the state of your choice from the North Central region.

9. Create a class book of interesting information about the region. Include interviews with people who have visited the area.

10. Construct a puzzle of the states in the North Central area using photocopied maps and contact adhesive paper.

11. After having studied an important person from your chosen state, place a short biography with photograph on a bulletin board map, according to birth place, area where person was influential, residence, or place of death.

Unit V Utilization of Sources

Utilization of Sources
Parts of a Nonfiction Book

FOCUS
Recognition of the parts of a book and uses of the parts of a book.

TEACHER PREPARATION
1. Review the information in the student activities.
2. Review any of the textbooks the students use to see which would make a good example. Ask that the students bring that particular book to class. Fill in title of that book on the activity sheet 16-b if you intend to reproduce it. If you do, that reproduced activity sheet can be done in class, and you may assign, if necessary for additional practice the activity sheet to be done again with another text book.
3. Complete the activity sheets; keep for handy classroom reference.

BACKGROUND INFORMATION
1. A lesson on parts of a book really helps the student understand all about a book; and in understanding, the student will be better able to use any nonfiction book.
2. Practice in using the index and cross references.
3. Get in the habit of having students do bibliographic citations on all reports, even book reports. We have included a generic bibliographic form. The students should know that the required form changes from school to school, and sometimes from instructor to instructor. They should also know that the citation form is not a listing, but is written on one line until the end of the line, then indented on the second and third.

CONCEPTS
• **Recognition and understanding of the parts of a book.**
• **Understanding the interrelationship of the parts of a book and the purpose of the research process.**
• **Recognition and use of the cross reference indicators:** *see* and *see also*.
• **Identification of the purpose of punctuation as used in an index.**

VOCABULARY
medium   spine/binding   appendix   acknowledgement   compiler   copyright   editor   frontispiece   glossary   illustrator   preface   table of contents   bibliographic citation

OBJECTIVES
The student will understand:
1. That once book selection for research has been made, that only through the appropriate use of a book's index will the student be provided with all the necessary pages concerning information in that book on a given topic in order to achieve optimum information retrieval.

2. That a book is a collection of pages bound or fastened on one side by a spine or a binding and is encased between two protective covers which in turn may also be protected by a dust cover.

3. That a nonfiction book, specifically a reference book or a content area book, is structured in an organized way to support reader comprehension.

4. That the general parts of a book to consist of: a title page; copyright page; table of contents; an introduction, foreword or preface; a body or text; an appendix; an index; a glossary; a bibliography; and an acknowledgement.

5. That the title of a book is the main idea or focus of the book.

6. That a title page includes a simple or descriptive title, name of the author, editor or compiler,

illustrator or photographer, publisher and place of publication.

7. That the copyright page includes the date of publication and owner of the copyright.

8. That the preface, foreword, or introduction of the book gives a general statement of the book's focus or theme.

9. That the table of contents reveals the organization of the parts of a book and is paginated in sequence.

10. That the table of contents indicates the divisions of sections to units to chapters and that all are titled.

11. That the body or text of the book contains a narrative explanation supportive of the general theme as set forth in the preface or foreword.

12. That the appendix of a book contains those visual aids which provide a knowledge that generally expands or gives background to the information as it is presented in the text.

13. The glossary to be a specialized dictionary of words specifically associated with the content of the book and that the words are defined in terms of their context as used in the book.

14. That the index of a book contains an alphabetical listing of topics, subtopics, and details. The topics are against the margin alphabetically, the subtopics and alphabetized and indented from the margin under the corresponding topic.

15. That a word is found more quickly through the use of the guide words when using the glossary.

16. That in an index, a comma between numbers (6,8) indicates two separate pages where a hyphen between numbers (12-16) indicates that those two pages and all the pages between are included and that a semicolon (;) separates topics and that a colon (:) indicates a list or separates entry word from the rest of the entry.

17. That the cross reference indicators are *see* and *see also* and that the same rules apply as in the card catalog and encyclopedia.

18. And identify a bibliography as a list of books or articles at the end of a book indicating an author's source.

19. That an author has written original material based on research while an editor or compiler brings others' written work into a collected form such as in a book or an encyclopedia.

20. That an illustrator is given credit for the drawings in a book, a photographer is given credit for photographs and a cartographer receives credit for the maps.

21. That visual aids may be borrowed with permission and original sources are given credit on an acknowledgement page.

MATERIALS NEEDED
Activity Sheets 16-a through 16-b and 16-b in optional student workbook.

ACTIVITIES
1. Read through and discuss the material focusing on using each of the parts as an efficient and effective part of research.
2. Having the same student text in hand, have students find the different parts of a book.
3. Use the context questions indicated by the Stop Sign as class participation or homework.

EXTENDED ACTIVITIES
1. Have a student or group of students make a display of books that have been personalized and autographed by the author.
2. Have a student or group of students make a display of books that have been cited in the acknowledgements or permissions of another book.

The Parts of a Nonfiction Book

In research, the principle medium of information is a book format, specifically nonfiction or reference. Once you have retrieved an appropriate book that is suitable to the purpose of an assignment, you must be prepared to use the parts of the book to locate the specific information needed to support the general purpose of the assignment. Appropriateness means: Are you able to read it? Is it about the Revolution and not the Civil War? Is it nonfiction and not a story? Suitable to the purpose of the assignment means: If what you need are the outcomes of the Revolution, the book on the reasons that the Revolution took place will not be suitable.

In a library setting a book is retrieved according to information as it appears on its spine or binding. Similar information will be found on the front or back cover of the book. Many times a book is covered with a dust cover or dustjacket to keep it clean. Upon opening a selected book or volume, the first page of print to which you will be exposed will be the title page. The title page contains the title, author, illustrator(if given), publisher(company that prints the book), and place of publication of the book. Sometimes instead of an author, the name or names of an editor or compiler might be given. To differentiate between the roles of the author and the editor/compiler, you should realize that an author has written original material based on his/her personal research while an editor/compiler brings the written works of others into collected forms such as in an encyclopedia.

In a nonfiction book, an illustrator is given credit for the drawings or illustrations in a book, a photographer is given credit for the photographs while a cartographer receives credit for the maps. The author or editor must obtain permission from his/her respective sources before using another person's work as a visual aid to support the body or text. This credit is usually presented on the acknowledgement page found in the back or in the front of the text.

Opposite the title page, many books offer a frontispiece which is an ornamental illustration, copy or picture. Not all books have a frontispiece. Directly behind the title page is the copyright page which provides the year or years in which the book was copyrighted and/or published. It also gives the owner of the copyright. The copyright page basically provides a history of the book up to the latest date of publication. From the title page and copyright page, you will be able to construct a bibliographic citation for the book.

1. What information can be found on a title page?
2. Explain the difference between an editor and an author.
3. A photographer, cartographer and illustrator provide what types of visuals?

4. What is the purpose of the acknowledgement page and of a copyright?

Often, following the copyright page is a preface, known as a foreword or introduction. Its purpose is to state the general theme or purpose of the book. The theme contained in the preface then will be fully developed in a written narrative form in the body or text portion of the book. The student should remember that there is a direct relationship among the title, preface and text of the book. A descriptive title states the main idea of the book, the preface states the book's theme or purpose, and the text or body of the book is a written and detailed explanation of both theme and purpose.

Still another section of a book is the table of contents. This provides you with an overview of the general information as presented in the text. It details in outline form the major topics and subtopics of the text through the headings and subheadings of the sections, units and chapters of the book. It also provides the corresponding page numbers, presented in number sequence. Also included in the table of contents will be the parts of the book other than the written text such as the glossary, atlas, appendix and index listed by corresponding page numbers as they appear in the text.

As mentioned before, in the text, the author develops his/her theme through the specific written discussion of topics and subtopics concerning the theme or message that he or she is presenting to you, the reader. It is important to note that very often the main idea or topics will be detailed by way of the headings of the sections, units or chapters: The bolder and larger the print, the more important the information.

A glossary is another section of a book. A glossary, alphabetical in organization by entry word, is a specialized dictionary that presents a simplified entry in terms of definitions presented. It focuses only on those definitions or meanings necessary to the specific understanding of the words as they are used in context in the book's text. In this way, you don't have to sift through the multiple meanings of a word as presented in a regular dictionary. In a glossary only those definitions that pertain to the word as it is used in context in the text are provided. You benefit in terms of time efficiency when working in a content area to use the book's glossary first when seeking a definition. If the word cannot be found in the glossary, you should turn to the dictionary as an alternative source.

As in a dictionary, the quickest way to locate an entry word in a glossary is through the use of guide words as found at the top of each page. The guide words are also the first and last words found on a page in a dictionary or a glossary.

Another section of a book is the atlas. The purpose of the atlas is to provide important maps which are necessary visual aids that are supportive of the geographic concepts as presented in the text. Very often, an author will provide extra maps that do not necessarily correspond to the text but provide general geographic understandings that are necessary to your knowledge to be an informed person of the day. An atlas is a very useful study skills tool.

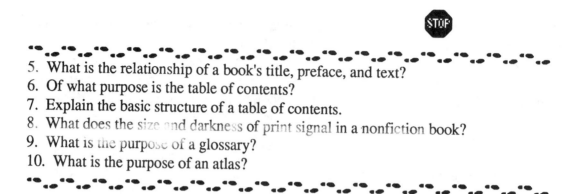

5. What is the relationship of a book's title, preface, and text?
6. Of what purpose is the table of contents?
7. Explain the basic structure of a table of contents.
8. What does the size and darkness of print signal in a nonfiction book?
9. What is the purpose of a glossary?
10. What is the purpose of an atlas?

Most nonfiction books will have at least one appendix. The appendix will provide extra materials of interest and information that will supply you with a general background of knowledge. Many of the basic ideas will not necessarily relate directly to the text. But, as in the atlas, the purpose is to present those general concepts supportive of a well-rounded, knowledgeable student: YOU.

In terms of effective usage, the index is one of the most important sections of a book to you as a researcher. Through the correct use of an index, you will be able to pinpoint exact chapters or pages dealing with your research topic. In order to do this, you must be able to generate multiple keywords or entry words and be able to use the cross references(*see; see also*) provided by the author.

The index, itself, is alphabetically organized first by topic then by subtopic. The topics are usually in bold print and are placed against the left margin. The cluster of subtopics are indented throughout the rest of the entry either in a vertical or horizontal pattern depending on the format of the index.

See examples:
Vertical pattern(*The World Book*)
Yellow Sea Y:559
   Huang He **H:389**
   Korea(The Land)**K:372** *with map-*

Horizontal pattern(*Collier's*)
Yellow Sea, sea, Asia **23-**
   691-a; 18-277b
--Maps **3**-Asia; **6**-China; **18-**
Pacific Ocean; **22**-U.S.S.R.
(Russia); **23**- World

Reprinted with permission, The World Book Encyclopedia, ©1989.

Permission of Macmillan,©1988

Since an index is always in alphabetical order, it is important that you identify the structure of the alphabetical order used as either word-by-word or letter-by-letter:

See examples:
Letter-by-letter
(Ignore spaces.)

Word-by-word
(Same first words are clustered.)

New Amsterdam
Newark
New Bedford
New Bern
Newbold
New Britain
Newburgh

New York
New Yorker
Newark
Newars
Newberry
Newbold
Newburgh

It is also important that you possess an understanding of the punctuation as found in an index entry. In an index, a comma between numbers (6,8) indicates two separate pages where a hyphen between numbers (12-16) indicates that those two pages and all the pages in between the two numbers of 12 and 16 are included. In some books the physical format of an index is of a vertical listing of topics and subtopics, though, many indices have horizontally structured entries.

In a horizontally structured entry a semicolon (;) separates topics while a colon (:) indicates a list or separates the entry from the rest of the entry. Review the examples that were listed under vertical and horizontal patterns.

You should also be aware that many entries will possess the cross reference indicators: *See* or *See also*. The purpose of the cross reference indicators are to support you in furthering your research in terms of providing you with other key words. The same rules apply to the words *see* and *see also* in a nonfiction index as they do in the card catalog or the index volume of a set of encyclopedia. The word *see* following an entry word indicates that the key word is not valid for the index. Others that are valid are provided for your use. The words *see also* indicate that while the located entry word is valid, if further information is required, other appropriate key words are also provided for your convenience. It is also suggested that you use the key words suggested by the author or editor of the book or series as well as your own generated list.

To use an index of any book, you should : (1) know a topic word, and, of course, multiple keywords for that topic word; (2) comprehend cross referencing; and (3) possess an understanding of the two types of alphabetizing.

A bibliography is also included in many nonfiction books. A bibliography is a listing books concerning a specific topic, subject or theme. It provides the necessary information in each bibliographic entry as to support the actual physical retrieval of the book represented by the entry. This assumes a parallel use of the card catalog. A bibliography also gives you an opportunity to check the author's sources in terms of expertise, if so desired.

One of the last pages in a nonfiction book will be the acknowledgement page where the author gives credit to other authors, illustrators, cartographers as well as others for the use of the various materials included in the book.

In all, a good understanding of the effective use of the parts of a nonfiction book will support a more time efficient approach to research as well as a lifetime of learning.

11. What is the importance of the appendix?
12. Of what use is the index?
13. Explain the basic structure of an index.
14. Explain the various types of punctuation found in an entry.
15. Explain cross referencing in an index.
16. What is the difference in the meanings of *see* and *see also*?
17. What is a bibliography and how can it be used in research?

The Parts of a Nonfiction Book

I. Title Page
    The title of the textbook
    Author
    Editor, compiler
    Illustrator, photographer
    Publisher
    Place of publication

II. Copyright page
    Date of copyright
    Owner of copyright
    Printing history

III. Acknowledgements   page

IV. Table of Contents   _____how many pages?

V. Introduction   _____Yes   _____No
           _____Page number

VI. Body Page_____to Page_____

VII. Appendix Page_____to Page_____
    Contents of Appendix_____

VIII. Index Page_____to Page_____

IX. Glossary Page_____to Page_____

X. Bibliography Page_____to Page_____

Bibliographic Citation:
    Author's Last Name, Author's First Name.   <u>Title</u>.   Place of Publication:
    Publisher, Copyright Date.

17

The Encyclopedia

FOCUS
This lesson will focus on the use of the encyclopedia.

TEACHER PREPARATION
1. Vocabulary first: Encyclopedia is a book or series of books with information on general topics or limited to specific topics. Encyclopedias is an acceptable plural. Index is an alphabetical arrangement of information. Both indexes and indices are acceptable plurals.

2. Find out what general encyclopedias are in the library in your school and how they are arranged.

3. Find out what specific encyclopedias are in your library and how they are arranged.

4. See what other encyclopedias the students have access to in the public library and prepare the students for using those also.

BACKGROUND INFORMATION
1. The library community uses reviews from *Booklist*, which contains Reference Books Bulletin; *Reference Quarterly*, known as *RQ*; *Library Journal*, and many others also, to ascertain the quality of new editions. Borrow a couple of the reviewing journals and read some reviews. You might also wish to share some some with the class.

2. Some general encyclopedias are *The World Book Encyclopedia*, *The New Book of Knowledge*, *Collier's Encyclopedia*, *Academic American Encyclopedia*, and *Merit Students Encyclopedia*. You might also find an encyclopedia printed in German, Spanish, or another language.

3. Some specialized subject encyclopedias are the *Encyclopedia of Human Evolution and Prehistory*; *Van Nostrand's Encyclopedia of Science*; *Encyclopedia of Science and Technology*.

CONCEPTS
- **An encyclopedia is comprised of one or more books or volumes.**
- **An encyclopedia could be general or specific.**
- **An encyclopedia might be ordered in three ways: alphabetical, chronological, or topical.**

VOCABULARY
encyclopedia volume spine alphabetically numerically topically format comprehensive bibliography

OBJECTIVES
The student will understand that :

1. An encyclopedia is comprised of one or more books or volumes containing information about people, places, things, or events. It may include general topics from a wide field of knowledge or may concentrate on reviewing one specific area in depth.

2. An encyclopedia is a set of volumes whose spines are alphabetically and/or numerically ordered when placed on a shelf.

3. An encyclopedia is the work of a great many people who are considered experts in the field in which

they are writing and their articles are compiled into volume format by an editor.

4. There are three types of encyclopedias: alphabetically ordered (A-Z); topically ordered (by author/editor/compiler's chosen order); or chronologically ordered (by time period, by year, by time era).

5. Most general encyclopedias which cover a wide range of topics are usually alphabetically ordered, while many specific topic encyclopedias are chronologically and/or topically ordered.

6. A combination of organizations are found in some encyclopedias, such the *Encyclopedia of American History* by Morris, in that it is chronological, then topical, then alphabetical in its biography section.

7. No matter how general the encyclopedia, it cannot contain all the information on any given subject, and that therefore the editors provide comprehensive bibliographies to suggest sources for further research.

9. The encyclopedia is a good starting point for research in that it will provide an overview of a topic and generate key words in text and through cross referencing.

10. Through the understanding of a general overview of a topic a student will be better prepared to narrow or expand a topic to research.

MATERIAL NEEDED
Activity Sheets 17-a.

ACTIVITIES
1. Read through Activity 17-a together in class.
2. Discuss various examples that you have brought to class or bring the class to the IMC and discuss the specific encyclopedias.
3. Arrange several encyclopedias on a table open to various visual aids in them: transparencies, diagrams, etc.
4. Let the students categorize and make lists of the various kinds of encyclopedias: all science encyclopedias, all encyclopedias that are broken alphabetically on the spine, etc.

EXTENDED ACTIVITIES
1. Perhaps a student might make an inventory of specific subject encyclopedias and how they are arranged.
2. Permit another student to make a bulletin board listing of specialized information necessary for different subjects that are available in different encyclopedias.

The Encyclopedia

An encyclopedia is a reference book made up of one or more volumes that contain information about people, places or events. It may include general topics from a wide field of knowledge or it may concentrate on reviewing one specific area in depth. The spine of each book or volume is alphabetically and/or numerically ordered when placed on a shelf. In an alphabetically ordered set of encyclopedias, volumes are marked with one letter such as "J" and all articles whose titles begin with that letter will be contained in that book. Some letters, though, represent too many articles to be placed in one book so the one volume is split into two. When this happens, the volume markings also are split. For example, one volume might be marked **C-Ch** and the other will be marked **Ci - Cz**. Some encyclopedias have an equal number of pages in each volume and the spine letters reflect the first and last entries: **Columbus - Descartes.**

The various articles are written by a great many people who are considered experts in the specific field in which they are writing. All of the articles written by each expert are pulled together into volume format by an editor. The editor also determines the encyclopedia's format according to his purpose. Encyclopedias are usually one of three basic types of organizations. They can by 1) alphabetically ordered (A-Z); 2) topically ordered (editor or author's chosen topic order); or 3) chronologically ordered (by time period, by year or time era). Most general encyclopedias, which cover a wide range of topics, are alphabetically ordered, though some encyclopedias dealing with specific topics are chronologically or topically ordered. Also, some encyclopedias are comprised of a combination of two or three of the organizations depending on their purpose.

It is important that you understand that no matter how general the encyclopedia, it can not contain all the information on a given subject. The editors, therefore, provide comprehensive bibliographies to suggest sources for further research. Still, though, the encyclopedia is a good starting point for research in that it will provide an overview of a topic and this, in turn, will help you to narrow or expand a chosen subject. It also will help you to generate other key words to help further your research.

1. What type of information is contained in an encyclopedia?
2. Name and explain the three basic types of formats used in the organization of encyclopedias.
3. Who writes the articles in an encyclopedia?
4. Why is it important to use the bibliography that often appears at the end of an article in an encyclopedia?
5. How might an encyclopedia help the student researcher?

The Encyclopedia Index
The Encyclopedia Article

FOCUS

This lesson is intended to help the student use the index of the encyclopedia and understand the basic format of an article.

TEACHER PREPARATION

1. Read material thoroughly.
2. Look over the indexes for all the encyclopedias.
3. Have examples of various encyclopedia indexes available for students to peruse.
4. Have specific science encyclopedia index and general encyclopedia index open to same scientific term. Show the similarities and differences.

BACKGROUND INFORMATION

1. We firmly believe in allowing and encouraging the student to read a comprehensive article in the encyclopedia on his/her topic before beginning research. We like to use the encyclopedia article as a starting point so that the student can obtain a working field of knowledge.
2. We feel mastery of the encyclopedia index will pave the way for understanding the efficient use of all types of indexes.
3. It's good practice for students to use bibliographic citation for encyclopedia articles. It guides them to look for signed articles.
4. Tell students that some encyclopedias have a one volume index for all volumes of the set while others have an index at the back of each volume plus a cumulative index.

CONCEPTS

- **Understanding of an encyclopedia index.**
- **Understanding of topics and subtopics in an index.**
- **Understanding of the part punctuation plays in an index.**
- **Understanding the effective use of encyclopedia article.**

VOCABULARY

encyclopedia alphabetical topical chronological index separate topic subtopic detail punctuation vertical horizontal format subheading heading signed unsigned visual legend spine cross reference

OBJECTIVES

The student will understand that:

1. An index in an encyclopedia may be found at the end of each volume or may be a separate volume index and will afford the most effective way to cross reference among volumes or to achieve information retrieval.

2. The index will provide volume numbers as well as page numbers for topics, subtopics, and details.

3. The punctuation and structure of an index in an encyclopedia are the same for any index in that a comma between two numbers indicates two separate pages (6,9) and a hyphen (6-9) would indicate the

two pages and all the pages between, a semicolon (;) often separates topics and a colon (:) often follows an entry word.

4. In an encyclopedia index, the index structure will present the entry topic word at the margin and the subtopics will be vertically listed alphabetically or presented horizontally and alphabetically separated by semicolons.

5. Each entry word in an index is expanded in narrative form on the corresponding pages indicated in a specific volume and that written explanations also known as an entry or article.

6. All entries have a simple or a descriptive title which helps the reader to identify the main idea or focus of the article.

7. Each article is divided by headings and subheadings which directly correspond to main topics, subtopics and supporting details.

8. Differentiation among topic, subtopic, and detail is indicated through the use of various size print in that the larger the print, the more important the information.

9. Guide words are found at the top of each page in the encyclopedia and they represent the first and last entries on the page and are used to rapidly find an entry in an alphabetically ordered encyclopedia.

10. The use of multiple key words in researching a specific topic or subject is important.

11. When the name of the author appears at the end of an article, it is known as "signed," but when no name appears it is known as "unsigned."

12. The visual aids presented in an encyclopedia text are to help the reader comprehend the written word and are not there for entertainment value.

MATERIAL NEEDED
Activity Sheets 18-a through 18-d and 18-b through 18-d in optional student workbook.

ACTIVITIES
1. Read through Activity 18-a and answer discussion questions. After reading, give each student 18-b and 18-c, which are pages from encyclopedia indexes with questions. Assign or do together orally. At this point, you may wish to have each student peruse some of the indexes you've brought to class.
2. Do Activity 18-d which consists of a series of questions corresponding to a page from an encyclopedia. Point out cross references and "signatures" of the articles' authors.

EXTENDED ACTIVITIES
1. Let students compare and contrast same topic in different encyclopedias which have been prepared for different focus and different audiences.
2. Let students do the same with an electronic encyclopedia.

The Encyclopedia Index

The most important volume in any set of encyclopedias, whether alphabetically, topically or chronologically organized, is the index. The index is usually a separate volume and, as in a nonfiction book, the index is alphabetically ordered by entry word or key word. Each entry word, in turn, begins a full entry which will provide volume numbers, page numbers, and cross references for each specific topic, subtopic or detail. The punctuation in the index of an encyclopedia is the same and has the same meaning as the punctuation in any index. The index can also be of a vertical or horizontal format and can be either letter-by-letter or word-by-word alphabetically ordered. The cross references also will be indicated by the terms *see* and *see also*.

When you select an appropriate entry word in an encyclopedia index for your topic, you should retrieve the correct volume by letter as indicated in the entry. Then turn to the correct page(s) as also presented in the entry. In the appropriate volume, on the correct page, you will find the entry or subject expanded in narrative form as a written explanation known as an article. (For explanation of punctuation, types of alphabetizing, index format, cross reference in an encyclopedia, see Lesson 16, Parts of a Nonfiction Book.)

1. Explain the organization of an index.
2. Explain the organization of an entry in an index.
3. In which two formats might you find the entries in an index?
4. What is the importance of cross referencing and punctuation in an index?
5. Why is knowledge of the difference between word-by-word and letter-by-letter important?

The Encyclopedia Article

Each article is also known as an entry as it appears in an encyclopedia. Each article will begin with a simple or a descriptive title which, in turn, will identify the main idea or the focus of the article.

The article will be divided by headings and/or subheadings which will be supportive of the main topic under discussion. The main headings will be in bold dark print and the subheadings will be in a lighter print. In fact, the darker and bolder the print, the more important the information. The simple or descriptive title will be the largest in print size in the article. In some articles, at the end, the name of the article's author is given and this is known as a "signed" article. Where the name of the author does not appear, the article is considered unsigned.

As in a dictionary, an alphabetically organized encyclopedia has guide words at the top or bottom of the page to help you to find more efficiently the page on which a research topic is located. As in a dictionary, the guide words represent the first and last entries or articles on a page or page spread.

To help you comprehend the text, many encyclopedias offer visual aids such as maps, graphs, charts, tables, diagrams, time lines, fact summaries, transparencies, etc. Under each visual aid is a legend which is a word, phrase or sentence that connects or links the visual to the text. A visual is an illustrated example of the information that also is written in the text.

You, as a researcher, are offered still other options to further research through the bibliography and related articles which are found at the end of each article. These bibliographies have been constructed by the author of the article or the encyclopedia's editor.

6. What information does size of print and boldness of print give to you as a researcher when reading the encyclopedia?

7. What is the difference between a signed and unsigned article?

8. Of what importance are the guide words in an alphabetically organized encyclopedia. How does this relate to the spine of the volume?

9. Name some of the various types of visual aids that can be found in an encyclopedia.

10. What is a legend and what is its importance in terms of the encyclopedia text?

11. Why is a listing of related articles or a bibliography important to you as a student researcher?

The World Book Encyclopedia Index

1. What is referenced for sailing in a catamaran?

2. a. What is referenced for sailfish?

   b. Where could you find a picture of a sailfish?

3. What is referenced for Eva Marie Saint?

4. What is referenced for Sagebrush State?

5. What is referenced for Margaret Olivia Slocum Sage?

6. What is referenced for drought in the Sahel?

7. What is referenced for safety fuse?

8. What is referenced for sailplane?

9. What is referenced for the Sailor's Church?

10. What is referenced for relationship of saffron and crocus?

BENITO RIVER
 map (1° 35′N 9° 37′E) 7:226
BENJAMIN 3:201
BENJAMIN (Texas)
 map (33° 35′N 99° 48′W) 19:129
BENJAMIN, ASHER 3:201 bibliog.
BENJAMIN, JUDAH P. 3:201–202
 bibliog.
 Civil War, U.S. 5:31
 Confederate States of America
 5:176
BENJAMIN, WALTER 3:202 bibliog.
BENJAMIN OF TUDELA 3:202
BENKELMAN (Nebraska)
 map (40° 3′N 101° 32′W) 14:70
BENN, ANTHONY WEDGWOOD
 3:202
 Labour party 12:157
BENN, GOTTFRIED 3:202 bibliog.
BENNET (Nebraska)
 map (40° 41′N 96° 30′W) 14:70
BENNETT (county in South Dakota)
 map (43° 15′N 101° 40′W) 18:103
BENNETT, ARNOLD 4:202 bibliog.,
 illus.
 realism (literature) 16:104
BENNETT, FLOYD 3:202
BENNETT, JAMES GORDON 3:202–203
 bibliog., illus.
BENNETT, JAMES GORDON, JR. 3:203
 bibliog.
BENNETT, MICHAEL 3:203
**BENNETT, RICHARD BEDFORD,
 VISCOUNT BENNETT** 3:203
 bibliog., illus.
 Canada, history of 4:86
BENNETT, RICHARD DYER- see
 DYER-BENNETT, RICHARD
BENNETT, RICHARD RODNEY 3:203–
 204 bibliog.
 English music 7:204
BENNETT, WILLIAM 15:526 illus.
BENNETT, WILLIAM STERNDALE 3:204
BENNETTSVILLE (South Carolina)
 map (34° 37′N 79° 41′W) 18:98
BENNING, FORT (Georgia) see FORT
 BENNING (Georgia)
BENNINGTON (Kansas)
 map (39° 2′N 97° 36′W) 12:18
BENNINGTON (Vermont) 3:204
 map (42° 53′N 73° 12′W) 19:554
BENNINGTON (county in Vermont)
 map (43° 4′N 73° 7′W) 19:554
BENNINGTON, BATTLE OF
 American Revolution 1:360
 Bennington 3:204
 Green Mountain Boys 9:348
 Stark, John 18:227
BENNINGTON COLLEGE 3:204
 American Dance Festival 1:338
BENNY, JACK 3:204 bibliog.
BENOIS, ALEKSANDR NIKOLAYEVICH
 3:204 bibliog.
 Ballets Russes de Serge Diaghilev
 3:48
BENOIT (Mississippi)
 map (33° 39′N 91° 1′W) 13:469
BENOIT, JOAN 3:204
BENOÎT DE SAINTE-MORE 3:204
BENQUE VIEJO (Belize)
 map (17° 5′N 89° 8′W) 3:183
BENSLEY (Virginia)
 map (37° 26′N 77° 26′W) 19:607
BENSON (Arizona)
 map (31° 58′N 110° 18′W) 2:160
BENSON (Minnesota)
 map (45° 19′N 95° 36′W) 13:453
BENSON (North Carolina)
 map (35° 23′N 78° 33′W) 14:242
BENSON (county in North Dakota)
 map (48° 0′N 99° 20′W) 14:248
BENSON, GEORGE
 jazz 11:389 illus.
BENSON, MARY
 basket 11:140 illus.
BENT (county in Colorado)
 map (38° 0′N 103° 0′W) 5:116
BENT, CHARLES
 Mexican War 13:354
BENT, THEODORE
 Zimbabwe Ruins 20:367
BENT PYRAMID 15:635
 Dahshur 6:7
BENTEEN, FREDERICK A.
 Little Bighorn, Battle of the 12:372
BENTHAM, JEREMY 3:204–205 bibliog.,
 illus.
 law 12:242
 Mill, John Stuart 13:425
 socialism 18:20
 state (in political philosophy)
 18:229; 18:232
 utilitarianism 19:497
BENTHONIC ZONE 3:205 bibliog.
 abyssal zone 1:67

bathyal zone 3:123
 deep-sea life 6:78; 6:79
 foraminifera 8:219
 littoral zone 12:373
 ocean and sea 14:331
 oceanography 14:345
 paleoecology 15:34
BENTINCK (family) 3:205 bibliog.
BENTINCK, LORD GEORGE
 Bentinck (family) 3:205
**BENTINCK, LORD WILLIAM
 CAVENDISH**
 Bentinck (family) 3:205
**BENTINCK, WILLIAM, 1st EARL OF
 PORTLAND**
 Bentinck (family) 3:205
**BENTINCK, WILLIAM HENRY
 CAVENDISH, 3rd DUKE OF
 PORTLAND**
 Bentinck (family) 3:205
BENTLEY, ARTHUR
 state (in political philosophy)
 18:232–233
BENTLEY, ERIC 3:205
BENTLEY, RICHARD 3:205
BENTLEYVILLE (Pennsylvania)
 map (40° 7′N 80° 1′W) 15:147
BENTON (Arkansas)
 map (34° 34′N 92° 35′W) 2:166
BENTON (county in Arkansas)
 map (36° 20′N 94° 15′W) 2:166
BENTON (Illinois)
 map (38° 0′N 88° 55′W) 11:42
BENTON (county in Indiana)
 map (40° 37′N 87° 19′W) 11:111
BENTON (county in Iowa)
 map (42° 5′N 92° 5′W) 11:244
BENTON (Kentucky)
 map (36° 52′N 88° 21′W) 12:47
BENTON (Louisiana)
 map (32° 42′N 93° 44′W) 12:430
BENTON (county in Minnesota)
 map (45° 40′N 94° 0′W) 13:453
BENTON (county in Mississippi)
 map (34° 50′N 89° 10′W) 13:469
BENTON (Missouri)
 map (37° 6′N 89° 34′W) 13:476
BENTON (county in Missouri)
 map (38° 20′N 93° 20′W) 13:476
BENTON (county in Oregon)
 map (44° 30′N 123° 25′W) 14:427
BENTON (Pennsylvania)
 map (41° 12′N 76° 23′W) 15:147
BENTON (Tennessee)
 map (35° 10′N 84° 39′W) 19:104
BENTON (county in Tennessee)
 map (36° 5′N 88° 7′W) 19:104
BENTON (county in Washington)
 map (46° 15′N 119° 35′W) 20:35
BENTON (Wisconsin)
 map (42° 34′N 90° 23′W) 20:185
BENTON, THOMAS HART (painter)
 3:205–206 bibliog., illus.
 Jefferson City (Missouri) 11:393
 Threshing Wheat 3:205 illus.
BENTON, THOMAS HART (political
 leader) 3:206 bibliog.
BENTON CITY (Washington)
 map (46° 16′N 119° 29′W) 20:35
BENTON HARBOR (Michigan)
 map (42° 6′N 86° 27′W) 13:377
BENTONIA (Mississippi)
 map (32° 38′N 90° 22′W) 13:469
BENTONITE
 clay minerals 5:46–47
BENTONVILLE (Arkansas)
 map (36° 22′N 94° 13′W) 2:166
BENTSEN, LLOYD 3:206
BENTWOOD ROCKING CHAIR 8:379
 illus.
BENUE RIVER
 map (7° 48′N 6° 46′E) 14:190
 Nigeria 14:189
BENZ (automobile) 2:365 illus.
BENZ, KARL 3:206 bibliog.
BENZALDEHYDE 3:206
BENZALKONIUM CHLORIDE
 antiseptic 2:68
BENZEDRINE see AMPHETAMINE
BENZENE 3:206 bibliog., illus.
 aromatic compounds 2:186
 chemical bond 4:314 illus.
 derivatives: Baeyer, Adolf von
 3:20–21
 molecular structure
 Kekulé structure, organic
 chemistry 14:435 illus.
 Kekulé von Stradonitz, Friedrich
 August 12:37
 phase equilibrium 15:223 illus.
 phenyl group 15:226
 pollutants, chemical 15:410
BENZIE (county in Michigan)
 map (44° 40′N 86° 0′W) 13:377

BENZODIAZEPINES
 Librium 12:319
BENZOIC ACID 3:207
BENZYLPENICILLIN see PENICILLIN
BEOGRAD see BELGRADE (Yugoslavia)
BEOWAWE (Nevada)
 map (40° 35′N 116° 29′W) 14:111
BEOWULF (epic) 3:207 bibliog.
 Scandinavia, history of 17:108
BEQUEST see TRUST; WILL (law)
BÉRAIN, JEAN 3:207 bibliog.
BÉRANGER, PIERRE JEAN DE 3:207
BERAT (Albania)
 map (40° 42′N 19° 57′E) 1:250
BERBER LANGUAGES
 Afroasiatic languages 1:174–175
 map
BERBERA (Somalia)
 map (10° 25′N 45° 2′E) 18:60
BERBÉRATI (Central African Republic)
 map (4° 16′N 15° 47′E) 4:251
BERBERS 1:145 illus.; 3:207–208
 bibliog., illus.
 Abd el-Krim 1:54
 Almohads 1:306
 Almoravids 1:307
 Kabyle 12:4
 Libya 12:321
 Moorish art and architecture 13:570
 Morocco 13:586
 North Africa 14:224
 Tuareg 19:325–326
BERBICK, TREVOR
 Ali, Muhammad 1:292
BERCHEM, NICOLAES PIETERSZOON
 3:208 bibliog.
BERCHER, JEAN see DAUBERVAL, JEAN
BERCHTESGADEN (West Germany)
 3:208
BERCZY, WILLIAM 4:89
BERDYAYEV, NIKOLAI 3:208 bibliog.
BEREA (Kentucky)
 map (37° 34′N 84° 17′W) 12:47
BEREA (Ohio)
 map (41° 22′N 81° 52′W) 14:357
BEREA (South Carolina)
 map (34° 53′N 82° 28′W) 18:98
BEREA COLLEGE 3:208
BEREGOVOI, GEORGY T. 3:208
BEREKUM (Ghana)
 map (7° 27′N 2° 37′W) 9:164
BERENGAR OF TOURS 3:208
BERENICE 3:208
BERENS RIVER (Manitoba)
 map (52° 22′N 97° 2′W) 13:119
BERENSON, BERNARD 3:208 bibliog.
 Gardner Museum 9:45
BERESFORD (South Dakota)
 map (43° 5′N 96° 47′W) 18:103
BERESFORD, BRUCE
 film, history of 8:87
BERETTYÓ RIVER
 map (46° 59′N 21° 7′E) 10:307
BEREZNIKI (USSR)
 map (59° 24′N 56° 46′E) 19:388
BERG, ALBAN 3:208–209 bibliog., illus.
BERG EN DAL (Suriname)
 map (5° 9′N 55° 4′W) 18:364
BERGAMO (Italy) 3:209
 map (45° 41′N 9° 43′E) 11:321
BERGAMOT 3:209
 mint 13:461
BERGANZA, TERESA 3:209
BERGEN (Belgium) see MONS
 (Belgium)
BERGEN (county in New Jersey)
 map (40° 53′N 74° 3′W) 14:129
BERGEN (New York)
 map (43° 5′N 77° 57′W) 14:149
BERGEN (Norway) 3:209
 map (60° 23′N 5° 20′E) 14:261
BERGEN, CANDICE 3:209
**BERGEN, EDGAR, AND McCARTHY,
 CHARLIE** 3:209
BERGEN-BELSEN (West Germany) see
 BELSEN (West Germany)
BERGEN OP ZOOM (Netherlands)
 map (51° 30′N 4° 17′E) 14:99
BERGENFIELD (New Jersey)
 map (40° 55′N 74° 0′W) 14:129
BERGER, MAURICE see BÉJART,
 MAURICE
BERGER, THOMAS 3:209
BERGER, VICTOR L. 3:209–210 bibliog.
 socialism 18:23
 Socialist party 18:25
BERGERAC, SAVINIEN CYRANO DE
 see CYRANO DE BERGERAC,
 SAVINIEN
BERGIUS, FRIEDRICH KARL RUDOLF
 3:210
BERGLAND (Michigan)
 map (46° 35′N 89° 34′W) 13:377
**BERGMAN, HJALMAR FREDRIK
 ELGÉRUS** 3:210

BERGMAN, INGMAR 3:210 bibliog.,
 illus.
 film, history of 8:86
 Von Sydow, Max 19:634
BERGMAN, INGRID 3:210 bibliog.;
 9:287 illus.
 Bogart, Humphrey 3:359
BERGMAN, SIR TORBERN 3:210
BERGMANN, GUSTAV 3:210
BERGONZI, CARLO 3:210
BERGOO (West Virginia)
 map (38° 29′N 80° 18′W) 20:111
BERGSON, HENRI 3:211 bibliog., illus.
 comedy 5:132
 process philosophy 15:561
BERIA, LAVRENTI PAVLOVICH 3:211
 bibliog.
 KGB 12:64
 Khrushchev, Nikita Sergeyevich
 12:69
BERIBERI 3:211 bibliog.
 Eijkman, Christiaan 7:92
 nutritional-deficiency diseases
 14:307
 thiamine deficiency, vitamins and
 minerals 19:619
BERING, VITUS JONASSEN 3:211
 bibliog., illus.
 Arctic 2:142 map
 explorations 7:336–337 map
 Northeast Passage 14:253
 Saint Elias, Mount 17:18
BERING ISLAND
 Commander Islands (USSR) 5:137
BERING LAND BRIDGE 3:212
 national parks 14:38–39 map, table
 prehistoric humans 15:512
 savanna life 17:99
BERING SEA 3:212 bibliog., map
 Bering Strait 3:212
 islands and island groups
 Commander Islands (USSR)
 5:137
 Pribilof Islands (Alaska) 15:534
 map (60° 0′N 175° 0′W) 19:388
 shellfish 17:255
BERING SEA CONTROVERSY 3:212
BERING STRAIT 3:212
 Bering, Vitus Jonassen 3:211
 map (65° 30′N 169° 0′W) 1:242
 Northeast Passage 14:253
BERINGIA see BERING LAND BRIDGE
BERINGOVA
 Commander Islands (USSR) 5:137
BERIO, LUCIANO 3:212 bibliog.
BERKELEY (California) 3:212
 education
 California, state universities and
 colleges of 4:38 table
 map (37° 57′N 122° 18′W) 4:31
 middle schools and junior high
 schools 13:412
BERKELEY (Missouri)
 map (38° 45′N 90° 20′W) 13:476
BERKELEY (county in South Carolina)
 map (33° 15′N 80° 0′W) 18:98
BERKELEY (county in West Virginia)
 map (39° 25′N 78° 0′W) 20:111
BERKELEY, BUSBY 3:213 bibliog.,
 illus.; 8:85 illus.
 illus.
BERKELEY, GEORGE 3:213 bibliog.,
 illus.
 idealism 11:30
 philosophy 15:245
 Smibert, John 17:366
BERKELEY, JOHN, LORD
 New Jersey 14:133
BERKELEY, SIR WILLIAM 3:213 bibliog.
 United States, history of the 19:437
BERKELEY HEIGHTS (New Jersey)
 map (40° 41′N 74° 27′W) 14:129
BERKELEY SPRINGS (West Virginia)
 map (39° 38′N 78° 14′W) 20:111
BERKELIUM 3:213
 actinide series 1:88
 element 7:130 table
 metal, metallic element 13:328
 Seaborg, Glenn T. 17:171
BERKMAN, ALEXANDER
 Goldman, Emma 9:235
BERKNER ISLAND
 map (79° 30′S 49° 30′W) 2:40
BERKOFF, DAVID 18:391 illus.
BERKS (county in Pennsylvania)
 map (40° 20′N 75° 50′W) 15:147
BERKSHIRE (England) 3:213–214
BERKSHIRE (county in Massachusetts)
 map (42° 27′N 73° 15′W) 13:206
BERKSHIRE HILLS 3:214; 13:208 illus.
 map (42° 20′N 73° 10′W) 13:206
BERKSHIRE MUSIC FESTIVAL 3:214
 bibliog.
 Boston Symphony Orchestra 3:410
BERLAGE, HENDRIK PETRUS 3:214
 bibliog.

Reprinted with permission of the ACADEMIC AMERICAN ENCYCLOPEDIA, 1989 edition, © Grolier, Inc.

Activity 18-c, *The Academic American Encyclopedia* Utilization of Sources

Answer these questions using the Academic American Index that's
labeled Activity 18-c.

The Academic American Encyclopedia, 1989

1. What is referenced for Frederick A. Benteen?

2. What is referenced for Bentwood Rocking Chair?

3. What is referenced for Battle of Bennington and John Stark?

4. What is referenced for foraminifera in the Benthonic Zone?

5. a. What is referenced for a bibliography on Ingrid Bergman?

6. a. What is referenced for the Berbers in Libya?

   b. What is referenced for a bibliography on the Berbers?

7. a. What is referenced for an illustration of a chemical bond for Benzene?

   b. What is referenced for chemical pollutants regarding Benzene?

   c. What is reference regarding benzene and an illustration for Kekulé structure?

8. What is referenced for prehistoric humans and the Bering Land Bridge?

9. What is referenced for the Pribilof Islands in the Bering Sea?

10. What is referenced for the Northeast Passage and the Bering Strait?

350   **Town**

brown towhee, and the green-tailed towhee—are found in the western United States. These birds resemble the rufous-sided towhee in size and habits.

Scientific classification. Towhees belong to the finch family, Fringillidae. The rufous-sided towhee is *Pipilo erythrophthalmus.*   Herbert Friedmann

See also **Bird** (picture: Birds' eggs).

Town is a community of closely clustered dwellings and other buildings in which people live and work. It may be large or small. Most of the people in the United States and Canada use the word *town* to refer to a municipal unit which is larger than a village and smaller than a city. In the New England states, the name *town* is given to a minor governmental division known in other parts of the United States as a township.   H. F. Alderfer

Related articles in *World Book* include:

Boom town	Local government	Township
Borough	Town meeting	Village

Town crier was a person appointed to make public announcements. The town crier was important in Europe, particularly in England, before newspapers were common, and was the "walking newspaper" of the American Colonies during the 1600's. The crier sang out the latest news at every corner, and announced the time of town meetings and other events of public interest. The town crier largely disappeared when the printing press, newspaper, and other forms of communication came into general use after the 1750's. Today, some British communities have a town crier.   Robert J. Taylor

Town meeting is held once a year by the voters of a town. The first town meetings were held in colonial days. Such a meeting is the purest form of democratic government known, because it is government by the people rather than by their elected representatives. Citizens 18 years of age or older may participate in town meetings. At the meetings, the township makes its decisions for the year to come. It passes ordinances and discusses township improvements and other business. The town clerk makes and keeps a record of the meeting. The town system is a typical New England institution, but it has been adopted elsewhere.   H. F. Alderfer

Town planning. See City planning.

Townes, Charles Hard (1915-   ), is a United States physicist. In 1951, he explained the basic principles that led to the development of the maser. A *maser* is a device that uses the energy of molecules or atoms to amplify radio waves. Townes helped build the first maser in 1953 (see **Maser**). In 1958, Townes and Arthur L. Schawlow proposed the *laser*, a device for amplifying light waves (see **Laser**). For his work, Townes shared the 1964 Nobel Prize in physics with two Russian scientists who also developed and improved masers.

Townes was born in Greenville, S.C. He taught physics at Columbia University from 1948 to 1961, when he became a professor of physics and provost of the Massachusetts Institute of Technology. In 1967, he became professor of physics at the University of California in Berkeley.   R. T. Ellickson

See also **Basov, Nikolai; Prokhorov, Alexander.**

Townsend, *TOWN zuhnd,* **Willard Saxby** (1895-1957), was one of the first black American labor leaders. He improved the wages and working conditions of *redcaps* (railroad baggage porters). Townsend helped redcaps gain a fixed salary, plus retirement and insurance benefits.

© *Chicago Sun-Times*
Willard Townsend

Townsend was born in Cincinnati, Ohio, and began working as a redcap there when he was 19 years old. In 1936, he was elected the first president of the Auxiliary of Redcaps, a union that belonged to the American Federation of Labor (AFL). In 1937, he became the first president of an independent union, the International Brotherhood of Redcaps. It became the United Transport Service Employees in 1940 and joined the Congress of Industrial Organizations (CIO) in 1942. Also in 1942, Townsend became the first black member of the CIO executive board. When the AFL and the CIO merged in 1955, he was named a vice president of the AFL-CIO.

Townsend was a vice president of the Urban League and an officer of the National Association for the Advancement of Colored People (NAACP). He was coauthor of *What the Negro Wants* (1944).   James G. Scoville

Townsend Plan, *TOWN zuhnd,* is an old-age pension plan proposed in 1934 by Dr. Francis E. Townsend of Long Beach, Calif. It provided that all U.S. citizens over 60 years of age be paid $200 a month. The funds were to come from a 2 per cent tax on the transfer or sale of goods. Supporters believed it would stabilize American prosperity, because those receiving pensions would be obligated to spend the money within a month. A modified version of the Townsend Plan was presented to the U.S. House of Representatives on June 1, 1939, but was voted down.   Robert J. Myers

Townshend, Peter. See Who, The.

Townshend, *TOWN zuhnd,* **Viscount** (1674-1738), pioneered in improving English agriculture. He retired to a Norfolk estate in 1730 after a successful political career. Townshend then introduced the turnip to English farms, for which he is known as "Turnip" Townshend. He practiced *marling* (fertilization) and *enclosure* (the use of fences). Townshend demonstrated the productivity of better cultivation in one of England's poorest farming districts. His given and family name was Charles Townshend.   C. B. Baker

Townshend Acts. See Revolutionary War in America (The Townshend Acts).

Township in the United States is a division of a county. It may be entirely rural, or include cities or towns. A township's governing body is usually a board of commissioners, supervisors, or trustees. It can pass ordinances and resolutions that have the force of law in the township. Routine administration is generally handled by a township clerk. In New England, most townships are called *towns,* and have more elaborate powers. See also **Local government; Town.**   H. F. Alderfer

Toxemia of pregnancy, *tahk SEE mee uh,* is a disease that attacks women during the later months of pregnancy or just after giving birth. It is also called *preeclampsia* (pronounced *pree eh KLAMP see uh*). The disease may result in the death of the mother, the fetus, or both. Its cause is unknown.

The World Book Encyclopedia Article

1. Who is the author of the article on Town meeting?

2. When was Willard Saxby Townsend born?

3. What are the cross references for Charles Hard Townes?

4. What is the reference for Town Planning?

5. What is the reference for Peter Townshend?

6. What are the related articles in World Book for Town?

7. Look carefully and see what is identical in the articles for Town, Town meeting, and Township.

8. What is the reference for Townshend Acts?

9. Who is the author for town crier?

10. What major reason does the article on the town crier give for the crier's disappearance?

11. Is there an unsigned article? If so, what is entry word?

Almanac

FOCUS
This lesson focuses on the uses of the almanac's index in researching.

TEACHER PREPARATION
1. Read the material thoroughly with a copy of the almanac in hand.
2. Work through the activities and keep answer sheet available for handy class reference.
3. Have *World Almanac* and other almanacs available for students to peruse.

BACKGROUND INFORMATION
1. The almanac is a neat package of concise facts.
2. Students sometimes shy away from using it because it's too bulky and seems too forbidding. Prove them wrong.

CONCEPTS
- **Understanding the nature of an almanac's format.**
- **Understanding the ease of use of the index.**

VOCABULARY
almanac annually summary   summaries topic subtopic detail margin hyphen chronologically

OBJECTIVES
The student will understand that:
1. The almanac is a compilation of summaries of information.
2. The general index for the World Almanac is found in the front of the book.
3. Topics, subtopics, and details are presented in the index.
4. Punctuation plays a role in reading the index.
5. The World Almanac contains an annual review of world events.

MATERIAL NEEDED
Activity Sheets 19-a through 19-b and 19-b in optional student workbook.

ACTIVITIES
1. Read through Activity 19-a orally using a transparency of an almanac page, pointing out left margin and indentation.
2. Point out topic, subtopic, detail.
3. Work through the other activities, either in class or as homework.

EXTENDED ACTIVITIES
1. With a world map on a table, let students randomly choose 3 areas by dropping 3 paper clips onto the map. Look up those three areas. List 5 facts for each. Put the three areas in order by ascending order of area in square miles.

2. Take a national, international, or general summary of facts from the chronology or the fact summary and list facts to visualize the amount of factual information stated.

3. Group students by category of summary they chose: national, international, general. Chart in chronological order preparatory to doing time line for bulletin board.

The Almanac

The World Almanac and Book of Facts is published annually in November. Its purpose is to present summaries of information on a variety of current topics of the day. It offers both a quick thumb index of topics as well as a quick reference index of a still more developed list of topics.

But, the most complete listing of information is presented in the general index found in the front of the book. The subjects are organized alphabetically by topic, subtopic, and detail. Topics are in bold print and are against the left margin on a two-column page. All subtopics are in a lighter print and are indented. Some subtopics are divided further into details and the details are also indented away from the subtopic margin. They are immediately recognizable by a hyphen.
Example:

Michigan
    Population
            -Black, Hispanic
            -Cities and towns
            -Counties

All topics, subtopics, and details correspond to specific page numbers of the book's text. Index use is of great importance as the text is topically organized and it would be impossible to retrieve all the possible information on a specific topic or division of the topic without its use. When the index page numbers are separated by a comma, two separate pages are indicated. Two pages separated by a hyphen, in turn, specify that those two pages and all the pages in between are included.
Example: 5,9 = (5 and 9);   5-9 = (5,6,7,8,9)

Along with the summaries of information found in the text, the *World Almanac* offers an Addenda which updates information presented up to the time of publication. Fact summaries are provided in the form of a selected top ten news stories of impact, and a chronological review of world events presented by month for an entire year (Nov-Oct) concerning the year prior to publication. It also contains a variety of lists, graphs, charts, and other visual aids presenting factual information.
    Using an almanac to its full advantage is an easy, yet fast way to update yourself of the many happenings, people, or places made famous during the year under review.

1. What is the purpose of the World Almanac?
2. Why is it important to use an index when using the World Almanac?
3. What is the difference between: (18,24) and (18-24)?
4. How might the World Almanac help you to have a better understanding of world events?

Name_____ **Activity 19-b**
Date_____

The World Almanac and Book of Facts

1. To what page would you turn for information on Victoria Day?

2. To what pages would you turn for information on electoral vote for President?

3. a. To what page would you turn for information on Virginia Beach?

   b. To what page would you turn for information on Mayor of Virginia Beach?

   c. To what pages would you turn for information on the population of Virginia Beach?

4. a. To what page would you turn for information on volume of geometric form?

   b. To what pages would you turn for information on volume of dry and fluid measure?

   c. To what pages would you turn for information on volume of sun and planets?

5. To what page would you turn for information on 1929 Stock Market Crash of Wall Street?

6. a. To what pages would you turn for information on voting by Washington, DC, residents?
   b. To what pages would you turn for information on voting in 1971 by 18 year olds?
   c. To what page would you turn for information on Voting Rights Act of 1965?

7. To what pages would you turn for information on War of 1812?

8. To what pages would you turn for information on Lech Walesea?

9. To what pages would you turn for information on Vernal Equinox?

10. To what pages would you turn for information on Visa Regulations?

11. a. To what page would you turn for information on wage loss from accident?
    b. To what pages would you turn for information on federal minimum hourly rate?
    c. To what page would you turn for information on wages and average starting salaries?
    d. To what other entry word are you referred for more information?

The Atlas

FOCUS
The lesson focuses on using the atlas's index in research.

TEACHER PREPARATION
1. Look over the variety of atlases available to you in your library.
2. Read thoroughly the material, do the activity sheets and keep them for handy class reference.
3. Although the activity is from an actual atlas index, we have tried to keep it generic as possible.

BACKGROUND INFORMATION
1. Many atlases exist. *The Earth and Man*, Rand McNally; *American Heritage Pictorial Atlas of United States History; The Times Atlas of Archeology; Maps on File* and *Historic Maps on File* from Facts on File; *The Times Atlas of World History;* to name just a few. *The New International Atlas* has maps of world cities. Display them for the students. Books such as *Great Historic Places in America* by David M. Brownstone, and the 2 volume *Encyclopedia of Historic Places* go great with an atlas display.
2. Don't forget the road maps that might be in the vertical file in your library, under your state counties, or different states and regions.
3. Although we have activities using an atlas index, you might want to key additional activities to a science, social studies or language arts project.
4. Standardized tests seek to implement map skills, such as reading the legend, and to infer geographic knowledge of terrain, latitude, crops, products, transportation.

CONCEPTS
*   **Understanding the use of an index in an atlas.**
*   **Understanding the format of an index in an atlas.**

VOCABULARY
visual atlas overview familiarization concise summaries   legend   alphabetically   coordinates geographic environmental

OBJECTIVES
The student will understand that:
1. An atlas is a collection of maps.
2. Usually an atlas has a focus.
3. The table of contents is important to gaining an overview.
4. A map key and a key to abbreviations are invaluable.
5. Global referencing is important, and perhaps even crucial to understanding.

MATERIAL NEEDED
Activity Sheets 20-a through 20-b and 20-b in the optional student workbook.

ACTIVITIES
1. After reading 20-a, answering the context questions, and working 20-b, you might wish to see if the students have individual atlases from another class. You could then work with the index in that book.
2. Although our focus is just on the index, we will be using the entire atlas in our Know Your Country questions.

EXTENDED ACTIVITIES
1. The names of places change, some more often than others. Permit a student to print the new Chinese province names in an old atlas.
2. Permit students to create addenda updating an old African atlas.
3. Permit students to research whether or not your city, county, or state has a sister locale somewhere in the world. Let them do a bulletin board on the two entities.
4. On a large wall map, flag the locations from the activities.

The Atlas

An atlas is a book of maps whose purpose is to provide visual information concerning general and specific land regions of the world. In learning to use an atlas, it is important that you develop a knowledge of a general overview of the book. This can be done easily through a study of the table of contents. You must then familiarize yourself with the general map key and abbreviations found in the front of the book. It is a good idea to use book marks to provide for easy usage of these two pages.

To understand a map, immediately become familiar with the map title to determine map focus and type (For example: North America - Climate). Also, read all concise fact summaries surrounding the map, and, of course, have a visual understanding of the individual map legend. Some atlases will indicate the area in relation to the globe. If the atlas does not do that, you should make a mental reference to a global area. It is also important to locate and understand the organization of the index.

An atlas index will be alphabetical by topic, subtopic, and detail. But, it is important that you determine whether a word-by-word or a letter-by-letter alphabetizing is used as in any index. A word-by-word alphabetizing recognizes spaces between words where a letter-by-letter approach does not.

Alphabetical by topic, then by subtopic and detail, the index provides the necessary information of page numbers and coordinates to be able to find a geographic place location on a map in the atlas. Sometimes the coordinates are simply numbers on the top and side of a page. At other times the coordinates are the actual longitude and latitude readings of the place location.

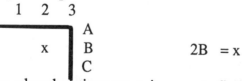

Either way, place locations are quite easy to find or locate on a map. An atlas is a valuable tool to understanding a people's culture because through map studies, physical and environmental challenges become readily apparent. It was these same physical problems that helped define a people as part of a geographic area or region.

1. In order to comprehend a map, list some of the areas with which you should become familiar before beginning.
2. Explain the workings of an atlas index.
3. Explain the structure of an entry in an atlas index.

Name ______________________ Date ____________

Introduction to Index

The index is divided into two parts for ease of access. The first part gives place names in the United States and the outlying territories of Puerto Rico, the Virgin Islands and the Panama Canal Zone. The second part of the index consists of place names from the rest of the world.

The number in bold type which follows each name in the index refers to the number of the map-page where that feature or place will be found. This is usually the largest scale on which the place or feature appears. Names in the U.S. are indexed to their state, which is not necessarily the largest scale.

The geographical co-ordinates which follow the place name are sometimes only approximate but are close enough for the place name to be located.

A solid square ■ follows the name of a country while an open square □ refers to a first order administrative area (states in the U.S.) A diamond ◇ refers to counties in the U.S. (parishes in Louisiana and census areas in Alaska).

Rivers have been indexed to their mouth or to where they join another river. All river names are followed by the symbol →.

Suvorov **179** 54 7N 36 30 E
Suvorov Is. = Suwarrow Is. **225** 15 0 S 163 0W
Suvorovo **167** 43 20N 27 35 E
Suwa **221** 36 2N 138 8 E
Suwa-Ko **221** 36 3N 138 5 E
Suwałki **152** 54 8N 22 59 E
Suwałki □ **152** 54 0N 22 30 E
Suwannaphum **204** 15 33N 103 47 E
Suwanose-Jima **219** 29 38N 129 43 E
Suwarrow Is. **225** 15 0 S 163 0W
Suwayq aş Şuqban **192** 31 32N 46 7 E
Suweis, Khalîg el **244** 28 40N 33 0 E
Suweis, Qanâl es **244** 31 0N 32 20 E
Suwŏn **215** 37 17N 127 1 E
Suykbulak **182** 50 25N 62 33 E
Suyo **210** 16 59N 120 31 E
Suzak **183** 44 9N 68 27 E
Suzaka **221** 36 39N 138 19 E
Suzdal **179** 56 29N 40 26 E
Suze, La **138** 47 54N 0 2 E
Suzhou **217** 31 19N 120 38 E
Suzu **219** 37 25N 137 17 E
Suzu-Misaki **219** 37 31N 137 21 E
Suzuka **221** 34 55N 136 36 E
Suzuka-Sam **221** 35 5N 136 30 E
Suzzara **162** 45 0N 10 45 E
Svalbard **12** 78 0N 17 0 E
Svalbarð **174** 66 12N 15 43W
Svalöv **172** 55 57N 13 8 E
Svanvik **174** 69 25N 30 3 E
Svappavaara **174** 67 40N 21 3 E
Svarstad **171** 59 27N 9 56 E
Svartenhuk Pen. **95** 71 50N 54 30W
Svartisen **174** 66 40N 13 50 E
Svartvik **172** 62 19N 17 24 E
Svatovo **180** 49 35N 38 11 E
Svay Chek **204** 13 48N 102 58 E
Svay Rieng **205** 11 5N 105 48 E
Sveio **171** 59 33N 5 23 E
Svendborg **173** 55 4N 10 35 E
Svene **171** 59 45N 9 31 E
Svenljunga **173** 57 29N 13 5 E
Svenstrup **173** 56 58N 9 50 E
Sverdlovsk, R.S.F.S.R., U.S.S.R. **182** 56 50N 60 30 E
Sverdlovsk, Ukraine S.S.R., U.S.S.R. **181** 48 5N 39 37 E
Sverdrup Chan. **95** 79 56N 96 25W
Sverdrup Is. **95** 79 0N 97 0W
Svetac **163** 43 3N 15 43 E
Sveti Ivan Zelina **163** 45 57N 16 16 E
Sveti Jurij **163** 46 14N 15 24 E
Sveti Lenart **163** 46 36N 15 48 E
Sveti Nikola, Prokhad **166** 43 27N 22 6 E
Sveti Nikole **166** 41 51N 21 56 E
Sveti Rok **163** 40 1N 9 6 E
Sveti Trojica **163** 46 37N 15 50 E
Svetlaya **218** 46 33N 138 18 E
Svetlogorsk **178** 52 38N 29 46 E
Svetlograd **181** 45 25N 42 58 E
Svetlovodsk **178** 49 2N 33 13 E
Svetlyy **182** 50 48N 60 51 E
Svetozarevo **166** 44 5N 21 15 E
Svidník **151** 49 20N 21 37 E
Svilaja Pl. **163** 43 49N 16 31 E
Svilajnac **166** 44 15N 21 11 E
Svilengrad **167** 41 49N 26 12 E
Svir → **176** 60 30N 32 48 E
Svishtov **167** 43 36N 25 23 E
Svisloch **178** 53 3N 24 2 E
Svitava → **151** 49 30N 16 37 E
Svitavy **151** 49 47N 16 28 E
Svobodnyy **185** 51 20N 128 0 E
Svoge **167** 42 59N 23 23 E
Svolvær **174** 68 15N 14 34 E
Svratka → **151** 49 11N 16 38 E
Svrljig **166** 43 25N 22 6 E
Swa **202** 19 15N 96 17 E
Swa Tende **253** 7 9 S 17 7 E
Swarzędz **152** 52 25N 17 4 E
Swastika **74** 48 7N 80 6W
Swatow = Shantou **217** 23 18N 116 40 E
Swaziland ■ **255** 26 30 S 31 30 E
Sweden ■ **174** 57 0N 15 0 E
Swedru **247** 5 32N 0 41W
Swellendam **254** 34 1 S 20 26 E
Swider → **152** 52 6N 21 14 E
Świdnica **152** 50 50N 16 30 E
Świdnik **152** 51 13N 22 39 E
Świdwin **152** 53 47N 15 49 E
Świebodzice **152** 50 51N 16 20 E
Świebodzin **152** 52 15N 15 31 E
Świecie **152** 53 25N 18 30 E
Świętokrzyskie, Góry **152** 51 0N 20 30 E
Swift Current, Newf., Canada **79** 47 53N 54 12W
Swift Current, Sask., Canada **88** 50 20N 107 45W
Swiftcurrent → **88** 50 38N 107 44W
Swilly, L. **135** 55 12N 7 35W
Swindle, I. **92** 52 30N 128 35W
Swindon **133** 51 33N 1 47W
Swinemünde = Świnoujście **152** 53 54N 14 16 E
Świnoujście **152** 53 54N 14 16 E
Switzerland ■ **147** 46 30N 8 0 E
Swords **135** 53 27N 6 15W
Syasstroy **178** 60 5N 32 15 E
Sychevka **178** 55 59N 34 16 E
Syców **152** 51 19N 17 40 E
Sydenham → **84** 42 33N 82 25W
Sydney, Australia **231** 33 53 S 151 10 E
Sydney, Canada **81** 46 7N 60 7W
Sydney L. **86** 50 41N 94 25W
Sydney Mines **81** 46 18N 60 15W
Sydney River **81** 46 7N 60 13W
Sydprøven **12** 60 30N 45 35W
Syke **146** 52 55N 8 50 E
Syktyvkar **176** 61 45N 50 40 E
Sylhet **202** 24 54N 91 52 E
Sylt **146** 54 50N 8 20 E
Sylva → **182** 58 0N 56 54 E
Sylvan L. **91** 52 21N 114 10W
Sylvan Lake **91** 52 20N 114 3W
Sylvania **88** 52 42N 104 0W
Sylvester **90** 55 0N 119 41W
Sym **184** 60 20N 88 18 E
Symón **105** 24 42N 102 35W
Synnott Ra. **228** 16 30 S 125 20 E
Syrdarya **183** 40 50N 68 40 E
Syrdarya → **184** 46 3N 61 0 E
Syria ■ **192** 35 0N 38 0 E
Syriam **202** 16 44N 96 19 E
Syrian Desert **186** 31 0N 40 0 E
Sysert **182** 56 29N 60 49 E
Syul'dzhyukyor **185** 63 14N 113 32 E
Syutkya **167** 41 50N 24 16 E
Syzran **179** 53 12N 48 30 E
Szabolcs-Szatmár □ **151** 48 2N 21 45 E
Szamocin **152** 53 2N 17 7 E
Szamos → **151** 48 7N 22 20 E
Szaraz → **151** 46 28N 20 44 E
Szarvas **151** 46 50N 20 38 E
Szazhalombatta **151** 47 20N 18 58 E
Szczawnica **151** 49 26N 20 30 E
Szczebrzeszyn **152** 50 42N 22 59 E
Szczecin **152** 53 27N 14 27 E
Szczecin □ **152** 53 25N 14 32 E
Szczecinek **152** 53 43N 16 41 E
Szczekocimy **152** 50 38N 19 48 E
Szczucin **152** 50 18N 21 4 E
Szczuczyn **152** 53 36N 22 19 E
Szczytno **152** 53 33N 21 0 E
Szechwan = Sichuan □ **216** 31 0N 104 0 E
Szécsény **151** 48 7N 19 30 E
Szeged **151** 46 16N 20 10 E
Szeghalom **151** 47 1N 21 10 E
Székesfehérvár **151** 47 15N 18 25 E
Szekszárd **151** 46 22N 18 42 E
Szendrö **151** 48 24N 20 41 E
Szentendre **151** 47 39N 19 4 E
't Harde **142** 52 24N 5 54 E
't Zandt **142** 53 22N 6 46 E
Ta Khli Khok **204** 15 18N 100 20 E
Ta Lai **205** 11 24N 107 23 E
Tabacal **124** 23 15 S 64 15W
Tabaco **210** 13 22N 123 44 E
Tabagné **246** 7 59N 3 4W
Ţâbah **192** 26 55N 42 38 E
Tabajara **123** 8 56 S 62 8W
Tabalos **122** 6 26 S 76 37W
Tabango **211** 11 19N 124 22 E
Tabar Is. **227** 2 50 S 152 0 E
Tabarca, Isla de **157** 38 17N 0 30W
Tabarka **241** 36 56N 8 46 E
Ţabas, Khorâsân, Iran **193** 32 48N 60 12 E
Ţabas, Khorâsân, Iran **193** 33 35N 56 55 E
Tabasará, Serranía de **112** 8 35N 81 40W
Tabasco, Baja Calif. N., Mexico **98** 32 30N 114 50W
Tabasco, Zacatecas, Mexico **105** 21 52N 102 55W
Tabasco □ **110** 18 0N 92 40W
Tabatière, La **79** 50 50N 58 58W
Tabatinga, Serra da **120** 10 30 S 44 0W
Tabayin **202** 22 42N 95 20 E
Tabāzīn **193** 31 12N 57 54 E
Tabelbala, Kahal de **240** 28 47N 2 0W
Taber **91** 49 47N 112 8W
Tabernas **157** 37 4N 2 26W
Tabernes de Valldigna **157** 39 5N 0 13W
Tabi **253** 8 10 S 13 18 E
Tabira **120** 7 35 S 37 33W
Tablas **210** 12 25N 122 2 E
Tablas Strait **210** 12 40N 121 48 E
Table B. = Tafelbaai **254** 33 35 S 18 25 E
Table B. **78** 53 40N 56 25W
Table Mt. **254** 34 0 S 18 22 E
Table Top, Mt. **230** 23 24 S 147 11 E
Tableland **228** 17 16 S 126 51 E
Tabogon **211** 10 57N 124 2 E
Tábor, Czech. **150** 49 25N 14 39 E
Tabor, Israel **189** 32 42N 35 24 E
Tabora **250** 5 2 S 32 50 E
Tabora □ **250** 5 0 S 33 0 E
Tabory **182** 58 31N 64 33 E
Tabou **246** 4 30N 7 20W
Tabrīz **192** 38 7N 46 20 E
Tabuelan **211** 10 49N 123 52 E
Tabuenca **156** 41 42N 1 33W
Tabuk, Phil. **210** 17 24N 121 25 E
Tabūk, Si. Arabia **191** 28 23N 36 36 E
Tacâmbaro de Codallos **107** 19 14N 101 28W
Tacaná, Volcán **110** 15 7N 92 6W
Tacheng **212** 46 40N 82 58 E
Tachibana-Wan **220** 32 45N 130 7 E
Tachick L. **92** 53 57N 124 12W
Tachikawa **221** 35 42N 139 25 E
Tach'ing Shan = Daqing Shan **214** 40 40N 111 0 E
Tachira **118** 8 7N 72 15 E
Táchira □ **118** 8 7N 72 15W
Tachov **150** 49 47N 12 39 E
Tácina → **165** 38 57N 16 55 E
Tacloban **211** 11 15N 124 58 E
Tacna **122** 18 0 S 70 20W
Tacna □ **122** 17 40 S 70 20W
Tacotalpa **110** 17 36N 92 49W
Tacotalpa → **110** 17 50N 92 52W
Tacualeche **105** 22 49N 102 25W
Tacuarembó **125** 31 45 S 56 0W
Tacupeto **100** 28 49N 109 11W
Tacutu → **119** 3 1N 60 29W
Tademaït, Plateau du **241** 28 30N 2 30 E
Tadent, O. → **241** 22 25N 6 40 E
Tadjerdjeri, O. → **241** 26 0N 8 0W
Tafelbaai **254** 33 35 S 18 25 E
Tafelney, C. **240** 31 3N 9 51W
Tafermaar **207** 6 47 S 134 10 E
Taffermit **240** 29 37N 9 15W
Tafí Viejo **124** 26 43 S 65 17W
Tafīhān **193** 29 25N 52 39 E
Tafiré **246** 9 4N 5 4W
Tafnidilt **240** 28 47N 10 58W
Tafraoute **240** 29 50N 8 58W
Taft, Iran **193** 31 45N 54 14 E
Taft, Phil. **211** 11 57N 125 30 E
Taga Dzong **202** 27 5N 89 55 E
Tagana-an **211** 9 42N 125 35 E
Taganrog **181** 47 12N 38 50 E
Taganrogskiy Zaliv **180** 47 0N 38 30 E
Tagânt **246** 18 20N 11 0W
Tagap Ga **202** 26 56N 96 13 E
Tagapula I. **210** 12 4N 124 12 E
Tagatay **210** 14 6N 120 56 E
Tagauayan I. **211** 10 58N 121 13 E
Tagbilaran **211** 9 39N 123 51 E
Tage **227** 6 19 S 143 20 E
Tággia **162** 43 52N 7 50 E
Taghrīfat **241** 29 5N 17 26 E
Taghzout **240** 33 30N 4 49W
Tagish **76** 60 19N 134 16W
Tagish L. **76** 60 10N 134 20W
Tagkawayan **210** 13 58N 122 32 E
Tagliacozzo **163** 42 4N 13 13 E
Tagliamento → **163** 45 38N 13 5 E
Táglio di Po **163** 45 0N 12 12 E
Tagna **118** 2 24 S 70 37W
Tago **211** 9 2N 126 13 E
Tago, Mt. **211** 8 23N 125 5 E
Tagomago, I. de **157** 39 2N 1 39 E
Tagua, La **118** 0 3N 74 40W
Taguatinga **121** 12 16 S 42 26W
Tagudin **210** 16 56N 120 27 E
Tagula **227** 11 22 S 153 15 E
Tagula I. **227** 11 30 S 153 30 E
Tagum **211** 7 33N 125 53 E
Tagus = Tajo → **155** 38 40N 9 24W
Tahakopa **235** 46 30 S 169 23 E
Tahala **241** 34 0N 4 28W
Tahan, Gunong **205** 4 34N 102 17 E
Tahānah-ye sūr Gol **197** 31 43N 67 53 E
Tahara **221** 34 40N 137 16 E
Tahat **241** 23 18N 5 33 E
Tahdziú **111** 20 12N 88 57W
Tāherī **193** 27 43N 52 20 E
Tahiti **226** 17 37 S 149 27W
Tahora **234** 39 2 S 174 49 E
Tahoua **247** 14 57N 5 16 E
Tahsis **92** 49 55N 126 40W
Tahta **244** 26 44N 31 32 E
Tahuamanu → **122** 11 6 S 67 36W
Tahulandang **207** 2 27N 125 23 E
Tahuna **207** 3 38N 125 30 E
Taï **246** 5 55N 7 30W
Tai Shan **215** 36 25N 117 20 E
Tai Xian **217** 32 30N 120 7 E
Tai'an **215** 36 12N 117 8 E
Taibei **217** 25 4N 121 29 E
Taibus Qi **214** 41 54N 115 22 E
T'aichung = Taizhong **217** 24 12N 120 35 E
Taidong **217** 22 43N 121 9 E
Taieri → **235** 46 3 S 170 12 E
Taiga Madema **241** 23 46N 15 25 E
Taigu **214** 37 28N 112 30 E
Taihang Shan **214** 36 0N 113 30 E
Taihape **234** 39 41 S 175 48 E
Taihe, Anhui, China **214** 33 20N 115 42 E
Taihe, Jiangxi, China **217** 26 47N 114 52 E
Taihu **217** 30 22N 116 20 E
Taijiang **216** 26 39N 108 21 E
Taikang **214** 34 5N 114 50 E
Taikkyi **202** 17 20N 96 0 E
Tailem Bend **232** 35 12 S 139 29 E
Tailfingen **147** 48 15N 9 1 E
Taimyr = Taymyr, Poluostrov **185** 75 0N 100 0 E

203

The Atlas

Answer these questions using the index from the *Prentice-Hall American World Atlas*, which is labeled Activity 20-b.

1. According to Introduction to the Index, what is said concerning rivers?

2. According to Introduction to the Index, what does a solid square symbolize?

3. According to Introduction to the Index, what does an open square symbolize?

4. According to Introduction to the Index, what does a diamond symbolize?

5. According to the Index, where is Tabriz and what are its coordinates?

6. According to the Index, where is Switzerland? What else can you tell about it?

7. According to the Index, what and where is Tahuamanu.

8. According to the Index, where is Taikkyi?

9. According to the Index, what and where is Sydenham?

10. According to the Index, what and where is Szechwan?

READERS' GUIDE

FOCUS
This lesson will focus on using the *Readers' Guide* and doing so more effectively and more efficiently.

TEACHER PREPARATION
1. Read thoroughly all the material. Make a transparency to use in teaching.
2. Have copies of *Readers' Guides* available for students to look at and use.
3. If *Readers' Guide* is available in another format, demonstrate it.

BACKGROUND INFORMATION
1. The long-time reference aid to general periodical article indexing, *Readers' Guide*, is published by H. W. Wilson, who also publishes specific periodical indexes, such as Library Literature, Education Index, etc.
2. The H. W. Wilson Company is effectively broadening its technological market by putting its indexing on CD ROM and having it available on-line.
3. *Readers' Guide Abstracts* are available in print also giving a summarization of the article along with the citation. They are also available in microform.
4. In addition to generating key words, the students should be made aware that use and convention sometimes changed what a key word should be. RUSSIA became SOVIET UNION with *see also* USSR.; ESP in one issue and EXTRA SENSORY PERCEPTION in another. So the key would be to "keep looking."

CONCEPTS
- **Understanding the use of the *Readers' Guide*.**
- **Understanding the format of information in the *Readers' Guide*.**

VOCABULARY
magazine   periodical   entry   topic   subtopic   detail   reference   abridged overview   visual aids

OBJECTIVES
The student will understand:

1. That the *Readers' Guide to Periodical Literature* is an index of articles in magazines and periodicals in print.

2. That many schools have an abridged version of the *Readers' Guide* and that it is a shortened version in that only a selected number of magazines are used.

3. That the *Readers' Guide* offers a page which indicates an organizational pattern of the accumulated volumes and that this information corresponds to the markings on the appropriate spines or bindings of specific individual volumes.

4. That the *Readers' Guide* offers a listing of the abbreviations of all the periodicals and magazines indexed as well as a separate listing of the general abbreviations used in the index and should be consulted to effectively use the information provided in the indices.

5. That it is necessary that the student review the pertinent information regarding each magazine indexed through the appropriate section and to also review the explanation of the suggested uses of the guide.

6. That there is a section in the *Readers' Guide* called Book Review, indexed by the author of the specific fiction/nonfiction book as reviewed in the various magazines listed in the *Readers' Guide*.

7. That the *Readers' Guide to Periodical Literature* is updated throughout the year with paperback editions published prior to the printing of the cumulative hard cover volume.

8. That the *Readers' Guide* is an alphabetical listing of topics/subjects and authors that correspond to articles contained in commonly used magazines.

9. That the physical placement of entries as topics, subjects, or authors in the *Readers' Guide* is against the margin and that each page contains two columns and therefore two margins.

10. That the size and boldness of print of topics and subtopics are the same although topics are placed against the left margin while subtopics are centered in the column; yet details, in italics, are also column-centered.

11. That all cross references are placed against the margin, just below the topic or subtopic to which they correspond and are indicated by the cue words *see* and *see also* to be followed by a listing of applicable key words.

12. That the detail *about* centered and in italics indicates that articles about the entry word which named a subject/person are to follow and that the subject is alphabetized within the index by last name.

13. That a *Readers' Guide* entry includes in order: the entry word; complete magazine article title; the author's name (if given); indication of any visual aids; the abbreviated name of the magazine or periodical, more recently given in italics; the volume number of the magazine, if given, separated from the page number by a colon; and an indication of the month, day, year of the issue in an abbreviated form.

14. The importance of using the listing of magazine abbreviations to determine an unrecognizable abbreviation from the entry.

15. That the following abbreviations and their corresponding words are commonly used in the *Readers' Guide*: por/portrait, map/map, bibl/bibliography, il/illustration.

16. That any unrecognizable abbreviation will be defined in the general list of abbreviations found in the front of the volume.

17. That next to a newspaper index, the most current information on any subject can be found through the use of the indexing of the *Readers' Guide* or specialized periodical indices, such as the *Education Index*, the *Business Index*, the *Art Index*.

18. That the *Readers' Guide* is found in the reference section of any library and does not circulate.

MATERIAL NEEDED
Activity Sheets 21-a through 21-c and 21-b through 21-c in optional student workbook.
Transparency (optional)
Copies of the *Readers' Guide* or *Abridged Readers' Guide*

ACTIVITIES
1. Teach with activities 21-a and 21-b using a transparency to highlight points you are making.
2. Assign activity 21-c to be done in class so you can monitor the students' progress.
3. Using 21-b as a screen, assign other activities with other pages to be done in class or as homework.

EXTENDED ACTIVITIES
1. Have a student buddy up with a lower grader and retrieve articles for the younger student's report.
2. Have the students make citations from the information given.
3. Develop list of magazines which are stored in the media center. Make list for distribution.
4. Discuss importance of union catalog of serials.

The Readers' Guide to Periodical Literature

The Readers' Guide to Periodical Literature is a subject index of articles found in magazines and periodicals in print. It is located in the reference section of the library and does not circulate. Many schools have a shortened version called an *Abridged Readers' Guide* that indexes only a selected number of magazines and periodicals. Both the complete Readers' Guide and the abridged version are updated throughout the year with paperback editions referencing subjects covered in current magazine articles. The paperback editions allow you, as the student researcher, to access the most current information on any subject, except, of course, for the information contained in the daily or weekly newspaper. At the end of each year, all the information provided in the paperbacks is combined into one alphabet and in one hardcover volume.

Each volume has a series of sections that will provide you with the necessary information to successfully use the Guide. One such section provides an overview of the many magazines referenced in the index. Two other sections explain many of the general abbreviations used in the Guide as well as the specific magazine abbreviations used in each entry. Another section gathers some of the many fiction and nonfiction book reviews that are referenced in the Guide.

Physically, each page of the index is divided into two columns creating two separate left margins. Topics, subjects or entry words are immediately recognizable in that they are in a bold print and are place directly against the left margin of a column.

Subtopics are of a lighter and less bold print and are column-centered. A division of a subtopic would be a detail. The detail would be presented in italics and would be column-centered under the subtopic.

Example:

Football
    equipment
        helmets

1. What is the purpose of the Readers' Guide?
2. How does the abridged version compare to the complete, unabridged, Readers' Guide?
3. Of what value are the paperback editions?
4. How is the Readers' Guide updated on a yearly basis?
5. Explain the physical description of the page in terms of: column, entry word, topic, subtopic, detail.

The Readers' Guide to Periodical Literature

It is important to understand that under each topic, subtopic or detail, many entries can be listed. Each entry represents one article in one magazine. Just as many articles from many different magazines can be listed under one topic or subtopic, all the articles from one magazine issued on one date will be scattered throughout the index according to the subject of each article.

All entries pertaining to a specific topic, subtopic or detail would be placed directly under the corresponding key word. A special detail, *about*, which is always column-centered and in italics indicates that all entries that follow underneath are *about* a specific person. That person will be located in the index alphabetically by last name.

The cross reference cue words of *see/see also* are also used in the Guide and have the same meaning as in any index. That is, a *see* followed by a series of key words indicates that the original key word is not valid for the index and the other provided must be used to locate information on that specific topic. The words *see also* indicate that the original key word is valid and will provide some information through the entries but to find all the information as indexed in the volume, the new cross reference key words should also be utilized. The cue words *see* and *see also* will be found next to or below the corresponding topic, subtopic or detail.

Example:

LIGHT COMMUNICATION SYSTEMS
    See also
   Fiber optics
   Lasers--Communication use
LIGHT COOKING *See* Low calorie cooking
LIGHT-EMITTING DIODES *See* Diodes

Each entry represents one article from one magazine. It can be found once in the index or many times according to the number of times it is cross referenced under various topics, subtopics, or detail key words. This is up to the Guide's authors.

Specifically, each entry contains information in the following order:
1. the entry word
2. complete magazine article title
3. the author's name, if given
4. indication of visual aids, if any
5. the abbreviated name of the magazine or periodical (more recently given in italics)
6. the volume number of the magazine
7. the page numbers
8. indication of month, day, year of issue in abbreviated form.

If visual aids or a bibliography are found in an article referenced in the Readers' Guide, the corresponding entry will indicate through the use of the following abbreviations: por/portrait, map/map, bibl/bibliography, and il/illustration.

Example:

LUMBER INDUSTRY
> *See also*
> Weyerhaeuser Company
> > **Federal aid**
> Timber! K. E. Franklin. *The New Republic* 200:12-14
> > Ja 2 '89

LUNAR BASES
> Moon base made easy. il *Popular Mechanics* 166:14 Ja
> > '89

Remember, the Readers' Guide is very important because next to a newspaper index, the most current information on any subject can be found through the correct use of a magazine and periodical index.

6. Of what importance is the word *about* in the guide?
7. Explain cross referencing in the Readers' Guide index.
8. Describe the contents of an entry in the guide.
9. List the visual aids and their abbreviations that might be found in an entry for the Readers' Guide.

556   **ABRIDGED READERS' GUIDE TO PERIODICAL LITERATURE 1987**

Light airplanes *See* Airplanes, Light
Light bulbs
Casting light on the latest in bulbs. D. H. Dunn. il
Bus Week p104 F 9 '87
Light-bulb savers: not a bright idea [work of Alexander
Emanuel] D. Stover. *Pop Sci* 230:34 My '87
Light bulbs in art *See* Light in art
Light communication systems
See also
Fiber optics
Lasers—Communication use
Light cooking *See* Low calorie cooking
Light-emitting diodes *See* Diodes
Light filters
Cokin creative filter system. K. Bloom. il *Petersens
Photogr Mag* 16:48-50 Je '87
Supafrost diffusion filters. R. Rosen. il *Petersens Photogr
Mag* 16:52-3 My '87
Light in art
See also
Sunlight in art
Neon. il *Natl Geogr World* 140:36-9 Ap '87
A vision in high visibility, Eric Staller believes in traveling
lit [use of light bulbs] M. Small. il por *People Wkly*
28:137-9 O 19 '87
Light of day [film] *See* Motion picture reviews—Single
works
Light production in animals and plants *See* Bioluminescence
Light rail systems
Trolleys—by any other name. C. Skrzycki. il *U S News
World Rep* 102:46 Ap 6 '87
Light shows
Equipment
The lava light returns [Eye of the Storm] S. A. Booth.
il *Pop Mech* 164:14 S '87
Light verse *See* Poetry
Lightbody, Andy
Terror-proof tourism [excerpt from The terrorism survival
guide] *Harpers* 275:24 Jl '87
Lighthouse tenders
Turn out the lighthouse, the party's over: keeper Joe
Larnard stoically awaits automation [Boston Light]
R. Arias. il pors *People Wkly* 28:86-8 S 21 '87
Women of the lights. E. De Wire. il *Am Hist Illus*
21:42-9 F '87
Lighthouses
Turn out the lighthouse, the party's over: keeper Joe
Larnard stoically awaits automation [Boston Light]
R. Arias. il pors *People Wkly* 28:86-8 S 21 '87
Conservation and restoration
The great lighthouse giveaway. N. Cutner. il *Life* 10:36-42
Ag '87
#4   The tide is turning for old beacons adrift at land's
end [cover story] D. G. Hanson. bibl (p145) il
Smithsonian 18:98-106+ Ag '87
Lighting
See also
Automobiles—Lighting
Discotheques—Lighting
Electric lamps
Photography—Light and lighting
Skylights
Control
See also
Electric switches
Lighting, Outdoor
How to install outdoor lights: easier than you think!
C. M. Stowers. il *Better Homes Gard* 65:78+ My '87
Low-voltage outdoor lighting. G. D. Cook. il *Better Homes
Gard* 65:50 O '87
Lightning
See also
Space flight—Lightning hazards
Lightning: nature's terrible swift sword. J. Sedgwick.
il *Read Dig* 131:23-5+ Ag '87
#3   Whistling for lightning's rhythm [research by William
C. Armstrong] S. Weisburd. *Sci News* 131:372 Je 13
'87
Lih, Lars T.
Gorbachev and the reform movement. bibl f *Curr Hist*
86:309-12+ O '87
Lila Acheson Wallace Wing *See* Metropolitan Museum
of Art (New York, N.Y.). Lila Acheson Wallace Wing
Lilla, Mark
The body politic. *New Repub* 197:14-16 S 28 '87
Lillie, John M., 1937-
about
Edelman: a new Lucky strike? K. M. Hafner. il por
Bus Week p49 F 23 '87

Lilly (Eli) and Company *See* Eli Lilly and Company
Lillywhite, Harvey B.
Snakes under pressure [cover story] il *Nat Hist* 96:58-67
N '87
Lily Tomlin: the film behind the show [film] *See* Motion
picture reviews—Single works
L'Image Graphics
The couple with the hippest greeting cards in town
[T. Barnes and W. Wilson] P. Finch. il pors *Bus
Week* p80 Je 8 '87
Liman, Arthur L.
about
'I'm not a potted plant'. A. Press. il pors *Newsweek*
110:21-2 Jl 20 '87
Sparring partners. J. V. Lamar, Jr. il pors *Time* 130:23
Jl 20 '87
Limericks
There was an old lady from Spain . . . B. Dubivsky.
il *N Y Times Mag* p40-1 My 10 '87
Limitation of arms *See* Disarmament
Limited Editions Club
Matchmakers. R. Bass. il *Art News* 86:9-10 F '87
Limited partnership
See also
Boston Ventures Management Inc.
Master limited partnership
Mesa Limited Partnership
Securities Groups
Stranger Partnership Fund
Cutting the risks in the restaurant game. T. Carson.
il *Bus Week* p120-1 Ag 17 '87
#1   Hooking up to a cable-TV limited partnership. M. Ivey.
il *Bus Week* p152 Je 8 '87
Limited partnerships drastically limited performance. il
Money 16:14 D '87
Limited partnerships for those who love long shots
[research and development limited partnerships] G.
Weiss. *Bus Week* p180 Jl 20 '87
The next land boom [raw land syndicators] J. B. Quinn.
il *Newsweek* 109:56 Mr 2 '87
Were STC's optical disks just a mirage? [suit brought
by limited partnership investors against Storage Tech-
nology Corp.] M. Ivey. il *Bus Week* p67 Je 15 '87
What partnership sponsors are peddling now. *Money*
16:14 Ap '87
Taxation
Building a cozy tax shelter with historic rehabs [real
estate limited partnership] T. Segal. il *Bus Week* p118
S 7 '87
#2   A 'PIG' can help with tax-shelter losses [passive income
generators] B. Hitchings. *Bus Week* p94 Ap 20 '87
Propping up paper losses [passive income generators]
H. Wheelwright. *Money* 16:159 Jl '87
Limousine service
See also
Execucoach (Firm)
Limulus *See* Horseshoe crabs
Lin, Florence
Shanghai secrets. il *N Y Times Mag* p63-4 S 27 '87
Lin Data Corporation
Why Nashua looks even richer now [acquisition of Lin
Data] G. G. Marcial. *Bus Week* p126 Jl 20 '87
Linck, Robert
about
Trapped in the wreckage of Flight 1713, Robert Linck
survives to fly home again. A. Richman. il pors *People
Wkly* 28:98-102 D 21 '87
Lincoln, Abraham, 1809-1865
about
My father, Mr. Lincoln and me. E. Ziegler. il *Read
Dig* 130:35-40 F '87
Fiction
Lincoln: fiction & fact [interview with W. Safire] A.
M. Schlesinger. il pors *Am Herit* 38:84-9 D '87
A modern vote for Abraham Lincoln [interview with
W. Safire] A. P. Sanoff. il por *U S News World
Rep* 103:57 Ag 24 '87
Safire on Lincoln and 'Freedom'. J. Kroll. il pors
Newsweek 110:56-7 Ag 31 '87
Historiography
Looking for Lincoln in the 1980's. G. S. Boritt. bibl
il pors *N Y Times Book Rev* 92:1+ F 8 '87
Press conferences
Lincoln meets the press [imaginary conference with
Lincoln's responses based on actual statements] W.
Safire. il *N Y Times Mag* p28-9 Ag 23 '87
Lincoln, Carl Eric, 1946-
M*A*S*H's Maine man. il pors *50 Plus* 27:42+ Mr
'87

The Readers' Guide to Periodical Literature

#1
Topic:
Subtopic:
Detail:
Title of article:
Author:
Title of Magazine:
Illustrated?
Volume #:
Page #'s:
Date of issue:
Cross reference(first two):

Extra information:

#2
Topic:
Subtopic:
Detail:
Title of article:
Author:
Title of Magazine:
Illustrated?
Volume #:
Page #'s:
Date of issue:
Cross reference(first two):

Extra information:

#3
Topic:
Subtopic:
Detail:
Title of article:
Author:
Title of Magazine:
Illustrated?
Volume #:
Page #'s:
Date of issue:
Cross reference(first two):

Extra information:

#4
Topic:
Subtopic:
Detail:
Title of article:
Author:
Title of Magazine:
Illustrated?
Volume #:
Page #'s:
Date of issue:
Cross reference(first two):

Extra information:

Horseback riding *See* Horsemanship
Horseback trips
Horseback camping [British Columbia] il map *Natl Geogr World* 141:7-13 My '87
Toward happier trails. J. Zumbo. il *Outdoor Life* 180:70+ N '87
Horsemanship
See also
Polo
A boy who climbed the marigold [P. Burkarth's participation in horseback riding program for the handicapped] A. Jones. il pors *Read Dig* 130:96-100 F '87
"Running Christ against the bandits" [horsemen carry on Easter tradition in Chile] C. Caviedes. il *Nat Hist* 96:44-53 My '87
The triumph of Mikko Mayeda [multiple sclerosis victim becomes a competitive equestrian] V. Scott. il por *Good Housekeep* 204:40 Mr '87
Horsepower (Mechanics)
Torque and horsepower. R. Grable. il *Mot Trend* 39:106-7 S '87
Horses
Breeding
Betting too big on the blood [catalog entry for thoroughbred horse at Keeneland Selected Yearling Sale] C. Flake. *Harpers* 274:58-9 My '87
Building a winning horse with biotech [embryo transfer used on Grand Prix jumpers] S. Budiansky. il *U S News World Rep* 103:63 N 2 '87
For a real day at the races, buy a horse. D. Cook. il *Bus Week* p162-3 My 11 '87
High-tech horses [embryo transplants] J. Horgan. il *Sci Am* 257:29-31 S '87
Old foes, new race [breeding stallions Alydar and Affirmed at Calumet Farm] W. Nack. il *Sports Illus* 66:44-6+ Je 8 '87
Training
See also
Horses, Wild—Training
Treatment
Bill Graham reins in the creeps who kill horses for profit. D. Van Biema. il pors *People Wkly* 28:46-8 Jl 20 '87
Horses, Fossil
Life's little joke [evolution] S. J. Gould. il *Nat Hist* 96:16+ Ap '87
Horses, Miniature
Little horse, big deal—protestors cry 'There goes the neighborhood' [P. Fairchild fights to keep her miniature horse in Thousand Oaks, Calif.] il pors *People Wkly* 27:96-7 Je 1 '87
Horses, Race
A high-stakes dream [Look To The Top] B. Weber. il por *N Y Times Mag* p62 Ag 2 '87
In the groove at long last [champion sprinter Groovy] W. Nack. il *Sports Illus* 67:50-3 O 19 '87
The long run for the roses [history of Demons Begone, early favorite to win the Kentucky Derby] L. Rosellini. il *U S News World Rep* 102:64-5 My 4 '87
Auctions
See Auctions
Breeding
See Horses—Breeding
Handicapping
See Horse race betting
Horses, Wild
The final roundup for America's wild horses? M. Satchell. il *U S News World Rep* 102:68-9 Mr 2 '87
Training
These cowboys are convicts [taming wild mustangs at Colorado State Penitentiary] J. Willwerth. il *Time* 130:20 Ag 31 '87
Horses in art
Exhibitions
Susan Rothenberg. J. Bell. il *Art News* 86:147 My '87
Horseshoe crabs
Diving for horseshoe crabs. il *Natl Geogr World* 141:20-3 My '87
Horticulture
See also
Gardens and gardening
Vegetable gardens and gardening
Horticulture as a profession
Turning your green thumb into a new career [cover story] S. Brewer. il *50 Plus* 27:27-31 O '87
Horticulture therapy *See* Gardens and gardening—Therapeutic use
Horton, Earle
about
Flying high with Church's Chicken. il pors *Ebony* 42:72+ Jl '87

Horton, Mark
The Swahili corridor. il maps *Sci Am* 257:86-8+ S '87
Horton, Yogi, d. 1987
about
Luther Vandross' drummer killed in 17-story leap. il por *Jet* 72:53 Je 29 '87
Hosang, Ulric
about
$3 million lotto win 'numbs' Queens man. il por *Jet* 72:24 Ag 24 '87
Hosenball, Mark
Autopen presidency. *New Repub* 196:16-18 My 11 '87
The culture of lying [cover story] *New Repub* 197:16-18 Jl 13-20 '87
The Khashoggi memo. *New Repub* 196:14+ F 2 '87
Leak-a-boo. *New Repub* 197:23-5 O 12 '87
Spooked. *New Repub* 197:13-14 Ag 31 '87
(jt. auth) See Isikoff, Michael, and Hosenball, Mark
Hosiery
Baby Steps are the socks of choice for toddlers who don't want to hit the skids early [marketed by V. Reisman and R. Lerner] il *People Wkly* 28:183 N 16 '87
I dreamed I saved a swimmer in my Maidenform pantyhose [protection from jellyfish] S. Brownlee. il *Discover* 8:52 Ag '87
Hoskins, Bob, 1942-
about
Cockney charisma. W. Boyd. il pors *N Y Times Mag* p52+ D 6 '87
Hoskins, Joe
about
Detroit football coach files $10 million job suit. *Jet* 71:46 Mr 9 '87
Hospital care
See also
Children—Hospital care
Children—Preparation for hospital and medical care
Infants, Newborn—Hospital care
Intensive care units
Malpractice
Monitoring (Medical care)
Costs
See also
AIDS (Disease)—Costs
The rising cost of health care: what it means to the nation, the elderly, and you [cover story; special issue] il *Sch Update* 119:2-12+ Ap 20 '87
Hospital Corp. of America
HCA may breathe new life into ESOPs. G. Weiss. il *Bus Week* p94 Je 15 '87
Physician, heal thy chain [plan to sell Hospital Corp. of America hospitals to employee-owned company] S. Ticer. *Bus Week* p52 Je 1 '87
Hospital equipment industry
See also
Baxter Travenol Laboratories Inc.
Hospital interns *See* Interns (Medicine)
Hospital management industry
See also
Gateway Medical Systems Inc.
Hospital Corp. of America
Humana Inc
Prognosis: empty beds and falling profits. J. O. Hamilton. il *Bus Week* p102 Ja 12 '87
Hospital patient representatives
Patient reps: the Rx for hospital hassles. I. Pave. il *Bus Week* p164 Je 22 '87
Hospital patients
Civil rights
See also
Hospital patient representatives
Psychology
Patients' best friend [pet room at the Swedish American Hospital in Rockford, Ill.] il *Prevention* 39:8 Ap '87
Psychiatric 'stretch' in the hospital [research by George Fulop and others] *Sci News* 132:94 Ag 8 '87
Visitors
See Hospitals—Visitors
Hospital ships
See also
Americares Foundation
Hospitality
See also
Entertaining
Guests
Hospitals
See also
Children—Hospitals
Hospital care
Nursing homes

The Readers' Guide to Periodical Literature

1. Locate the topic: **Horsemanship**
   a. Name the cross reference topic
   b. What is the triumph of Mikko Mayeda?

2. Locate the topic: **Horses**
   a. List the three subtopics.
   b. What is the cross reference for the subtopic: training?
   c. Who wrote the one article under the subtopic: treatment?

3. If you were interested in **Horticulture** as a profession, to which magazine, volume, and issue should you turn?

4. If you were interested in articles on **Hospitality**, which cross references are suggested?

5. If you wanted information on **Horses in Art**, to which magazine, volume, and date of issue should you turn?

6. If you wanted information on **Mechanical Horsepower**, to which magazine, volume, and date of issue should you turn?

The American Heritage Index

FOCUS

The focus of this lesson is the use of the *American Heritage Index* and the companion *A Chronological Subject Guide to American Heritage.*

TEACHER PREPARATION

1. Check your library to see if both publications and index(es) are to be found.
2. Read through material.
3. Have two issues of *American Heritage* available for the students to see: a recent paper cover and a hard bound copy from 1979 or before. Your library might, of course, have the soft covers bound in volumes.
4. Have the *Index* and the *Guide* available in class.
5. A new index covering the five years from December 1982 to December 1987 is now available.

BACKGROUND INFORMATION

1. If ever there was a magazine that needed to be included in a book talk, this is it. Pull out the June, 1983, issue for an historical overview of baseball, pp. 65-79. Or football, p. 102, in September, 1988. How about the 10 greatest American cars: February, 1986, pp. 32-41, to find out why "It's a Duesie!" is still an acceptable accolade? Or show the picture on p. 4 in December, 1976, to see if the students can figure out why the pioneer woman is collecting buffalo chips. Or even if they know what buffalo chips are? If they don't, refer them to the article in October, 1979, pp. 28-29. The article in April, 1983, (pp. 49-64) on the ill-fated whaler, The *Essex*, is gripping enough to be read on Hallowe'en. You'd better read it first---survival via cannibalism!
2. Using this index is truly a case of "If you can't find it the first time, look, look again." Under "New Jersey," there's a subtopic about a "duel between Burr and Hamilton, June 74:99-100." That reference does not appear under Burr. Therefore, you must reiterate to the students the necessity of checking and rechecking. Emphasize the rewards in terms of wealth of material.

CONCEPTS

• Understanding that articles in American Heritage can be retrieved through the use of the American Heritage Index.
• Understanding that although American Heritage is about American history, the articles are not relegated to items about the distant past.
• Understanding that the use of the Index represents a challenge for them.

VOCABULARY

index supplement   supplementary   specific   companion   structure   parentheses   chronological
quotation marks   cross referencing

OBJECTIVES

The student will understand that:

1. The *American Heritage Index* is an index that corresponds to the *American Heritage* magazine, a bimonthly magazine of American history chronicling past and present events.

2. The *American Heritage Index* covers the years from December, 1954, through October, 1982, and that a supplementary two-year index covers the years from December, 1982, through October, 1984. A new five year index covers the years from December, 1982, through December, 1987.

3. Although *American Heritage* magazine covers current topics of today, it also offers articles that construct a broad overview of topics of the past as seen through the eyes of the historian.

4. The *American Heritage Index* alphabetically references entries through subject, author and article title, and that each illustration can be found by artist, title, and subject.

5. Structurally, each entry is offered on a three-column page with the entry word against the left margin of each column, with the rest of the entry indented.

6. Each entry contains author or illustrator, article title, issue by month, volume number and page.

7. Volume number and pages are separated by a colon, that the article title is in quotation marks and that the title of any article or book from any source other than *American Heritage* will be indicated through italics rather than quotation marks.

8. Subject entries are then divided alphabetically into subtopics, and the subtopic entry will be indented and will include subtopic entry word, volume number and page.

9. All pages containing illustrations will be so indicated through the use of bold print.

10. Subject entries of people, places or things that are not immediately recognizable are often defined according to occupation or importance within the entry, e.g. Diga Diga Doo song.

11. A companion volume to the *American Heritage Index* is *A Chronological Subject Guide to American Heritage.*

12. In *A Chronological Subject Guide To American Heritage* is a structure that encompasses eleven broad headings which are subdivided into sections that include the areas of social, cultural, military, political and economic knowledge of the time period as discussed in selected articles representing these aspects of American history.

13. Each selected article is then represented as an entry under the appropriate topic then subtopic, and that each entry includes the title of the article as it appears in the *American Heritage* magazine, the author, the date of the magazine issue, in parentheses the volume and number, the page/pages and a short summary statement of the focus of the article.

14. To effectively use the *American Heritage Index* the student must generate multiple key words or topic/subtopic areas as a cue system for cross referencing is not used extensively in the structure of the index.

MATERIAL NEEDED
Activity Sheet 22-a through 22-c and 22-b through 22-c in optional student workbook.

ACTIVITIES
1. Discuss 22-a after reading. Have copies of the periodical and index available.

2. Discuss the context questions, indicated by the Stop Sign.

3. Discuss or assign 22-b and 22-c after reading. Have copies of the periodical and guide available.

5. Discuss the context questions, indicated by the Stop Sign.

EXTENDED ACTIVITIES
1. Let the students do a time line based on *Chronological Guide.*

2. Assign each student a different week during the year during which he/she will be responsible for an intriguing story from American Heritage. Develop basic format for a one-side-of-paper presentation that can be hung on bulletin board until the next week.

The American Heritage Index

The *American Heritage Index* is the index for the *American Heritage* magazine. The magazine, published every two months, offers a broad overview of major events concerning America's past as well as her present. The index covers the years of publication from December, 1954, through October, 1982. A supplementary two year index updates through October, 1984. A new five year index covers the years December, 1982, through December, 1987. It details subjects covered in the *American Heritage Magazine* during those specific times. Another addition to the basic index and supplement is a companion index titled *A Chronological Subject Guide to American Heritage*. This also will be discussed in detail.

The Basic Index

The *American Heritage Index* alphabetically references entries through subject, author and title. Each illustration also can be found by the artist's last name, title or subject.

It is important for you to remember that to use the *American Heritage Index* to its best advantage you must list and use many key or entry words for topics or subtopic areas. This is because the see/see also cross referencing cue word system is not used extensively in the structure of the index. It is therefore up to you as the individual researcher to effectively use the index.

Structurally, each entry is offered on a three column page with the entry word placed against the left margin of each column with the rest of the entry indented. Each entry, in turn, contains the name of the author or illustrator, article title, issue by month, volume number and page. The volume number and pages are separated by a colon, the article title is in quotation marks but the title of any article or book from any source other than *American Heritage* will be indicated through italics.

Example:
"LA SALLE AND THE DISCOVERY OF THE GREAT WEST," selection from *The Discovery of the Great West*, book by Francis Parkman, Apr 57:4,6, 8-15, 18, 71-91.
"LA SALLE ON THE MISSISSIPPI," porfolio of paintings by George Catlin, Apr 57:**4-19**

Subject entries are alphabetical. Subtopics of subject entries are clustered alphabetically and are structurally indented under the main topic. The subtopic entry contains the same type of information as the main entry.

All articles containing illustrations are indicated through bold print. Subject entries of people, places or things that are not immediately recognizable are often defined

The American Heritage Index

according to occupation or importance within the entry.

example:
STARKOFSKY, employee in Triangle Waist Company fire, Aug 57:57
STEBBINS, N. L. photograph of the *General Slocum*, excursion steamer, by, Oct
  79:**62-63**

1. What is the focus of American Heritage Magazine?
2. What is the general organization of the American Heritage Index?
3. Since the *see/see also* cue system is not used extensively in the index, how should
you cross reference when using the index?
4. Describe the structure of an entry.

5. Why are some names defined according to occupation or importance in the index?

A Chronological Subject Guide to American Heritage

As previously mentioned, a companion guide to the *American Heritage Index* is *A Chronological Subject Guide to American Heritage*. The purpose of the guide is to present a chronological view (by time period) of American history. It is structured to focus on one general and ten chronologically listed subject headings detailing America's growth. Each heading is divided into areas concerning the social, cultural, military, political and economic happenings of each time period.

In this guide, each entry is structured to correspond to a selected article in the American Heritage Magazine. Each entry is placed first in terms of one of the eleven broad areas and then under the appropriate subtopic.

The entry, itself, includes the title of the article as it appears in the *American Heritage Magazine*, the author, the date of the magazine issue, in parentheses will be the volume and number, the page or pages and a short summary statement of the focus of the article.

example:

3/THE ERA OF THE REVOLUTION: 1763 - 1783

MILITARY HISTORY
The Girls Behind the Guns Fairfax Downey Dec. 56 (VIII-1) 46. Molly Pitcher

The American Heritage Index

and Molly Corbin, first-rate cannoneers.

SOCIAL AND CULTURAL HISTORY

Why Washington Stood Up in the Boat George F. Scheer Dec. 64 (XVI-1)17. Memoir of an artist who modeled for Leutze's painting.

A Medical Profile of George Washington Rudolph Marx Aug. 55(VI-5) 42. A doctor analyzes Washington's medical history and concludes that today the general would be considered unfit for duty.

This index will be of great value to you when researching America's past or present.

6. Describe the basic physical structure of *A Chronological Subject Guide to American Heritage.*

7. Describe the elements of an entry.

8. When would you use the Chronological Guide rather than the *American Heritage Index?*

9. How might both guides benefit you as a student researcher?

The American Heritage Index

Use the page labeled Activity 22-b which is from the *American Heritage Index* and fill in answers:

#1
Name/topic:
Subtopic:
Date of issue:
Page #:
Illustrated?:

#2
Name/topic:
Subtopic:
Date of issue:
Page #:
Illustrated?:

#3
Name/topic:
Subtopic:
Date of issue:
Page #:
Illustrated?:

#4
Name/topic:
Subtopic:
Date of issue:
Page #:
Illustrated?:

#5
Name/topic:
Subtopic:
Date of issue:
Page #:
Illustrated?:

#6
Name/topic:
Subtopic:
Date of issue:
Page #:
Illustrated?:

#7
Name/topic:
Subtopic:
Date of issue:
Page #:
Illustrated?:

#8
Name/topic:
Subtopic:
Date of issue:
Page #:
Illustrated?:

7/THE EMERGENCE OF MODERN AMERICA: 1865–1914

SOCIAL AND CULTURAL HISTORY *(continued)*

American Gothic Wayne Andrews Oct. 71 (XXII-6) 26. The late-19th-century revival of Gothic style in architecture and furniture.

Urban Pollution—Many Long Years Ago Joel A. Tarr Oct. 71 (XXII-6) 65. The impact of horses (pro and con) on 19th-century urban life.

#4 *A Conquest of Solitude* Robert V. Bruce April 73 (XXIV-3) 28. Alexander Graham Bell and Helen Keller.

The Colossus of His Kind: Jumbo James L. Haley Aug. 73 (XXIV-5) 62. Story of the great circus elephant.

Eliot of Harvard Alexander Eliot Aug. 74 (XXV-5) 4. The career of the Harvard president.

1876: The Eagle Screams Lynne Vincent Cheney April 74 (XXV-3) 15. The story of the Philadelphia Exposition celebrating the 100th anniversary of the Declaration of Independence.

Scott Joplin Rudi Blesh June 75 (XXVI-4) 26. The career of the ragtime composer.

#1 *Mrs. Frank Leslie's Illustrated Newspaper* Lynne Vincent Cheney Oct. 75 (XXVI-6) 42. The careeer of Miriam Follin, actress turned publisher.

#3 *How Mother Got Her Day* James P. Johnson April 79 (XXX-3) 14. The story of Anna Jarvis and her campaign for a holiday to celebrate mothers.

FOREIGN AFFAIRS, 1867–1914

#2 *Seward's Wise Folly* Robert L. Reynolds Dec. 60 (XII-1) 44. The purchase of Alaska, 1867.

The Needless War with Spain William E. Leuchtenburg Feb. 57 (VIII-2) 32. Origins of the Spanish-American War.

The Sham Battle of Manila Leon Wolff Dec. 60 (XII-1) 65. The aftermath of Dewey's capture of Manila in the Spanish-American War.

Under Fire in Cuba William Ransom Roberts Dec. 77 (XXIX-1) 78. A volunteer's account of the war with Spain.

American Characters: Winfield Scott Schley Richard F. Snow Dec. 82 (XXXIV-1) 92. Portrait of a naval officer in the Spanish-American War.

Last of the Rough Riders V. C. Jones Aug. 69 (XX-5) 42. The recollections of Jesse Langdon, a veteran of T.R.'s regiment in the Spanish-American War.

How We Got Guantanamo Robert D. Heinl, Jr. Feb. 62 (XIII-2) 18. Cuba in 1898—the Marines take America's first overseas base.

53

A Chronological Subject Guide to American Heritage

#1
Topic
Subtopic
Article Title
Author
Magazine
Date
Page
Summary

#2
Topic
Subtopic
Article Title
Author
Magazine
Date
Page
Summary

#3
Topic
Subtopic
Article Title
Author
Magazine
Date
Page
Summary

#4
Topic
Subtopic
Article Title
Author
Magazine
Date
Page
Summary

The National Geographic Index

FOCUS
The focus of this lesson will be using the *National Geographic Index*.

TEACHER PREPARATION
1. Check to see which volumes of the index are available to you. A 1989 copyright index is available.
2.. Check to see how far back the *National Geographic* are retained.
3. Read material thoroughly and use the index to locate some material.

BACKGROUND INFORMATION
1. Usually, libraries will have back issues of *National Geographic* because someone is always donating issues.
2. *National Geographic* contains readable prose and interesting maps. It's usually a magazine in which you can get a disinterested reader engrossed.
3. *The Index* is easy to teach and easy to use.

CONCEPTS
- **Understanding that the National Geographic has its own separate index.**
- **Understanding that the index is easy to use.**

VOCABULARY
categories access alphabetically prior index supplement revised previous format indices acronym overview interfiled

OBJECTIVES
The student will understand that:

1. The purpose of the *National Geographic Index* is to allow access to the articles written concerning over 7000 categories covering many of the events of the period from 1947 to 1983, as depicted in the *National Geographic* magazine. The 1989 copyright edition covers the 100 years from 1888-1988.

2. A companion edition to the 1947-1983 index has been published covering the years 1888-1946.

3. Index supplements are published two times a year covering six issues each to update all categories.

4. The *National Geographic Index* provides a section which offers an overview of the history of the National Geographic Society, medals awarded by the Society, and an indication of their interrelated publications.

5. The *National Geographic Index* has an alphabetical listing of subjects, topics, and names.

6. All subjects are in bold print against the left margin and that there are three left margins on the page as each page is divided into three columns.

7. All subtopics are indented and are of a lighter print than the topic.

8. All entries are ordered alphabetically by the first most important word in the title of the article, book, map or television show, dropping *a, an, the,* when it appears at the beginning.

9. The *National Geographic Index* offers cross referencing through the words *see* and *see also*.

10. The *see* entry is placed to the right of the invalid entry word and the replacement, valid, entry words will immediately follow.

11. The *see also* cross reference appears at the end of all the entries for a given topic or subtopic and will supply alternative entry words to help further research.

12. All acronyms will be cross referenced by *see* and will refer to the original upon which the acronym was based.

13. An entry in the *National Geographic Index* will include the entry word or phrase, the complete article title, the author, the photographer/illustrator, number of illustrations included in article, indication if a map is included, pages, and issue date by month and year.

14. All large colored maps that are offered as supplements are also listed in the index in a separate section and are alphabetically placed by map title with a narrative description of the geographic content of each in the 1947-1969 edition, while they are interfiled with all entries in the 1947-1983 edition.

15. A revised publication copyright date 1984 was printed to cover the years 1947-1983 and now includes books and television as well as the articles and maps of the previous issues. The new copyright date of 1989 is available.

16. All entries including articles, books, television shows, and maps are alphabetically interfiled by individual title of each under the appropriate topics and subtopics.

17. All articles, books, television shows, and maps are coded in the margin by the entry to differentiate one from the other at a glance.

MATERIAL NEEDED
Activity Sheets 23-a through 23-c and 23-b through 23-c in optional student workbook.
National Geographic issues
National Geographic Index

ACTIVITIES
1. Read through Activity 23-a orally in class using transparency of index page to highlight items being discussed.
2. Use context questions indicated by Stop Sign as in-class activity or homework.
3. Activities 23-b and 23-c are replications of an index page, along with questions.

EXTENDED ACTIVITIES
1. Using Ectagraphic Visualmaker or any copy camera stand, permit student or group to make a slide presentation for illustrating class project using photos from *National Geographic*. Correlate with another subject.

2. Permit student or group of students to correlate historical fiction reading list with any applicable articles from *National Geographic*. For example: Albrecht, Lillie V. *The Spinning Wheel Secret*. NY: Hastings House, 1965; and McDowell, Bart, "Deerfield Keeps a Truce With Time," *National Geographic*, June, 1969, pp 780-809.

3. Develop a list of acronyms and identify the full name.

The National Geographic Index

The *National Geographic Index* is an index whose purpose is to enable you, as the student researcher, to alphabetically access according to subject or topic any article(s) written in the *National Geographic Magazine.* Over 7000 categories are alphabetically listed by subject, topic or name. Although one index in print covers the period of time from 1947-1983, a companion edition also indexes the additional period of time from 1888-1946. An index with a copyright of 1989 covers the 100 years from 1888 to 1988, comprising the information from all of the prior publications.

Also, at this time, index supplements are published two times a year and cover six issues of *National Geographic.* These supplements update all corresponding categories. The revised publication copyright dates of 1984 and 1989, also include in the listings references for books and television shows as well as the usual magazine articles and maps also presented in the previous issues. All articles, books, television shows and maps are differentiated from one another through a coding system of figures and colors. The code is placed in the margin next to the beginning of the entry, a key is in place at the bottom of every other page and recognition of entry type becomes obvious at a glance.

The physical presentation or format of a page in the index consists of a page divided into three columns. Subjects, topics, and names are placed in bold print two spaces to the left of the left margin of a column. All entries, in turn, are in line against the left margin under the corresponding subject. All subtopic entry words have a print lighter than the topic but darker than the entry. All subtopic entry words are in line and are indented 2(two) spaces to the right of the topic entry word.

Example:
NAPOLEON I:
• Napoleon. By John J. Putman. Photos by Gordon W. Gahan. 142-189, Feb. 1982
• St. Helena: the Forgotten Island. By Quentin Keynes. 265-280, Aug. 1950
• Sunny Corsica: French Morsel in the Mediterranean. By Robert Cairns. Photos by Joseph J. Scherschel. 401-423, Sept. 1973

1. How are the entries listed in the National Geographic Index?
2. If you were interested in locating a particular National Geographic television show on a specific topic, to which index would you turn?
3. Of what value to you, the student researcher, is the coding system per entry used in the 1947-1983 index and in the 1888-1988 index?
4. Explain the physical appearance of a page in regard to: topic, subtopic, columns.

The National Geographic Index

All entries, including magazine article titles, books, television shows and maps are interfiled alphabetically by the individual title of each under the appropriate topic or subtopic. To order, all entries are placed alphabetically by the first most important word in the title of the article, book, map or television show, dropping *a, an, the* when it appears at the beginning. The 1989 copyright *Index* covering the years 1888-1988 arranges the topic entries alphabetically but puts the subtopic entries in chronological order beginning with the most current date of publication.

As in most indices, *The National Geographic Index* offers cross referencing through the cue words of *see* and *see also*. The *see* entry is placed to the right of the invalid entry word and the replacement, valid entry words, will immediately follow.

examples:
CIVILIZATIONS, Early. *See* Early Civilizations
MYXOMYCETES. *See* Slime Mold

The *see also* cross reference, in turn, appears at the end of all the entries for a given topic or subtopic and will supply alternative entry words to help further research.

example:
PAINTING: *See also listing under* Art Galleries; Rock Art

Also cross referenced will be all acronyms by *see*. You then will be referred to the original words upon which the acronym was based.

example:
NASA. *See* National Aeronautics and Space Administration

An entry in *The National Geographic Index* will include the entry word or phrase, the complete article title, the author, the photographer or illustrator, number of illustrations in an article, indication if a map is included, pages, and issue date by month and year.

In addition, all large, colored maps that are offered as supplements also are listed in the index. In a separate section, they are placed alphabetically by map title with a narrative description of the geographic content of each in the 1947-1969 edition, while they are interfiled with all entries in the 1947-1983 edition.

The National Geographic Index also provides a section which offers an overview of the history of the National Geographic Society, medals awarded by the Society and an indication of their interrelated publications.

5. How are the articles listed under each topic and subtopic?
6. Of what importance are the cue words: *see/ see also*? How do they relate to acronyms?
7. List the elements of an entry in National Geographic.
8. How are the large, colored supplementary maps of a particular region indexed?
9. Why will you not find information on any other magazine in this index?

● Articles ◆ Books ▲ Maps ● Television

417

Activity 23-b, *National Geographic Index*   Utilization of Sources

The National Geographic Index

Use the index page labeled Activity 23-b to answer the questions:

#1
Topic:
Type of entry:
Title:
Author:
Photographer:
Date of Issue:
Page #'s:
Extra Information:
Cross References:

#2
Topic:
Type of entry:
Title:
Author:
Photographer:
Date of Issue:
Page #'s:
Extra Information:
Cross References:

#3
Topic:
Type of entry:
Title:
Author:
Photographer:
Date of Issue:
Page #'s:
Extra Information:
Cross References:

#4
Topic:
Type of entry:
Title:
Author:
Photographer:
Date of Issue:
Page #'s:
Extra Information:
Cross References:

#5
Topic:
Type of entry:
Title:
Author:
Photographer:
Date of Issue:
Page #'s:
Extra Information:
Cross References:

#6
Topic:
Type of entry:
Title:
Author:
Photographer:
Date of Issue:
Page #'s:
Extra Information:
Cross References:

● Solving the Riddles of Wetherill Mesa. By Douglas Osborne. Paintings by Peter V. Bianchi. NGS research grant. 155-195, Feb. 1964
● 20th-century Indians Preserve Customs of the Cliff Dwellers. Photos by William Belknap, Jr. NGS research grant. 196-211, Feb. 1964
● Your Society to Seek New Light on the Cliff Dwellers. NGS research grant. 154-156, Jan. 1959

WETLANDS:
● Can We Save Our Salt Marshes? By Stephen W. Hitchcock. Photos by William R. Curtsinger. 729-765, June 1972
◆ *Explore a Spooky Swamp.* 1978
● Florida's Booming–and Beleaguered–Heartland. By Joseph Judge. Photos by Jonathan Blair. 585-621, Nov. 1973
● Island, Prairie, Marsh, and Shore. By Charlton Ogburn. Photos by Bates Littlehales. 350-381, Mar. 1979
● Marsh Dwellers of Southern Iraq. By Wilfred Thesiger. Photos by Gavin Maxwell. 205-239, Feb. 1958
● Mississippi Delta: The Land of the River. By Douglas Lee. Photos by C. C. Lockwood. 226-253, Aug. 1983
● The People of New Jersey's Pine Barrens. By John McPhee. Photos by William R. Curtsinger. 52-77, Jan. 1974
● Rare Birds Flock to Spain's Marismas. By Roger Tory Peterson. 397-425, Mar. 1958
● San Francisco Bay: The Beauty and the Battles. By Cliff Tarpy. Photos by James A. Sugar. 814-845, June 1981
● Sea Islands: Adventuring Along the South's Surprising Coast. By James Cerruti. Photos by Thomas Nebbia and James L. Amos. 366-393, Mar. 1971
● Sudan: Arab-African Giant. By Robert Caputo. Included: The Sudd swamp. 346-379, Mar. 1982
● The Swans of Abbotsbury. By Michael Moynihan. Photos by Barnet Saidman. 563-570, Oct. 1959
● Trouble in Bayou Country. By Jack and Anne Rudloe. Photos by C. C. Lockwood. 377-397, Sept. 1979
● Water Dwellers in a Desert World. By Gavin Young. Photos by Nik Wheeler. 502-523, Apr. 1976
● Western Grebes: The Birds That Walk on Water. By Gary L. Nuechterlein. NGS research grant. 624-637, May 1982
● *See also* Corkscrew Swamp; Everglades; Okefenokee Swamp

WETMORE, ALEXANDER:
● Board of Trustees, member. 595, May 1947; 344, Sept. 1948; 65A-65B, July 1954; 364, Mar. 1956; 835, Dec. 1959; 883, Dec. 1960; 555, Oct. 1964; 485, Oct. 1966; 839, Dec. 1970; 151, Aug. 1975; 227, Aug. 1976
● Board of Trustees: Trustee Emeritus. 672, May 1978
● Committee for Research and Exploration, Vice Chairman. 705, June 1947; 175, Feb. 1960; 532, Oct. 1965; 489, Oct. 1967; 881-882, Dec. 1967

● Editorial. By Gilbert M. Grosvenor. 151, Aug. 1975
● Hubbard Medal recipient (1975). 151, Aug. 1975
Author:
● Re-creating Madagascar's Giant Extinct Bird. 488-493, Oct. 1967

WHALES:
● *Calypso* Explores for Underwater Oil. By Jacques-Yves Cousteau. Photos by Louis Malle. NGS research grant. 155-184, Aug. 1955
● Editorial. By Gilbert M. Grosvenor. 721, Dec. 1976
☛ The Great Whales. 439, Oct. 1977; cover, Feb. 1978; Emmy Award. 1, Jan. 1979
● Hunting the Heartbeat of a Whale. By Paul Dudley White and Samuel W. Matthews. NGS research grant. 49-64, July 1956
◆ *Namu.* Announced. 726-728, Nov. 1973
● Whales of the World. 722-767, Dec. 1976
I. The Imperiled Giants. By William Graves. 722-751; II. Exploring the Lives of Whales. By Victor B. Scheffer. 752-767
▲ "Whales of the World." Painting supplement. Map on reverse, *The Great Whales: Migration and Range.* Dec. 1976
● *See also* Belugas; Blue Whales; Bowhead Whales; Gray Whales; Humpback Whales; Killer Whales; Right Whales; *and* Dolphins

WHALING:
● The Azores, Nine Islands in Search of a Future. By Don Moser. Photos by O. Louis Mazzatenta. 261-288, Feb. 1976
● Editorial. By Gilbert M. Grosvenor. 721, Dec. 1976
● The Last U. S. Whale Hunters. By Emory Kristof. 346-353, Mar. 1973 "Ocean mammals are to us what the buffalo was to the Plains Indian." By Lael Morgan. 354-355
● Martha's Vineyard. By William P. E. Graves. Photos by James P. Blair. 778-809, June 1961
● A Naturalist in Penguin Land. By Niall Rankin. 93-116, Jan. 1955
● *Nomad* Sails Long ·Island Sound. By Thomas Horgan. 295-338, Sept. 1957
● Off the Beaten Track of Empire. By Beverley M. Bowie. Photos by Michael Parker. 584-626, Nov. 1957
● Peoples of the Arctic. 144-223, Feb. 1983
I. Introduction by Joseph Judge. 144-149; II. Hunters of the Lost Spirit: Alaskans. By Priit J. Vesilind. Photos by David Alan Harvey. 150-197; III. People of the Long Spring. By Yuri Rytkheu. Photos by Dean Conger. 206-223, Feb. 1983
▲ *Peoples of the Arctic; Arctic Ocean,* double-sided supplement. Feb. 1983
● To Europe with a Racing Start. By Carleton Mitchell. 758-791, June 1958
● Whales of the World. 722-767, Dec. 1976
The Imperiled Giants. By William Graves. 722-751

● *See also* Faeroe Islands; Nantucket; Western Australia

WHARTON, CHARLES HEIZER:
Author:
● Seeking Mindanao's Strangest Creatures. 389-408, Sept. 1948

WHAT a Place to Lay an Egg! By Thomas R. Howell. NGS research grant. 414-419, Sept. 1971

WHAT About Nuclear Energy? By Kenneth F. Weaver. Photos by Emory Kristof. 459-493, Apr. 1979

WHAT Causes Earthquakes. By Maynard M. Miller. 140-141, July 1964

WHAT Future for the Wayana Indians? By Carole Devillers. 66-83, Jan. 1983

WHAT I Saw Across the Rhine. By J. Frank Dobie. 57-86, Jan. 1947

WHAT'S Black and White and Loved All Over? By Theodore H. Reed. Photos by Donna K. Grosvenor. 803-815, Dec. 1972

WHAT'S Happening to Our Climate? By Samuel W. Matthews. 576-615, Nov. 1976

WHAT Is It Like to Walk on the Moon? By David R. Scott. 326-331, Sept. 1973

WHAT'S So Special About Spiders? By Paul A. Zahl. 190-219, Aug. 1971

WHAT Six Experts Say. Contents: Statements from John F. O'Leary, Hans H. Landsberg, Steven C. Wilson, Robert B. Stobaugh, Fred L. Hartley, Amory B. Lovins. 70-73, *Special Report on Energy* (Feb. 1981)

WHAT the Moon Rocks Tell Us. By Kenneth F. Weaver. 788-791, Dec. 1969

WHAT Voyager Saw: Jupiter's Dazzling Realm. By Rick Gore. Photos by NASA. 2-29, Jan. 1980

WHAT Was a Woman Doing There? By W. E. Garrett. 270-271, Feb. 1966

WHAT We've Accomplished in Antarctica. By George J. Dufek. 527-557, Oct. 1959

WHAT You Didn't See in Kohoutek. By Kenneth F. Weaver. 214-223, Aug. 1974

WHATEVER Happened to TVA? By Gordon Young. Photos by Emory Kristof. 830-863, June 1973

WHEAT AND WHEAT GROWING:
● Can the World Feed Its People? By Thomas Y. Canby. Photos by Steve Raymer. 2-31, July 1975
● Canada's Heartland, the Prairie Provinces. By W. E. Garrett. 443-489, Oct. 1970
● North Dakota Comes into Its Own. By Leo A. Borah. Photos by J. Baylor Roberts. 283-322, Sept. 1951
● North With the Wheat Cutters. By Noel Grove. Photos by James A. Sugar. 194-217, Aug. 1972

WHEATLEY, HAROLD G.: Author:
● This Is My Island, Tangier. Photos by David Alan Harvey. 700-725, Nov. 1973

● Articles ◆ Books ▲ Maps ▪ Television

555

The National Geographic Index

Use the index page labeled Activity 23-c to answer the questions:

1. Locate the topic: **Whales**
   a. Write the title of the television show.

   b. In which issue was a picture from this show a magazine cover?

   c. State a title of a book about the topic.

   d. List the title and date of issue of a map on the subject of the Great Whales.

   e. List the first two cross reference topics for the topic whales.

   f. What is the title of the article written by Paul Dudley White and Samuel W. Matthews, published July, 1956? On what page(s) will it be found?

2. Look up the name **Alexander Wetmore**.
   a. In what year did he receive the Hubbard Medal?

   b. In which issue and on what pages was the honor reported?

   c. What is the title of the article that Wetmore authored?

3. Look up the topic: **Wetlands**
   a. Write the title of the one book cited. In what year was it published?

   b. List the three cross reference topics listed for this subject.

4. Look up the topic: **Whaling**
   a. Who wrote the article The Azores, Nine Islands in Search of a Future?

   b. Who was the photographer for that article?

   c. Name the title of the map supplement printed in Feb., 1983, on this subject.

   d. List three cross references given for this topic.

Magazine Article Summaries

FOCUS

The focus of this lesson will be on using one form of periodical article abstracts: Ebsco's *Magazine Article Summaries*.

TEACHER PREPARATION

1. See if your library has MAS, or any form of abstracting service.

2. Read the material thoroughly, preferably with MAS in hand. Work through the activity sheets and keep for handy class reference.

3. If knowledgeable about your class's other assignments, customize the work sheets to include topics that they would be working on.

BACKGROUND INFORMATION

1. Any article abstracting service tries to get the essence of the article. It is not to omit getting the article and reading it, but to make more efficient researchers.

2. MAS is extremely easy to use, and because of its 200 sources, tends to cover more than your school library can.

CONCEPTS

• *Magazine Article Summaries* **is an abstracting service.**

• **Using abstracts is time efficient.**

VOCABULARY

summaries   inset   entry   heading   subheading   cross references   cover story

OBJECTIVES

The student will:

1. Understand the organization and index use of *Magazine Article Summaries*.

2. Utilize magazine summaries found in MAS in a decision-making process when working with MAS.

MATERIAL NEEDED

1. *Magazine Article Summaries*.

2. Activity Sheets 24-a through 24-c and 24-a through 24-c in optional student workbook.

ACTIVITIES

1. Read through material and discuss using transparency.

2. Answer context questions for homework or in class.

3. Do activity sheets.

EXTENDED ACTIVITIES:

1. Bulletin Board showing relationship of brown index pages to white.

2. Have student or group of students list some of the periodicals used. See how many can be borrowed to be brought in and displayed.

Magazine Article Summaries

Magazine Article Summaries, also known as MAS, is a weekly index that references over 200 current magazines and periodicals. Its publication year runs from January to December. Organizationally, MAS's contents are divided into white pages of article summaries and brown pages of index references. All are combined into one large yellow binder that includes cover story highlights that are so recent that they are not included in the cumulative index. The index is updated every two months, and replaces all other indices for that year. The white pages contain article summaries that are published weekly and are current within two weeks of related magazine cover dates. Each weekly issue of the white pages is chronologically organized into the binder by date of issue.

The INDEX

MAS's index is cumulative and is updated six times a year. The index provides easy access to the most current of events. It is alphabetically organized by heading, then by subheadings. The subheadings are to lead you to the most precise aspect of a topic that is needed by you to meet the requirements of your research.
Example:

> **Artificial satellites**
> --Oceanographic use
> ---Japan

Since MAS uses a controlled vocabulary (Sears List of Subject Headings) a cross reference cue system of _see_ and _see also_ is built into the index. This is to provide you with a vocabulary strategy that you might employ to locate easily the more appropriate heading as used in the index. The word _see_ indicates that your chosen vocabulary heading is not valid for the index. The words following _see_ should be utilized. The phrase _see also_ indicates that your topic word is valid but the use of the words following _see also_ will supply still more information on your topic.

Each index entry provides the following information: heading, subheading(s), column number, paragraph number, and asterisk if a cover story.
Example:

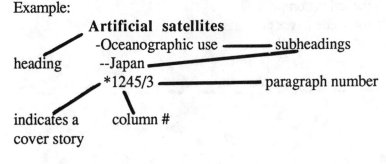

A heading is a main topic and the subheadings are subtopics of that topic. The asterisk indicates a cover story whose topic was very developed by the related magazine. The column and paragraph numbers reference you to the related magazine article citation and summary located in the white pages of the binder.

The WHITE PAGES

The white pages arrive at the library on a weekly basis. Each page is divided into three columns and each column is numbered consecutively from January through December. Each column contains up to ten entries but only complete entries with article summaries are counted as paragraphs.

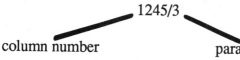

1245/3

column number   paragraph number(the third entry in that column to have a summary)

Each white page entry includes a heading, subheading, article, title, article summary comprised of up to 100 words, complete magazine title, cover date, number and type of illustration, starting page of article and total number of pages covered in the article. Insets, or short articles within an article, are also indicated with a one sentence focus. Well-developed summaries offer the advantage of knowing the main idea or focus of the article before the magazine is taken from the shelf. This increases work and time efficiency. Instructions for use are found throughout MAS. It is an extremely useful tool for you, the student researcher.

1. What is the purpose of Magazine Article Summaries?
2. Describe the basic organization of MAS.
3. Of what is a reference in the index comprised?
4. Of what is a reference in the white pages comprised?
5. Of what benefit is the citation summary?
6. What is an inset?

FRUIT brandies
   See Brandies, Fruit
FTC
   See US. Federal Trade Commission
FUEL
   See also
   Alcohol as fuel
FUEL consumption
   See Automobiles--Fuel consumption
FUEL, Liquid
   See Gasoline
FUJI Neopan 1600 (Photography film)
   422/6
FULBRIGHT, J. William
   381/7
FUMBLING the Future (Book)
   73/5
FUNDAMENTALISM, Christian
   73/6, *422/7
FUNDAMENTALISM, Islam
   *73/6
FUNDAMENTALISM, Judaism
   73/6
FUQUA Industries Inc.
   See also
   Intermark Inc.--Acquisitions &
FURET, Francois
   See also
   La Revolution (Book)
FURNACES, Gas
   -Rating
   366/5
FURNACES, Oil
   -Rating
   366/5
FURNITURE
   -Buying & selling
   22/3
FURNITURE industry
   See also
   Hickory Chair Co.
FUTURE life
   361/4
FUTURES
   282/2
   See also
   Chicago Mercantile Exchange
   Wine futures
FUTURES Center (Philadelphia, Pa.)
   361/5
G.I. Joe (Doll)
   406/2
GABEL, Hortense
   308/1
GABLE, John Clark
   190/3
GAF Corp.
   -Securities
   147/5
GALAPAGOS Islands. description &
travel
   291/7
GALAXIES
   361/6
   -Computer models
   362/1
   -Observations
   *190/4
GAMBLING
   See also
   Dog racing
GAME & game birds
   476/1
   See also
   Duck hunting
GAME shows
   See also
   Wheel of Fortune
GAMES
   See also
   Chess
   Olympic games
   Tennis
   Video games
   Word games
GAMES, Olympic
   See Olympic games

GANDHI, Indira
   -Assassination
   157/4
GANDHI, Rajiv
   292/1
GARBAGE
   See Refuse & refuse disposal
GARDENING
   190/5
   See also
   Agricultural genetics
   Flower gardening
   Gardening catalogs
   Landscape gardening
   Vegetable gardening
   -Books & reading
   423/1
   -Equipment & supplies
   See also
   Tillers, Rotary
GARDENING catalogs
   *22/4
   See also
   Seed catalogs
GARDENS
   See also
   Achnacloich (Argyll, Scotland)
   Arduaine at Kilmelford (Argyll
   , Scotland)
   Crarae (Argyll, Scotland)
   -Australia
   22/5
   -Case studies
   190/6, 423/2
   -Fort Worth (Tex.)
   243/6
GARDNER, Charles
   325/6
GARRIOTT, Richard
   423/3
GAS companies
   See Public utilities
GASES
   See also
   Poisonous gases
GASOLINE
   -Taxation
   191/1, 362/2
GASTRONOMY
   See Food
GEBEL-Williams, Gunther
   476/2
GEDDES, Graham
   22/5
GEESE, Snow
   -Migration
   191/2
GEETING, Doug
   363/1
GEMAYEL, Amin
   131/4
GEMS
   See also
   Tucson Gem & Mineral Show
GENE splicing
   See Genetic engineering
GENERAL Dynamics Corp.
   See also
   F-16 (Airplane)--International
   cooperation
GENERAL Electric Co.
   See also
   Kidder Peabody Group Inc.
   -International aspects
   244/1
   -Management
   391/5
GENERAL Motors Corp.
   See also
   New United Motor Manufacturing
   Inc.
   Smith, Roger
   -Industrial relations
   423/4
   -Performance
   362/3, 423/5
GENESIS (Drama)
   420/5

GENESIS Health Ventures Retirement
& Rehabilitation Centers
   See also
   Intergenerational Latchkey
   Program
GENETIC Basis of Human Disease
(Report)
   362/4
GENETIC counseling
   See also
   Muscular dystrophy--Genetic
   aspects
   Prenatal diagnosis
GENETIC engineering
   See also
   Genetically-engineered
   organisms
   -Actions & defenses
   476/3
   -Research
   *23/1
GENETIC recombination
   362/5
   See also
   Genetic engineering
GENETICALLY-engineered human cell
transplants
   -Government policy
   23/2
GENETICALLY-engineered organisms
   244/2
GENETICALLY-engineered plants
   170/3, 423/6
GENETICS
   362/4, *424/1
   See also
   Agricultural genetics
   -Research
   292/3
GENIUS
   476/4
GENTILES & Jews
   See Jews & Gentiles
GEOGRAPHY
   See also
   Boundaries
GEOGRAPHY, Political
   See Boundaries
GEOLOGY
   See also
   Earthquakes
   Rocks
GEOLOGY, Economic
   See also
   Mines & mineral resources
GEOPOLITICS
   See also
   Boundaries
GEORGE Washington Preparatory High
School (Los Angeles, Calif.)
   365/5
GEOSTATIONARY Operational
Environmental Satellite (GOES)
   476/5
GERMANY (West).
   See also
   Cities & towns
GERMANY (West). commercial policy
   244/3
GERMANY (West). foreign policy
   244/4
GERMANY (West). industries
   See also
   Chemical industry
GERMANY (West). politics &
government
   476/6
   See also
   Kohl, Helmut
GERMANY (West). role in NATO
   244/5
GESELL, Gerhard
   476/7
GIAMATTI, Bartlett
   398/1
GIANT (Book)
   83/3
GIBBONS, Barry
   245/4

Activity 24-b, *Magazine Article Summaries*

Utilization of Sources

Magazine Article Summaries, 1989

Directions: Use the index page on MAS on page labeled Activity 24-b to answer all questions in terms of column numbers, pages numbers or cross references.

1. To what are you referred when you look for information on Political Geography?

2. To what are you referred when you look for information on G. I. Joe doll?

3. To what are you referred when you look for information on gardening catalogs? What other information is available?

4. To what are you referred when you look for information on politics and government in West Germany?   What other information in available?

5. a. To what are you referred when you look for information on galaxies?

   b. Is there an additional reference for computer model?

   c. Is there a cover story on observation of galaxies?

6. To what are you referred when you look for cover story information on genetic engineering?

7. To what are you referred when you look for information on economic geology?

8. To what are you referred when you look for information on gardens in Fort Worth, Texas?

9. To what are you referred when you look for information on migration of snow geese?

10. To what are you referred when you look for information on gasoline taxation?

3677

Discusses television star Malcolm-Jamal Warner's book 'Theo and Me: Growing Up Okay.' By H.G. Chua-Eoan
(Time, 11/7/88, 1c, p129, 1/4p)

THIRD parties (US politics)
America needs a new political party now.
Opinion. Argues in favor of formation of a third progressive political party in the US. How the new party would break up the political monopoly held by the Republican and Democratic parties. Deadening role of television in US politics; Role of Democratic and Republican lobbyists; Disenchantment of black voters. By W. Greider
(Rolling Stone, 11/17/88, 1 illustration, p57, 4p)

#3 TOURNAMENT of Roses Parade, 1989--Centennial
Rough cut.
Describes how Waterford Crystal designed and made the crystal bowl to commemorate the centennial of the Tournament of Roses parade in Pasadena, Calif. Blowing of the bowl and pedestal; Cutting the glass. By B. Weber
(New York Times Magazine, 10/30/88, 1 illustration, p102, 1p)

TRAVEL trailers & campers See also Espre 176

TROTSKY, Leon See also Gorbachev, Mikhail--Reform policies, Civil rights

TRUCKS See also Dodge D250

TRUCKS--Rating
What's New? '89 towing.
A preview of 1989 light trucks for trailer-towing enthusiasts. Among the new-model changes, Mazda, Mitsubishi, and Toyota are boosting towing capacities, while General Motors is introducing the 454 V-8 in vans. By J. Johnston
(Trailer Life, Nov88, 8bw, p84, 4p)

TURKEYS--Cookery
Turkey roasting guide.
Provides information on what size turkey to buy, how to prepare turkey for stuffing and roasting, roasting directions, and time chart. How to test for doneness; Turkey hotline telephone number.
(Better Homes & Gardens, Nov88, 1c, 1 table, p182)

TURNER, John See also Elections--Canada

TWIGG family--Actions & defenses
My child or your child?
Report on the latest developments in the case of Ernest and Regina Twigg, who claim their baby was switched with Barbara and Robert W. Mays' daughter in the maternity ward at Hardee Memorial Hospital in Florida nine years ago. Background; Legal battles. By C. Leerhsen
(Newsweek, 11/7/88, 1c, p103, 1p)

U2 (Rock performers) See also Rattle & Hum
(Music recording)

UNIFORMS, Football
#2 Do black shirts make bad guys?
Discusses whether there is any real connection between football team reputations, playing style and the color of their uniforms.

3678

Examines if black uniforms reflect a color bias that affects what players do or how referees judge their actions. By J. Horn
(Psychology Today, Nov88, 4c, p19, 3p)

UNITED Nations
*Peace in our time?
Discusses recent United Nations settlements and how the world is moving toward peace in reaching such agreements. Persian Gulf war; Afghanistan; Vietnam; Conflicts around the world; United Nations role; US; Soviet Union. By M. Woollacott
(World Press Review, Oct88, p24, 1p)

UNITED Nations
*Instrument of persuasion.
Discusses how the United Nations has become an instrument of persuasion, of setting the stage for peaceful negotiation. Unsuccessful history; Superpowers' (US and Soviet Union) role with the UN. By A. Parsons
(World Press Review, Oct88, 1 cartoons, p22, 2p)

UNITED Nations
*A star is reborn.
Discusses the United Nations' role as a peacekeeping organization. Ideals; Perception; Past history; New positive attitudes; Problems with the attitude of US and its financial situation. By A. Gowers
(World Press Review, Oct88, p14, 2p)

UNITED Nations See also United Nations--Role of US

#1 UNITED Nations--Role of US
*A majority of two.
Discusses the Soviet Union and US involvement with the United Nations and their attitudes toward the organization. US Republican and Democratic attitudes toward the UN. By C.C. O'Brien
(World Press Review, Oct88, 1bw, p15, 2p)

UNITED STATES. Central Intelligence Agency--Administration
Spy vs. spy.
Discusses leadership changes at the Central Intelligence Agency (CIA), if Vice President George Bush wins the presidency.
(Time, 11/7/88, p30, 1/16p)

UNITED STATES. Congress See also Political action committees

UNITED STATES. Drug Enforcement Administration
More smack, less crack?
Discusses the fear of members of the US Drug Enforcement Administration that peace in Afghanistan will result in greater production of opium.
(Time, 11/7/88, 1c, p42, 1/16p)

UNITED STATES. Federal Aviation Administration--Regulations
Cracking down.
Discusses the Federal Aviation Administration's proposal of a rule requiring the 7,200 rivets on older model 737 airplanes be replaced.
(Time, 11/7/88, 1c, p105, 1/3p)

UNITED STATES. Federal Savings & Loan Insurance Corp.
Who will pick up the check?

3679

Discusses the attempt by one of the country's largest savings and loans to get out of paying a 150 fee hike to the Federal Savings and Loan Insurance Corporation, which will use the money to rescue poorly managed, insolvent banks.
(Time, 11/7/88, p101, 1/4p)

UNITED STATES. Federal Savings & Loan Insurance Corp. See also Great Western Financial Corp. --Finance

UNITED STATES. Military Academy See also Holleder Center (West Point, N.Y.)

UNITED STATES. National Oceanographic & AtmosphericAdministration See also Meteorological satellites

UNITED STATES. Postal Service See also Express service

UNITED STATES. Postal Service--Addresses & essays
#4 The United States Postal Service crisis.
Discusses the importance to all Americans of the US Postal Service and the crisis it's facing from competition and rising costs; also, the efforts being made in marketing, productivity, and restructuring to help the service out. Suggests a full Congressional review of the Postal Reorganization Act of 1970 to determine service needs and operation criteria. Problems; Suggestions. By R.K. Brack Jr
(Vital Speeches, 10/15/88, p22, 4p)

UNITED STATES. climate
What's wrong with our weather.
Discusses the changes in US weather during the past decade, as winters have become colder and summers warmer. Around the world other countries are also experiencing changes, as researchers look into them. Many believe carbon dioxide will devastate the world within a century, with the 'greenhouse effect.' Greenhouse effect dangers; Other possible causes of changing weather; Research. By L. Ponte
(Reader's Digest, Nov88, 2 illustrations, p71, 6p)

UNITED STATES. commerce See also European Economic Community--Policies, 1992

UNITED STATES. commerce--Asia
Asia's export upstarts face high winds from..
The final days of the Reagan Administration are bringing unexpected new pressures on Asia's most prosperous developing nations. The US and Thailand are headed for a showdown on software and patents. The Treasury Department lashed Taiwan and South Korea for manipulating their currencies, and Washington is threatening to revoke trade privileges for Thailand and Malaysia unless they institute labor reforms. By W.J. Holstein
(Business Week, 11/7/88, 2c, p52, 2p)

UNITED STATES. commerce--Japan
Japan in America.
Discusses the lethargy with which the Japanese have opened their markets to US money and products. Trade. By M.W. Karmin
(US News, 11/7/88, p65, 1/4p)

UNITED STATES. commercial policy--Political aspects

November 7, 1988 - 3677-3679

Magazine Article Summaries

Directions: Use the page on MAS on page labeled Activity 24-c to answer the questions. You have been referred to Columns 3677, 3678, 3679. Answer your questions in terms of what you see on the page.

#1
Entry subject
Magazine article
Author
Magazine title
Date of issue
page it begins on
how many pages is article
illustrations?
what kind and how many?
cover story?

#2
Entry subject
Magazine article
Author
Magazine title
Date of issue
page it begins on
how many pages is article
illustrations?
what kind and how many?
cover story?

#3
Entry subject
Magazine article
Author
Magazine title
Date of issue
page it begins on
how many pages is article
illustrations?
what kind and how many?
cover story?

#4
Entry subject
Magazine article
Author
Magazine title
Date of issue
page it begins on
how many pages is article
illustrations?
what kind and how many?
cover story?

The Statesman's Yearbook

FOCUS
The focus of this lesson will be on a particular reference book: *The Statesman's Yearbook*.

TEACHER PREPARATION
1. Ascertain whether or not your library has the *Statesman's Yearbook*.
2. Read the material thoroughly.
3. Work through the activities and keep for handy reference.

BACKGROUND INFORMATION
1. An almanac-sized book, the *Yearbook* provides quick, easy, current information on countries, states and international organizations.
2. It is similar to *The Worldmark Encyclopedia*, but much more compact.
3. It is similar also to *Clements' Encyclopedia of World Governments*, but the *Yearbook* offers bibliographies at the end of most articles.

CONCEPTS
- **Understanding the effective use of the *Statesman's Yearbook*.**
- **Understanding the format and table of contents of the *Statesman's Yearbook*.**

VOCABULARY
comprehensive   informational   format   punctuation   organization   knowledgeable

OBJECTIVES
The student will understand that:
1. *The Statesman's Yearbook* is a research tool concerning countries, states and international organizations.
2. *The Statesman's Yearbook* is divided into two parts; one on international organizations, the second on countries.
3. *The Statesman's Yearbook* has two indexes.
4. The articles in *The Statesman's Yearbook* have a similar format.

MATERIAL NEEDED
Activity Sheets 25-a through 25-b and 25-b in the optional student workbook.

ACTIVITIES
1. Read through 25-a and answer the questions.
2. Assign 25-b, which is a page from the index.

EXTENDED ACTIVITIES
1. One of the indexes is of products of countries. Research the various ingredients and natural resources needed for a product, such as: cars, shoes, televisions or furniture. From which countries will you be able to gain all your necessary components. How will you transport them? Trace a route on a map showing how you would get the raw material to the factory? Optional: What manufacturing processes and machinery would be needed?
2. List all the International Organizations headquartered in your state.
3. Select five places you'd like to visit. Research those organizations that would be most helpful to you prior to leaving and give reasons why.
4. Pick a product: such as a specific cereal or candy. List the ingredients and then chart the possible countries from which the ingredients came.
5. Place international organizations on map. Develop key.
6. Pick 6 states or 6 countries. Develop chart with 5 categories of comparison and contrast.

The Statesman's Yearbook

The Statesman's Yearbook is a research tool for the student. It provides easy retrieval of information concerning international organizations, countries, and states of the world. It is a fine partner to an atlas. It is divided into two parts. Part I offers information on the International Organizations of the World and Part II provides information on the countries of the world. It includes specific information on each of the fifty states as well as the United States as a country. Also included are states and territories of countries other than the United States. A comprehensive table of contents offers you, the researcher, a total overview of the book.

Two indices are also offered. Both are alphabetically organized by topic and subtopic. Topics are at the margin while subtopics are indicated by a hyphen and an indentation to the right. Punctuation means the same as in any index. A comma (,) refers to separate pages (19,24 = 19 and 24) while a hyphen (-) refers to the two pages mentioned and all the pages in between (19-24 = 19,20,21,22,23,24). One index focuses on places and International Organizations while the other index is an index of the products of the countries.

Each article possesses a similar informational format that includes the areas of : history, area, population, climate, defense, international relations, economy, energy, natural resources, industry, trade, communication, justice, religion, education, and welfare.

In addition, at the end of most articles, is a bibliography of related books to help you, the student researcher, in terms of furthering investigation of a subject or topic. If an organization is mentioned, its current address is given.

1. Why would a yearbook of this type be a good partner to an atlas?
2. Why is it important to be knowledgeable of the table of contents in a book such as the Statesman's Yearbook?
3. Why is knowledge of the use of an index important to information retrieval in any nonfiction book?

4. When might this book benefit you, the student researcher?

Use with index page 1664 from **The Statesman's Yearbook.**

1. What is referenced for Roswell?

2. What is referenced for Rota?

3. What is referenced for Ruse?

4. What is referenced for Reims?

5. a. What is referenced for Rhodesia?

   b. What is referenced for Northern Rhodesia?

   c. What is referenced for Southern Rhodesia?

6. What is referenced for Rift Valley?

7. a. What is referenced for Renaix?

   b. Go to that reference. What is it?

8. What is referenced for government and representation of Rhode Island?

9. What is referenced for Rosario, Honduras?

10. What is referenced for education in Rhode Island?

Current Biography

FOCUS
This lesson will focus on the use of *Current Biography* as a research tool.

TEACHER PREPARATION
1. Ascertain if your library has *Current Biography*.
2. Read the material thoroughly, work through the activity sheets, and keep your answers for handy classroom reference.

BACKGROUND INFORMATION
1. *Current Biography* is issued in paperback and then a cumulative hardbound yearbook copy is available for purchase.
2. The yearbook index is cumulative for ten years, ending with the year that has zero in it.
3. The scope of subject matter is interesting to share with the students.

CONCEPTS
• Using *Current Biography* to find biographical information about currently famous people.
• *Current Biography* is easy to use.

VOCABULARY
current biography   cumulative index   bibliography

OBJECTIVES
The student will understand:
1. The purpose of *Current Biography*.
2. The organizations of *Current Biography*.
3. The basic type of information presented in *Current Biography*.
4. The difference between a one year, and a ten-year cumulative index.

MATERIAL NEEDED
1. Activity Sheets 26-a through 26-b and 26-a through 26-b of optional student workbook.
2. Optional: Back Issues of *Current Biography*.

ACTIVITIES
1. Read and discuss 26-a.
2. Assign the context questions indicated by the Stop Sign for in-class work or for homework.
3. 26-b is a page from the index and will be used for the activities.

EXTENDED ACTIVITIES
1. Permit students, who have generated a list of famous people from a particular field of endeavor, to look up and list those people and their addresses in a bulletin board activity about careers: Baseball players, musicians, government leaders, writers, journalists, etc.

2. Using those addresses, letters could be written for language arts assignment.

3. When assigning biography book reports, have the students do a short report on someone currently famous in the same field as the subject of their book.

4. Pick 6 figures in the same subject field and do comparison/contrast chart with 5 areas to be compared.

Current Biography

Current Biography is published once a year in a yearbook format and is comprised of all prior eleven monthly issues. Its purpose is to present a concise but accurate factual representation of people who have achieved a leadership role in their field of expertise. The information is timely, in that the original source, the person under discussion, is given the opportunity to update and correct any errors before the annual yearbook is published. The writers of the *Current Biography* entries also maintain the objectivity of their work through a careful screening of the many nonfiction sources of information in which the subject is discussed. It is through these efforts that the writers of *Current Biography* present a well-documented and timely overview of their topic.

Current Biography is alphabetically organized by the last name of the subject of the article. Each article or entry includes the person's complete name, date of birth and an address. The entry's text details the person's background and his or her impact upon the field or fields in which he/she is famous. Each entry ends with a bibliographic listing of nonfiction sources on which the article is based. A picture of the subject is usually included.

Current Biography offers a section of obituaries of subjects who have appeared in the *Yearbooks* previously. This again supports *Current Biography's* goal of presenting the most updated information possible on a subject. To help you, the researcher, a listing of key abbreviations used is given in the front of the book. Other indices also included list the biographical references used and the periodicals and newspapers consulted. Also offered is a listing by field classification of the people who appear in *Current Biography*. To facilitate information retrieval, the paperback monthly issue's index is cumulative to the end of the year, and the *Yearbook's* index is cumulative throughout ten-year periods ending in years that have a zero at the end. In addition, there is a new index, *Current Biography Cumulated Index 1940-1985,* which cumulates and supersedes all previous indexes, and which can be consulted in order to locate a name within that period of time.

1. What is the purpose of *Current Biography*?
2. What types of indexes are available?
3. How might *Current Biography* be used by you, the student researcher?

Dart, Justin W(hitlock) obit Mar 84

Dassault, Marcel (Bloch) obit Jun 86

D'Aubuisson, Roberto Jul 83

Dausset, Jean May 81

Davis, Al(len) Jul 85

Davis, Andrew May 83

Davis, James C(urran) obit Feb 82

#1 Davis, Patti Nov 86

Davis, Peter (Frank) Feb 83

Day, Dorothy obit Jan 81

Dayan, Moshe obit Jan 82

Dean, William F(rishe) obit Oct 81

Debray, (Jules) Régis Jun 82

Debus, Kurt H(einrich) obit Nov 83

Decker, Mary Oct 83

Decter, Midge Apr 82

Defferre, Gaston obit Jun 86

Deighton, Len Sep 84

de Kiewiet, Cornelis W(illem) obit Apr 86

de Kiewit, Cornelis W(illem) See de Kiewiet, C. W. obit

#10 De Kooning, Elaine (Marie Catharine) Jul 82

De Kooning, Willem Sep 84

De La Madrid (Hurtado), Miguel Apr 83

Del Tredici, David Mar 83

De Mille, Agnes Jan 85

Demme, Jonathan Apr 85

De Montebello, (Guy-)Philippe (Lannes) Apr 81

Dempsey, Jack obit Jul 83

Dempsey, William Harrison See Dempsey, Jack obit

Densen-Gerber, Judianne Nov 83

Denton, Jeremiah A(ndrew) Jr. May 82

De Palma, Brian Sep 82

De Rochemont, Richard (Guertis) obit Sept 82

Dershowitz, Alan M(orton) Sep 86

Deukmejian, (Courken) George, Jr. Jun 83

#7 DeVries, William C(astle) Jan 85

Dewey, Charles S(chuveldt) obit Feb 81

Dial, Morse G(rant) obit Jan 83

Diamond, Neil May 81

Diana, Princess of Wales Jan 83

Dickinson, Angie Feb 81

#6 Dietz, David obit Apr 85

Dietz, Howard obit Sep 83

Dillard, Annie Jan 83

Diller, Barry (Charles) Apr 86

Dillon, Matt May 85

Dingell, John D(avid) Jr. Aug 83

DiSalle, Michael V(incent) obit Nov 81

Dodds, Harold W(illis) obit Jan 81

Dodge, Cleveland E(arl) obit Feb 83

#2 Doe, Samuel K(anyon) May 81

Doenitz, Karl obit Feb 81

Dohnányi, Christoph von Oct 85

Dole, Elizabeth Hanford Jun 83

Dolin, Anton obit Jan 84

Domenici, Pete V(ichi) Jun 82

#9 Donovan, Raymond J(ames) Jan 82

Dorticós (Torrado), Osvaldo obit Aug 83

Douglas, Donald W(ills) obit Mar 81

Douglas, Melvyn obit Sep 81

Douglas, Thomas C(lement) obit Apr 86

Downey, Morton obit Jan 86

Drabble, Margaret May 81

Drew, George A(lexander) obit May 84

Druckman, Jacob May 81

Drummond, (James) Roscoe obit Nov 83

Duarte (Fuentes), José Napoleón Sep 81

Dubinsky, David obit Jan 83

Dubos, René J(ules) obit Apr 82

Dubuffet, Jean obit Jul 85

Dunne, John Gregory Jun 83

Durant, Will(iam James) obit Jan 82

Duras, Marguerite Nov 85

Durrell, Gerald May 85

Eastland, James O(liver) obit Apr 86

Eckstein, Gustav obit Nov 81

Eckstein, Otto obit May 84

#4 Eco, Umberto Apr 85

Edwards, Blake Jan 83

Edwards, James B(urrows) Nov 82

Edwards, Joan obit Oct 81

Edwards, (W.) Don(lon) Mar 83

Egan, William Allen obit Jul 84

Ehricke, Krafft A. obit Feb 85

Eisenhower, Milton S(tover) obit Jul 85

Eliade, Mircea Nov 85 obit Jun 86

Elizabeth, Queen Mother of Great Britain Aug 81

Ellerbee, Linda Oct 86

Ellis, Perry Jan 86 obit Jul 86

Emerson, Faye obit May 83

Enders, John F(ranklin) obit Jan 86

Engstrom, E(lmer) W(illiam) obit Feb 85

Erlander, Tage (Fritiof) obit Aug 85

Ernst, Jimmy obit Apr 84

Ershad, Hussain Muhammad Nov 84

Ervin, Sam(uel) J(ames), Jr. obit Jun 85

Estes, Simon Aug 86

Ethridge, Mark (Foster) obit Jun 81

Evans, Harold (Matthew) Apr 85

Evans, Linda Mar 86

Evans, Luther H(arris) obit Feb 82

Evren, Kenan Apr 84

Fabius, Laurent Feb 85

Fagerholm, Karl-August obit Jul 84

Fagg, Fred D(ow) Jr. obit Jan 82

Falwell, Jerry Jan 81

Farrar, Margaret (Petherbridge) obit Aug 84

Farrington, (Mary) Elizabeth Pruett obit Sep 84

Fassbinder, Rainer Werner obit Aug 82

#3 Feinsinger, Nathan P(aul) obit Jan 84

Feld, Irvin obit Nov 84

Feldstein, Martin (Stuart) May 83

Ferguson, Homer obit Mar 83

Ferraro, Geraldine A(nne) Sep 84

#8 Feynman, Richard P(hillips) Nov 86

Field, Henry obit Mar 86

Fielding, Temple (Hornaday) obit Jul 83

Fierstein, Harvey Feb 84

Fischl, Eric Jun 86

Fishback, Margaret obit Nov 85

Fisher, M(ary) F(rances) K(ennedy) Sep 83

Fisher, Welthy (Blakesley Honsinger) obit Feb 81

Fisk, James Brown obit Oct 81

Fitzgerald, Albert J. obit Jul 82

Fitzgerald, Ed obit Jun 82

#5 FitzGerald, Garret Aug 84

Fitzgerald, Robert (Stuart) obit Mar 85

Fitzsimmons, Frank E(dward) obit Jul 81

Fleming, Lady Amalia obit Apr 86

Flesch, Rudolf (Franz) obit Nov 86

Florinsky, Michael T(imofeevich) obit Jan 82

Flory, Paul J(ohn) obit Nov 85

Flutie, Doug Oct 85

Fo, Dario Nov 86

Folon, Jean-Michel Feb 81

Activity 26-b, *Current Biography*   Utilization of Sources

Current Biography Yearbook, 1986

#1
Name:
Date of Issue:
Obit Indicated:

#2
Name:
Date of Issue:
Obit Indicated:

#3
Name:
Date of Issue:
Obit Indicated:

#4
Name:
Date of Issue:
Obit Indicated:

#5
Name:
Date of Issue:
Obit Indicated:

#6
Name:
Date of Issue:
Obit Indicated:

#7
Name:
Date of Issue:
Obit Indicated:

#8
Name:
Date of Issue:
Obit Indicated:

#9
Name:
Date of Issue:
Obit Indicated:

#10
Name:
Date of Issue:
Obit Indicated:

DID YOU KNOW?

FOCUS

The focus of this lesson is to have the students aware of the many and varied sources available to them.

TEACHER PREPARATION

1. Go through all the activities to see if your library has all the sources in here. It might help for you to do the assignment first so you can aid the students. THIS IS NOT AN EASY LESSON!!

2. Pick and choose the ones you need.

3. For the ones you have chosen, check the editions. Although we have tried to be judicious in the choice of questions and current in the source, it is possible that your library's edition might have different answers than the ones included in the answer key.

4. We have followed a basic format of having the student answer index questions for #1. For number #2, if possible, we had them survey another part of the book. Numbers #3 and #4 usually go together: number #3 is an index question and the answers from that must be used in number #4. There are a few instances, that, because of the format of the book, question #4 can stand alone.

5. It is possible that you might want your students to be familiar with all the sources indicated here even though your library might not have all of them. You could assign a few activity sheets for completion at the local or county library. PLEASE alert the staff at the library(ies) of your assignment. In fact, common courtesy dictates sending them copies of the activities. Of course, if you went and checked out their reference shelves yourself, you could meet with the staff at that time.

BACKGROUND INFORMATION

1. We have found that students nearly always want to stay with the familiar, the tried and true.

2. Many sources suffer from lack of use because fear of the unknown on the part of the students.

3. The questions represent a range of difficulty. The lessons do require hands-on use of the sources.

4. The lessons are set up in a card format with "did you know. . ." information on them.

5. The call numbers of the books have deliberately been left blank.

CONCEPTS

- **Reference sources need to be used in order to be appreciated.**
- **Use of the index is definitely encouraged.**
- **Understanding the format of the book helps information retrieval.**
- **Understanding that the researcher needs to input some searching.**

VOCABULARY

organization   alphabetical   cross references topical appendices glossary

OBJECTIVES

The student will understand:

1. That reference sources need to be assessed for format and organization.

2. That the index or indices in reference sources need to be used.

3. That additional material in reference books sometimes occurs in the beginning or in the appendices.

MATERIAL NEEDED

The activities in Lesson 27 are indicated by page number, not a suffix on the lesson number. You may use any or all as described under Teacher Information.

ACTIVITIES

1. You can use on an individual basis or you can set up a rotating schedule of use of all books for all students. There are enough sources to do that. Just remember: This is a **DIFFICULT** assignment for the majority of students. We have indicated some extremely difficult ones in the answer key and an especially EASY one. You might assign one per pupil and then let each do a "show and tell" on that reference for the rest of the class.

2. The first order of business is for the student to fill in the library call number for the book.

3. Retrieve the book and use it to answer the questions.

4. You must decide before you begin the lesson whether or not you want the students to pull the books from the shelves and put them back when they are done. You may wish the first class to do that and then leave those out for the next classes. Or you may wish to take all the books into a classroom. In that situation, you could arrange them in Dewey order on a cart.

EXTENDED ACTIVITIES

1. It's always nice to see the students enjoy some of the sources. You can arrange for oral discussions of the sources when the students have completed the lessons.

2. You might have one of the students survey the class to ascertain which new source they liked best.

3. Of course, the best thing that might happen is that the student will FIND a new reference source that's not on one of the activities and tell the class about it. A suggestion instead of an assignment that sometimes works.

Did you know?

Encyclopedia of the Third World

Did you know. . .

> —— Kurian, George Thomas
> ——   Encyclopedia of the Third World. NY:
>   Facts of File, 1987. Third edition.
>   3 v.
>   That the Encyclopedia of the Third World is
> comprised of three volumes and is paged continuously?
> The information presented is organized according to a
> format that allows for comparative studies of many land
> areas. Supportive to the use of the set are the 17
> appendices which also offer multiple charts, graphs, and
> tables of comparative information. In the first volume are
> a table of contents covering all three volumes, and an
> article on the use of the encyclopedia. Also included are
> lists of acronyms and abbreviations dealing with aspects of
> the third world, an overview of the type of information
> contained in the basic organizational format of each article
> and the sources from which the editors compiled the data.
> As in any encyclopedia, an index is included for efficient
> and effective retrieval of information. Visual aids are found
> throughout and a comprehensive bibliography is included.
>
>   O

Encyclopedia of the Third World
1. Using the index for the *Encyclopedia of the Third World*, find references for
whales._____
2. Using the table of contents of the *Encyclopedia of the Third World*, find the
address for the World Bank/International Bank for Reconstruction. Turn to p. 23 and
write the address._____
3. Using the index of the *Encyclopedia of the Third World*, find a reference for yak
hair. _____
4. Look up that reference, and find which country it's in. _____

Did you know?

Past Worlds: Times Atlas of Archaeology

Did you know. . .

Past Worlds: The Times Atlas of
Archaeology. Maplewood, NJ: Hammond,
1988.
    319 pp.
        That Past Worlds: The Times Atlas of
Archaeology has an introduction, a table of contents, a list
of world-wide contributors, a chronology table that is
divided geographically? In addition, it has a glossary, a
bibliography divided by subheading of content and text
indication. It has an index that pinpoints name, area, and
description along with page. The index also includes "also
called, also spelled, sometimes called, now called,"
versions of names. The book's extensive use of graphics
include an actual aerial view of the ziggurat in the sacred
enclosure at Ur and an aerial view of Sigirya in Ceylon(Sri
Lanka) which resembles Masada and Machu Picchu. The
cutaway diagrams include a long barrow burial mound and a
waterpowered multi-story mill.

Past Worlds; The Times Atlas of Archaeology
1. Using the index of *Past Worlds; The Times Atlas of Archaeology*, find the page
reference for Shillacoto and what it is. _____
2. Using the table of contents of *Past Worlds; The Times Atlas of Archaeology*, find
the page number on which Part Three: The Agricultural Revolution starts. _____
3. Using the index of *Past Worlds; The Times Atlas of Archaeology*, find the page
references for textiles. _____
4. Go to the two pages referenced together. According to the map legend, what four
items are represented? _____

Name_____

Date_____

Did you know?

Atlas of the Third World

Did you know. . .

> Kurian, George.
>   Atlas of the Third World. NY:
> Facts of File, 1983.
>   381 pp.
>   That the purpose of the Atlas of the Third World is
> to present thematic profiles of third world countries
> through map studies and country profiles?

○

Atlas of the Third World

1. Using the index of *Atlas of the Third World*, look up Baghdad. What pages are referenced? _____

2. Look up Panama in the *Atlas of the Third World*. What is the name of the biggest lake in the Canal Zone? _____

3. Using the index of *Atlas of the Third World*, look up Irrawaddy River. What pages are referenced? _____What country is the Irrawaddy River pictured in?

_____

4. On those pages, what is the population in persons/square mile in the area of the only city shown? _____

Did you know?

Roget's Thesaurus

Did you know. . .

> —— Lewis, Norman, editor.
>   New Roget's Thesaurus of the English Language. NY: Putnam, 1964.
>   552 pp.
>
>   That the New Roget's Thesaurus of the English Language is an alphabetically organized dictionary of synonyms? Although it supplies some antonyms, its purpose is to supply appropriate alternative word choices. No definitions are provided. Cross referencing is indicated through words in capital letters. A synonym choice in capital letters refers you to that word as an entry word where you will find a supply of other alternative words that match that meaning. When you use a thesaurus, keep a dictionary at hand to provide you with necessary definitions in order to make sure that your choice is appropriate and correct.
>
> O

Roget's Thesaurus

1. In *Roget's Thesaurus*, look up shoulder. As a verb, what are some of the synonyms? _____

2. In *Roget's Thesaurus*, what are some of the synonyms for hotel? _____

3. As what part of speech does *Roget's Thesaurus* list grim? _____

4. Look up overstate in *Roget's Thesaurus*. What is one of the synonyms? _____

Did you know?

United States Energy Atlas

Cuff, David J. & Young, William J.
United States Energy Atlas.   NY:
Macmillan(Free Press), 1980.
416 pp.

Did you know. . .

That the purpose of the United States Energy Atlas is to outline the location, distribution, and amount of all energy sources in the US?   An introduction explains the correct use of the atlas which is topically arranged into three parts. The appendices include a glossary of terms, geologic time scales and suggested references and readings. There is an index and, due to the topical organization of the text, utilization of the index is encouraged to support efficient use of the atlas.

United States Energy Atlas
1. In the index of the *United States Energy Atlas*, what are the page references for the Alaskan pipeline? _____
2. In the table of contents of the *United States Energy Atlas*, what is the page number for the glossary?_____
3. In the index of the *United States Energy Atlas*, what are the page references for Three Mile Island? _____
4. Go to the second page referenced. What are on that page?_____
_____

Did you know?

Annals of America

> ─── Adler, Mortimer J., editor.
> ─── Annals of America. NY: Encyclopedia
> Britannica, 1968 to present.
> 21 volumes
>
> That the Annals of America is comprised of 21
> volumes and a separate index? Its purpose is to present
> great issues in American life in chronological order through
> original source material. Its separate volume index,
> covering V. 1 -V. 19, is divided into three different indices.
> The first index is a listing of all the tables of contents of
> all the volumes to date. The second index is a proper name
> index. The third index presents authors and sources.
> Volumes 19-21 each have a separate index in their
> respective volumes.

Did you know. . .

The main index also offers an explanation of the use of the additional two volumes of the set known as Conspectus I and Conspectus II. Conspectus I & II present 25 major subjects or issues concerning American history. Each subject is covered as a whole. The issue is introduced through an historical essay. Following the essay is an outline of the topic which is keyed to specific primary source reference materials found in the set of Annals.*

Following the outlines are cross references that apply to other chapters in Conspectus I & II, the Encyclopedia Britannica and the Compton's Encyclopedia. Lastly, recommended readings for the user, are presented in a bibliographic format.

*NOTE:

An example of the outline format:
Topic: National Character
  Subtopic: Period Phases of American Character
    Detail: A focus on Anglo Saxon heritage
    Source material of: T. Jefferson, John Jay, Henry Cabot Lodge, Jean deCrèvecoeur

Annals of America

1. Using the 1971 or 1975 index of *Annals of America*, look up Revolution of 1800. What volume and page number are referenced? _____

2. Using the 1971 or 1975 index of *Annals of America*, look up John Winthrop. What are the references on his exclusion of heretics?_____ What does the CII stand for? _____

3. Using the 1971 or 1975 index of *Annals of America*, look up World War I. What is the reference for *Lusitania*?_____Go to that volume and page number and look for the author of that article. Who is it?_____Read the introductory paragraph to find the author's occupation. What is it? _____

4. Using the index in Volume 21 of *Annals of America*, look up air traffic controllers strike. What is the page reference?_____Look up the article. What is the format of this primary source material? _____

Did you know?

Lands and Peoples

Did you know. . .

Lands and Peoples. Danbury, CT: Grolier, 1987.

6 v.

That the series Lands and Peoples is comprised of six volumes? Its purpose is to help you study the lands and peoples of the entire world. Each volume is topical and the topic is indicated on the volume spine. The organization of the text information is alphabetical by entry as indicated by the table of contents found in each volume. Each volume also contains visual aids and a geographic glossary. The last volume contains an index for the series and a complete bibliography which is coded to support selection of extended readings for the young reader. A separate section consists of a chronological listing of dates dealing with the major events of the history of the world.

○

Lands and Peoples

1. In the index of *Lands and Peoples*, look up Tabasco. What volume and page number are referenced to find Olmec carvings? _____

2. Use the table of contents in Volume 1 of *Lands and Peoples* to find Burkina. What page?_____   According to the **Facts and Figures** part of the article that starts on that page, what is the official name of the country?_____ According to the **Land and Economy** heading, what are the three major rivers in Burkina? _____

3. Use the table of contents in volume 5 of *Lands and Peoples* to find Barbados. What is the page referenced?_____

4. According to the article on Barbados that starts on that page number, under the heading of the **Land and Economy**, how long does the summer last?_____

Did you know?

Encyclopedia of Black America

Did you know. . .

Low, W. Augustus & Clift, Virgil A., editors.
Encyclopedia of Black America. NY: McGraw Hill, 1981.
921 pp.

That the purpose of the Encyclopedia of Black America is to present information about famous Black Americans through biographical sketches and factual information about events that impacted on Black America? It is a good source for the study of American history as well as the study of Black history. Text entries and the index are alphabetically organized. Cross references can be found in both the index and at the end of the individual articles.

Encyclopedia of Black America

1. In the index of the *Encyclopedia of Black America*, find a page reference for Charles Henry Turner._____Go to the page referenced. What were his main occupations?_____

2. In the table of contents of the *Encyclopedia of Black America,* on what page does the list of contributors start? _____

3. In the index of the *Encyclopedia of Black America*, find reference for pathologists. How many are listed?_____

4. Go to the reference for the second person. What page is it?_____Who is she, by name and specialty, and what year was she born?_____
_____

Did you know?

The Encyclopedia of American History

Did you know. . .

Morris, Richard B.
The Encyclopedia of American History.
NY: Harper & Row, 1976.
5th edition

That the Encyclopedia of American History is divided into three sections? The basic chronology of American events is offered as a first section to provide an overview of American history. A second section contains a topical organization and includes nonpolitical aspects of popular issues of the day and are presented chronologically by time periods. A third section, a biographical section, provides information of famous Americans.

It has an index and instructions for use. It also includes a listing of maps and charts dealing with American history.

○

Encyclopedia of American History

1. Using the index of *Encyclopedia of American History,* look up Icarian communities. What is the page reference?_____

2. In *Encyclopedia of American History,* look up the biography for John Milton Hay. What is the page number? _____Where and when was he born? _____

3. Use the table of contents of *Encyclopedia of American History* to look up SCIENCE, INVENTION and TECHNOLOGY in **Part 2 Topical Chronology** . What page number is referenced?_____Under that heading, what page number is referenced for **Invention and Technology?**_____Go to the beginning of that topic, what does it say happened in 1790-91. _____

4. Is there a further reference in those words? _____ Go to that page, and find out what it is. _____

Did you know?

Encyclopedia of World Biography

Did you know. . .

McGraw Hill Encyclopedia of World
    Biography. Palatine, IL: Jack Heraty,
1988.
12 v. + 4v supplement entitled Encyclopedia
of World Biography
        That the McGraw Hill Encyclopedia of World
Biography is comprised of 16 volumes? Its purpose is to
present biographical information about famous people
throughout history. Volumes 1-11 are the basic set.
Volume 12 is an index and Volumes 13-15 are
supplements. Volume 16 is an index and study guide. The
index contains a study guide which is chronological and
geographical by topic, then alphabetically ordered. The
index includes volume and page numbers and, at times, an
explanatory phrase indicating the importance or fame of the
entry.
        The text is alphabetically ordered by article. Each
article includes a biographical sketch, cross references
where they apply, and a picture if available.

McGraw-Hill Encyclopedia of World Biography
1. Using the index of *McGraw-Hill Encyclopedia of World Biography,* look up Nat
Love. Who is he and what volume and page number? _____
2. In *McGraw-Hill Encyclopedia of World Biography*, look up Maria Montessori.
Where and when was she born? _____
3. Using the index of *McGraw-Hill Encyclopedia of World Biography*, look up
nicknames. Who was known as the Sharpshooter? _____
4. Look up the reference. What are the volume number and page
number?_____What was the real name? _____

Did you know?

Bulfinch's Mythology

Did you know. . .

| | Bulfinch, Thomas.
  Bulfinch's Mythology; the age of fable;
the age of chivalry; legends of Charlemagne;
illus. by Elinore Blaisdell. Crowell [©1970]
    957 pp. col illus maps

        That Bulfinch's Mythology is a dictionary of
fictional gods, goddesses, heroes and heroines? Each entry
represents a subject from one of the Western European
mythological tales. The book was written over 100 years
ago. The index is combined with a glossary where the
entry words are syllabicated, accented and cross referenced.
There is also a listing of archeological sites in a separate
appendix.

Bulfinch's Mythology
1. Using the index of *Bulfinch's Mythology*, find who Ozanna is and the page reference for him. _____
2. Using the table of contents of *Bulfinch's Mythology*, on what page does the Introduction to King Arthur and his Knights start? _____
3. Using the index of *Bulfinch's Mythology* look up Muses. Who were they and what page number is referenced? _____
4. Look up the page number that is referenced in #3. What are the names of the muses? _____

Did you know?

Who's Who in American History

____ Who was who in America.
____   Chicago: Marquis Who's Who, 1963 to
____ date

Did you know. . .

Index through 1989.

That the Who's Who in American History is an on-going series comprised of at least 10 volumes? The purpose of the series is to offer a very brief sketch of biographical information about those famous in American history. Who Was Who in America, 1897-1942 is the first volume in the series, whereas The Historical Volume covers the years 1607-1896 and actually precedes the first volume.

The volumes are chronologically ordered by time period, but the information in each individual volume is alphabetically ordered by the entry word which is the subject of the article.

The series has a separate volume index which can be used by the student to efficiently retrieve needed information on any topic or subtopic of American history..

○

Who was Who, Who is Who in America

1. Using the *Who was Who, Who is Who in America* Index 1607-1981 volume, what volume would Linda Gilbert be in? _____

2. Find William Slosson Lincoln in the Historical *Who was Who, Who is Who in America* volume. What was his basic occupation? _____

3. Using the first volume, 1897-1942 of *Who was Who, Who is Who in America*, look up James W. Pinchot. Who did he marry and when? _____

4. What are some of the things for which James W. Pinchot is famous?

       a. _____

       b._____

       c. _____

       d. _____

       e. _____

Did you know?

Worldmark Encyclopedia of the States

Did you know. . .

> _____ Worldmark Encyclopedia of the States.
> ===== NY: Worldmark Press, 1986.
>   690 pp.   Second Edition
>
>   That the purpose of the Worldmark Encyclopedia of
> the States is to provide information on every state and
> territory of the United States? A section provides a factual
> overview of the entire United States and the table of
> contents reveals that the specific state information is
> alphabetically organized by the entry name of the individual
> state. A listing of Presidents with notable events occurring
> in the respective administrations and a listing of Supreme
> Court Chief Justices and the major decisions of their courts
> are near the back of the volume. A glossary and
> bibliography are provided.
>
>   O

Worldmark Encyclopedia of the States

1. Using the table of contents of *Worldmark Encyclopedia of the States*, on what page would you find Puerto Rico? _____

2. Using the table of contents of *Worldmark Encyclopedia of the States*, find the glossary. What is the page referenced?_____What is the definition of ombudsman in the glossary? _____

3. Find Alaska in *Worldmark Encyclopedia of the States*. What pages? _____

4. Under **Famous Alaskans** in Alaska in *Worldmark Encyclopedia of the States*, who was Sheldon Jackson and what did he do? _____

Did you know?

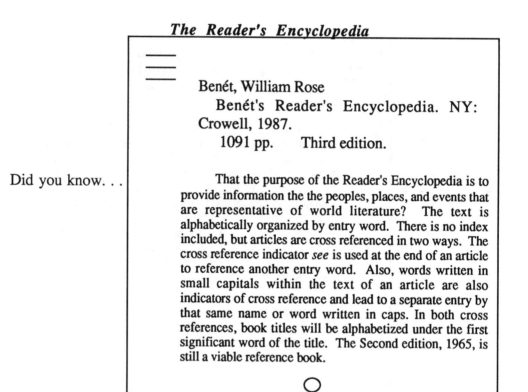

The Reader's Encyclopedia

Did you know. . .

Benét, William Rose
    Benét's Reader's Encyclopedia. NY: Crowell, 1987.
    1091 pp.   Third edition.

    That the purpose of the Reader's Encyclopedia is to provide information the the peoples, places, and events that are representative of world literature? The text is alphabetically organized by entry word. There is no index included, but articles are cross referenced in two ways. The cross reference indicator *see* is used at the end of an article to reference another entry word. Also, words written in small capitals within the text of an article are also indicators of cross reference and lead to a separate entry by that same name or word written in caps. In both cross references, book titles will be alphabetized under the first significant word of the title. The Second edition, 1965, is still a viable reference book.

Benet's Readers Encyclopedia, either edition
1. In *Benet's Readers Encyclopedia, either edition*, look up cyclic poets. What are they also called? _____
2. In *Benet's Readers Encyclopedia, either edition*, look up The Cry of the Children. Who wrote it and what is it about? _____
3. In *Benet's Readers Encyclopedia, either edition*, look up Hiawatha. What are the two cross references indicated? _____
4. Look up the person who is not the author. Why is he referenced? _____

Did you know?

Bartlett's Familiar Quotations

Did you know. . .

----   Bartlett, John, compiler.
====   Familiar Quotations.   Boston: Little,
Brown, 1968
1750 pp. 14th Edition

That Bartlett's Familiar Quotations is chronologically ordered by the last name of the person and that the time period covered spans centuries? There are two indices. The first is alphabetical by author. The second is alphabetical by the main entry word of the quote. Both indices reference page numbers in the text. The purpose of the book is to allow the user to retrieve the author of a quote, to locate the specific quote by a given author, to locate the full quote from an entry word, and to locate the citation of the quote.

○

Bartlett's Familiar Quotations

1. Using the main index of *Bartlett's Familiar Quotations*, what is the page and column reference for "sandwich men shuffling"? _____

2. Using the index of Authors in *Bartlett's Familiar Quotations*, what are the dates for Logan, Mingo Chief, and what is the page number referenced? _____

3. Using the index of Authors in *Bartlett's Familiar Quotations*, what is the page reference for Anne Morrow Lindbergh? _____ Why does her husband's reference occur in the text ten pages before hers? _____

4. Using the main index of *Bartlett's Familiar Quotations*, find entry for democracy. On what page are you? _____ Find reference to "everybody but me." What page and column? _____ Go to that page and list the author and source of that quote. _____   _____

Did you know?

Encyclopedia of Visual Arts

Did you know. . .

———
———
———

Gowing, Sir Lawrence, editor.
   Encyclopedia of Visual Art. Danbury,
CT: Grolier, 1983.
   10 Volumes.

   That the Encyclopedia of Visual Art is comprised
of 10 volumes? The purpose of the series is to present art
information in the areas of history, biography, and media
studies. The last volume contains the index for the series.
It also lists museums and galleries of the entire world. The
encyclopedia has a biographical dictionary of artists as well
as a glossary of art terms. Many visual aids are presented
throughout the entire series.

○

Encyclopedia of Visual Art

1. Using the index (volume 10) of *Encyclopedia of Visual Art*, what are the references
for Li Ssu-hsun? _____

2. According to the table of contents in Volume 1 of *Encyclopedia of Visual Art*, list,
by volume and page number, where the glossary is. _____ On what page
does the glossary actually begin?_____ Go there and list the
meaning of warp. _____

3. Using the index volume or the table of contents in Volume 1 of *Encyclopedia of
Visual Art*, what is the volume and page reference for a list of Museums and Galleries
of the World? _____ Using that list, what is the name of the
Museum in Gdansk, Poland? _____

4. According to the table of contents in Volume 1 of *Encyclopedia of Visual Art*,
which volumes contain biographical information on artists? _____

Did you know?

Atlas of the United States, Rand McNally

_____ Atlas of the United States. NY: Rand
_____ McNally, 1983.
192 pp.

Did you know. . .

That the purpose of the Rand McNally Atlas of the United States is to supply graphic information to support an awareness of the geographic, political, economic individuality of each state in the United States? The basic format allows for comparative studies, supported by many visual aids.

It is important that the student read all key and legend explanations as well as visual aid titles to most effectively use the atlas. The index provides access to specific locations through entries containing page numbers and coordinates comprised of both a letter and a number.

Rand McNally Atlas of the United States

1. Using the index of *Rand McNally Atlas of the United States*, what page is referenced for Zuni Indian Reservation? _____ What state is it in?_____

2. In *Rand McNally Atlas of the United States*, find Missouri. Interpreting the map in that article, what cities lie in the counties with the most persons per square mile?

_____

3. In *Rand McNally Atlas of the United States*, find Kansas. How many types of maps are shown? _____

4. Using one of those maps on Kansas, how many counties had 15 or more tornadoes in the years between 1961 and 1981._____

Did you know?

Science and Technology Illustrated

Did you know. . .

———— Science and Technology Illustrated. NY:
===== Encyclopedia Britannica, 1984.
————   28 volumes

     That Science and Technology Illustrated is a series comprised of 28 volumes and that it is continuously paged throughout the 28 volumes? It offers detailed scientific information, many visual aids, and an index in the last volume of the series. Its purpose is to present historical and current scientific knowledge covering many areas of science.

        ○

Encyclopedia Britannica Science and Technology Illustrated
1. Using the index, Volume 28, of *Encyclopedia Britannica Science and Technology Illustrated*, what is the volume and page number reference for lock-stitch machines?

_____

2. In *Encyclopedia Britannica Science and Technology Illustrated*, find the article on MASS. What is pictured? _____
3. Using the index for *Encyclopedia Britannica Science and Technology Illustrated*, what is the reference for intaglio? _____
4. Look that reference up. What is the title of the article in which is listed?

_____

Did you know?

New Book of Popular Science

Did you know. . .

⎯⎯   New Book of Popular Science. Danbury,
⎯⎯   CT: Grolier, 1984.
         6 Volumes

        That the purpose of the New Book of Popular Science is to provide information concerning science and technology? It is a series comprised of 6 volumes. Each volume contains information on one or more major scientific areas which are indicated on the spine of the book. The series is therefore topically ordered, and the last volume has an alphabetical index for the entire series. There is also a softcover index that references to the entire series. To effectively use this series, it is suggested that the index be used consistently when retrieving information.

○

New Book of Popular Science
1. Using the index in *New Book of Popular Science*, on what volume and page could an illustration of a mole be found? _____
2. In the table of contents for Volume 1 of *New Book of Popular Science,* find the page number on which **Computers and Mathematics** begin._____ Go to the next page. What's there? _____ On which page would a discussion of probability start? _____
3. Using the index in *New Book of Popular Science,* find a page and volume reference for Microscopes. _____
4. In that Microscope reference, find the volume and page reference for the illustration for Hooke's microscope. What is it? _____ Find it. According to the caption, what is the title of Hooke's book? _____

Did you know?

World Book Encyclopedia of Science

Did you know. . .

> ═══   World Book Encyclopedia of Science.
> ───   Chicago: World Book Enterprises, 1985.
>   7 Volumes.
>
>   That the World Book Encyclopedia of Science is a
>   series comprised of 7 volumes? Each volume covers a
>   separate scientific topic as indicated by the volume title
>   found on the spine of the book. Each volume also has its
>   own index, glossary and table of contents. Many visual
>   aids can be found throughout the series. Its purpose is to
>   present information in many areas of science. The
>   individual volumes are titled: The Plant World, Chemistry
>   Today, The Heavens, The Animal World, Physics Today,
>   The Planet Earth, and The Human Body.
>
>   ○

World Book Encyclopedia of Science
1. Using the index in *Chemistry Today*, give reference for Marsh test? _____
2. Using the glossary in *The Heavens*, define regolith. _____
3. Using the index in *The Plant World*, find the reference for Charles Macintosh.
_____

4. Go to that reference in *The Plant World*. What is he famous for?
_____

Did you know?

Occupational Outlook Handbook

Did you know. . .

U. S. Department of Labor.
  Occupational Outlook Handbook. U. S.
Government Printing Office, 1986.
  523 pp.

    That the Occupational Outlook Handbook is a
government document whose purpose is to provide
information to help support intelligent decision-making in
job or career choices?   The introduction provides
information on how to use the handbook. The index, with
cross references, allows you to retrieve information on any
career in terms of description, projected jobs, job outlook,
and changes in job supply.   Through a summary of
information, it details the nature of the job, working
conditions, average income, job potential and references
you to additional sources of information on each specific
career or job. The table of contents lists the jobs and
careers by occupation or specialty.

Occupational Outlook Handbook, 1986-87
1. Go to the index of *Occupational Outlook Handbook*, find the cross reference and
page number for zoologists. _____
2. Go to the table of contents for *Occupational Outlook Handbook*. Under Special
features, find page reference for Tomorrow's Jobs: An Overview._____
3. Go to the Dictionary of Occupational Titles (D.O.T.) Index of *Occupational
Outlook Handbook*. Find D. O. T. # 3061018. What is occupational title and page
number? _____
4. Go to the page referenced and find address for sources of additional information.
_____

Did you know?

What's What

Did you know. . .

> What's What; A Visual Glossary of the World. NY: Facts on File, 1981. 565 pp.
>
> That the What's What is a visual glossary, a picture dictionary? But unlike most dictionaries, this book is topically arranged. It has a table of contents and an index. Before the table of contents, there is a section on how to use the book. The text is a combination of drawings, photographs, and diagrams with all parts labeled. You can look up parts of oil drilling platforms or jewelry parts, parts of cars or parts of clothing.

What's What

1. Using the index of *What's What*, find the page reference for tank._____

2. Using the table of contents in *What's What*, find carriages under transportation. What kinds are listed? _____

3. In the index of *What's What*, find page reference for sundial._____

4. Go to that reference. What is the name of the structure that throws the shadow? _____

The Mountain Region of the U. S.

Draw in the other two countries which border ours. Check with an atlas to correct your drawing. Which state is completely bordered by the other states in this region? In this region, there is the only point in the United States which is common to four states. Where is it? Which four states join at that point?

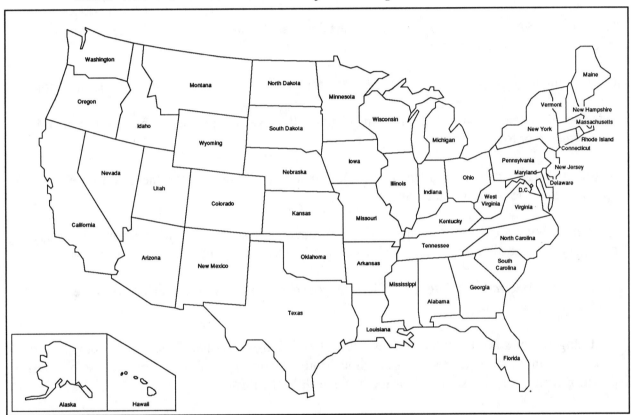

The Mountain Region of the United States

Montana = MT	WY = Wyoming
Colorado = CO	ID = Idaho
Utah = UT	NV = Nevada
Arizona = AZ	NM = New Mexico

1. Chart and categorize the main national parts, national recreation areas, national forests, national historic sites, and national monuments of all the states in the Mountain region of the United States.

2. Survey the school to find out how many people have visited any of the areas mentioned in the first activity. Graph your results.

3. Interview those people who have visited the areas. Consider those people in terms of knowledge, speaking voice, collection of slides or pictures, realia or artifacts. Recommend someone for a presentation to your class.

4. Using the *Readers' Guide to Periodical Literature* or *Magazine Article Summaries*, list the articles under the entry word of your state's name.

5. Using the *National Geographic Index*, chart the available articles and media about your chosen state from the Mountain region.

6. Using an atlas, graph the highest and lowest points of all eight states in the Mountain region.

7. Using the almanac, make a bulletin board chart of addresses and phone numbers of state chambers of commerce or tourist offices.

8. Using the almanac and a map of the Mountain states region, place the city locale and the approximate date of all the state fairs.

9. After having studied an important person from your chosen state in the Mountain area, write a two-day diary of some significant historical event that impacted on your state or on the region.

10. Using the *American Heritage Index*, look up your chosen state's name and list the references with volume and page numbers.

11. Using any or all of the reference resources, find information on at least two museums in your chosen state in the Mountain region. List name, address, phone, special collections, if possible. Write the information for inclusion in your media center's vertical file.

Using a CD-ROM

FOCUS
This lesson focuses on the theory and reasons for using CD-ROM.

TEACHER PREPARATION
1. Read through Background Information and the Student Notes.
2. Finish the activity sheets and keep at hand for ready reference during class.

BACKGROUND INFORMATION
1. The CD-ROM in use in your media center might have a brand name such as LePac or AutoGraphics for book search, WilSearch/WilsonDisc for periodical searching, or the Electronic Encyclopedia for encyclopedia searching.
2. You can tell the students that the technology is the same as their compact disc music.
3. The laser disc and laser disc players are basically the same technology.
4. If your media center's book catalog is completely electronic, explain to the students the process of retrospective conversion.
5. If your media center has not yet converted, explain what will be done, the reasons why, and the time table.
6. The activity sheets in this lesson are on the theoretical base. We have chosen to leave specific skills for each brand application up to the individual library.

CONCEPTS
- **CD-ROM is a useful technology.**
- **CD-ROM is not connected on-line outside the media center.**
- **CD-ROM is a tool for a more efficient search strategy and method.**

VOCABULARY
computer technology   compact disc   Read Only Memory   networking information explosion   interconnect   work station   union catalog   menu   citation faxed   facsimile machine

OBJECTIVES
The student will understand that:
1. The computer workstation will be labeled as to its specific function.
2. Compact disc technology allows the CD to have all the information that the card catalog used to have.
3. Compact disc technology allows the student the browsing use of other libraries' holdings.
4. Compact disc technology permits periodical searching.
5. Compact disc technology permits encyclopedia searching.

MATERIAL NEEDED
Activity sheets 28-a.

ACTIVITIES
1. Oral discussion in class after reading emphasizing quantities of resources available through technology.
2. Flow charting of retrieval techniques.
3. No specific activities are included in this lesson, primarily because there are so many different applications for CD-ROM.
4. Depending on which brand(s) and use(s) are available in your media center, tailor your retrieval activities to those.

EXTENDED ACTIVITIES
1. Permit the interested student the opportunity to understand what a MARC record is.
2. The student can extrapolate library service in future. They usually can think of things that adults can't.
3. Let the student list the kinds of benefits from all the new technology, such as CD, laser discs, fax machines, etc.

USING A CD-ROM

Computer technology has become a part of the everyday life of the people living in this country. One of the more interesting aspects for the student researcher is that it has helped harness a world experiencing an information explosion. Without the help of the technology of the computer, the tremendous expansion of knowledge that the world has experienced since World War II would be unmanageable due to sheer volume.

The main goal of the library has always been service. Its objective has been to bring needed information to the fingertips of its patrons. But, through the years, as knowledge has mushroomed, so has the number of books, journals and magazines in which it is stored. It has steadily become more difficult for the librarian to locate all the information available on a given subject because the physical boundaries of the library limited the storage area for materials; therefore, many of the books were not within reach. It became obvious that computer networking was the answer. Therefore, in order to meet its primary goal of service, the library has reached out to accept the challenge of the '90's: information retrieval.

Through computer networking on local, regional, state and national levels, many libraries have garnered forces to interconnect through data bases to allow patrons to ascertain <u>what</u> is available on a subject, <u>where</u> it is available and <u>how</u> one would go about retrieving it. Through the financial support of state and local communities, most libraries have implemented or are transitioning into the process of computer networking. This is the most efficient and effective method of information search and retrieval. It is necessary that you, as a student researcher, reach out to familiarize yourself with this new technology, as shortly it will be everywhere as are the telephone and television. It <u>is</u> the library of the future.

As already stated, many libraries are fully computerized in terms of search and retrieval. Still others are just at the beginning stages. In many cases, a combination of an updated card catalog and a series of computer work stations will be available to the library patron. The use of the card catalog has been fully explained so the student focus of this lesson will be the various aspects of a computer workstation.

A library that has begun to computerize information retrieval will have a variety of labeled computer workstations. Through the use of one or all of the stations you will be able to construct an information search according to the level of your research needs. Each station, in turn, will supply a computer and possibly a printer. In order to explain the purpose of each station, it is necessary to include some explanation and definitions.

CD-ROM
The first station under discussion is a CD-ROM retrieval service. CD-ROM stands

for Compact Disc-Read Only Memory. A compact disc is a spiral of pits of information that is about five miles long but is wrapped into a disc shape, approximately three to four inches in diameter. In terms of information, it has what is known as "read-only memory." That means that when you begin a search you will not be able to access information beyond that which has been placed on the disc. For example, if the disc contains information from a set of encyclopedia, any information asked beyond the limits of the encyclopedia can not be accessed or answered. The limits of a compact disc are impressive, though. For example, all the titles in the Library of Congress can fit on four compact discs and an entire twenty volume encyclopedia can fit on just one.

To work, a computer needs a compact disc driver, a compact disc and a software package. The software package helps you access the information from the compact disc to the computer screen through a series of commands punched into the computer by you. Currently, CD manufacturers are putting the software on the disc to make accessibility even more efficient. Just as each compact disc contains its own field of information called a data base, each software package contains its own command language. A computer's use is dependent upon both the compact disc and the software package. All three are interrelated. Simply stated, the result of the combined use of all three, as an interrelated unit, is to allow you, as the searcher, to access information from the disc in response to the commands that you have punched into the computer through the use of the instructions provided by the software package. As each user command is answered, you are in effect setting up a search strategy through the software package based on your selected topic and subtopic.

Your search strategy will be designed through the software package to narrow the field of information to be accessed. This will include only that part of the field of information on the disc that directly relates to the specific topic and subtopics that you have entered into the computer. Many search strategies are designed into the software package to select the best topic/subtopic keywords through the use of vocabulary lists and indices. Strategies to help narrow the output field of citations is also used in combining topic/subtopic keywords in the best possible way to support the objective of your research. This is all accomplished through screens of lists of choices known as menus.

The eventual output or search results can be presented in a variety of formats according to the type of information necessary to the objective of your research. Selection of format is, again, made through the lists of menus provided by the software package. For example, when using an encyclopedia on CD-ROM, output can be an actual article of information that can be printed on the printer or a listing of citations based on the use of the index. The format of the citation can even be specified to support the needs of your research.

As mentioned, each disc on CD-ROM is created with a different purpose in mind.

Discs are prepared to hold the citations of all the books in a particular library, or as an index to summaries/abstracts and citations of magazines, journals and other periodicals. And as mentioned before, a complete encyclopedia can be placed on one disc.

In place in some libraries is a computer work station housing a CD-ROM disc that lists only the library's own materials and resources and functions as a catalog for that library. Therefore the output or search results from this disc will be limited to only those materials located in that library. Difficulty will arise if your topic extends beyond the limits of the sources contained in your library.

1. How has computer technology allowed the library to grow and expand in meeting the needs of its patrons?

2. Explain the limits of the compact disc in terms of information.

3. Give examples of materials that can be found on CD-ROM in some libraries.

UNION CATALOG

Since many of the discs or data bases are limited by nature of the size of the library from which they are developed, it has become necessary to find a means by which a smaller library might expand its potential researching base. To increase the information available beyond the individual library another type of work station has been developed. This data base is called a union catalog, and it, too, is on a compact disc. It reaches out and includes all the participating member libraries of a specific region. All of the citations of materials in a union catalog region are cataloged on one disc, also providing information as to where these materials may be found within the region. If your library is a member, the actual source represented by the citation can be delivered to you through the delivery system outlined for the union catalog. In fact, if the material is concise, it can be instantly faxed to you. In time, entire states will be considered part of a union catalog region.

4. Explain the purpose of a union catalog.

5. How would you go about retrieving the materials found in a union catalog?

On-Line Accessing

FOCUS
The focus of this lesson will be a generic look at on-line accessing of databases.

TEACHER PREPARATION
1. If you are proficient in on-line accessing, you are ahead of the game. If you are not and someone else in the library is, you can become proficient at the same time your students will. If that makes you uncomfortable, learn before they do, and then you can do the teaching.
2. Read the material thoroughly, and work with the databases. Keep a list of the databases accessible to you along with their descriptors that need to be entered.
3. Narrowing a topic involves the same decisions that were discussed earlier in the lessons.

BACKGROUND INFORMATION
1. We have chosen to give search strategy based on a front-end software package that permits strategic decisions to be made without the costs associated with on-line.
2. If your library only has direct on-line searching, strategies must be pointedly taught before your students go on-line, so that economic searching becomes a goal also.
3. On-line accessing permits you to put the resources of the world at the fingertips of your students. Well, almost, anyway!
4. It is conceivable that your students are more computer literate than you are. That does not automatically mean that they understand the databases with which they'll be working better than you do. It just means that they might understand the techniques of the machinery better.
5. The database agencies have print documents that list all the sources on the database. These documents are invaluable. Learn how to use them.

CONCEPTS
•   **Using on-line accessing of databases usually improves the quantity of citations engendered.**
•   **Using excellent search strategy usually improves the quality of the citations engendered.**
•   **Using on-line accessing enlarges the area of your library resources.**

VOCABULARY
on-line   networking   union catalog   workstation   search strategy   citation Boolean
operators   passwords   thesaurus   Venn diagrams   database

OBJECTIVES
The student will understand that:
1. On-line databases are used to enlarge the resources available to him/her.
2. Search strategies must be employed to narrow the topic.
3. On-line searches may render full documents or citations of material that must be located through the use of the local library or through other means.

MATERIAL NEEDED
1. On-line workstation
2. Activity sheets 29-a through 29-b and 29-b in optional student workbook.

ACTIVITIES

1. Read through 29-a. Discuss it as a group. Use the Venn diagrams to aid understanding of the narrowing concept.

2. Activity 29-b is used to have the student understand what is in the local media center.

2. If applicable, use the worksheets that come with an on-line subscription package.

3. Students can be taught the mechanics of using on-line, but to comprehend the decision-making that goes along with narrowing a topic and getting source citations for just that, use this activity at a time when the students are doing reports.

EXTENDED ACTIVITIES

1. Draw a flow chart of the steps that you might take in developing strategies in the software package that is a pre-step to going on-line.

2. Draw a diagram of what is included in your library in terms of data bases.

3. Chart local libraries: find out which libraries have computerized their own collections to be a data base, which ones offer which on-line services; which ones offer union catalogs of serials, union catalogs of all resources, and how large is the union. Find out what you as a student have to do to access the resources from these local libraries. Share your knowledge on a bulletin board or on a data sheet to be duplicated and distributed.

4. If your school media center does not have any or all of the new technology, videotape a buddy using the resources at another library. Bring back film to show.

On-Line Accessing

On-line searching is still another informational networking system. It presents an even wider field of sources. CD-ROM limits your field of sources to the particular library in which you are working. Union cataloging opens the field to include all the sources found in your union catalog region. On-line, in turn, offers a national networking system to include multiple data bases throughout the country. It is call "on-line" because the networking connection is through a telephone line. The workstation for on-line consists of a telephone line, a computer and a printer. Next to a newspaper, it is the only way to access the most current information on any topic because the elapsed time of the publishing of the article in a magazine and its appearance as a citation in the on-line system is about four days. This is in sharp contrast to print indexes of magazines that are updated every few weeks. On-line is also more sophisticated than CD-ROM in that it can network multiple data bases at one time and this is called stringing. Once the entry strategies have been worked out, the databases searched, and the print button is activated, bibliographic information on a specific topic is available in your desired choice of format (author, title, journal, year of publication, catalog citation).

On-line is a way in which the librarian can assist you in becoming aware of what is available on your chosen topic. In some instances, basic abstracts are presented to help you further screen through available citations and help structure a base by which you will determine those sources that are necessary to successfully complete your report. In other words, so much will be available that you will want to make intelligent decisions about the source documents you will try to locate and retrieve.

At this point, you will have accessed enough bibliographic information to begin to locate your sources. In fact, depending upon the database with which you chose to work, you might already have in hand complete documents. The work stations in your own library including CD-ROM and your union catalog will help you pinpoint the locations of other needed materials. If the material can be found in the union catalog region, it can be delivered to your library or faxed to you if the material is concise enough. Screening of a union catalog in another region might help you locate still more sources. The research librarian of your own library will be able to help you structure the most appropriate retrieval strategy to locate your needed sources.

According to the individual rules of your library, on-line searching will be conducted by the librarian, the library staff, or by you. If the search is to be done by you, the librarian will allow you to enter the on-line system through a series of passwords that are unique to each library and database. These will not be shared with you as they are a form of a lock to the system. Once you've been accepted into the system you will be placed into a software program that will help you structure your search. At this point you will not be connected to any of the data bases and you library will not be charged for the time. This is a pre-step provided through the system to help students or newcomers to the program.

Through your interaction with the computer software program, structured in a command-response mode, you will be led through various strategies used to narrow your topic by way of a series of menus. This type of menu is of the same format as one you might find in a restaurant. It provides an indication of what is available to you so that you can make appropriate selections based on your research needs for your current topic.

As previously mentioned, for a search strategy to be as effective as possible, you must narrow or limit your topic and subtopic within the search strategy so that you will not be generating hundreds of useless citations. The software package helps you do this through an offering of a thesaurus of alternative subject headings used in the data base for your particular topic and subtopics. You will then be provided with a screen that will help you structure the use of the Boolean operators-- and, or, not--in combining your topics and subtopics. If you follow the instructions as given in the software package, these operators will help to narrow the field of citations to only those for which you are searching. Only those articles that are comprised of a discussion of the aspects of your topic and subtopics will be part of the search results. To understand what is happening as each operator of and, or, not is placed with the topic/subtopic, see the Venn diagrams that follow. The shaded area represents the final output of citations as the result of using this strategy.

A = topic   b, c, d = subtopics

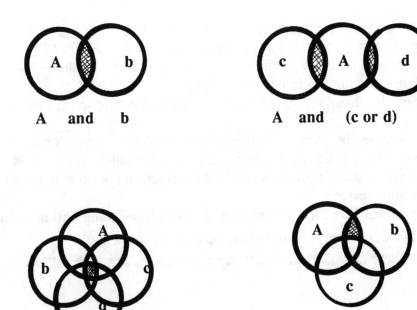

A   and   b

A   and   (c or d)

A   and   b   and   c   and   d

A   and   b (but not c)

In summary, when you've begun to organize your search strategy, the following steps will be utilized before you are on-line, connected to the multiple data bases.

A. The librarian enters a password(s).
B. You will be connected to a presearch strategy software program which will help narrow your search through:
   1. Appropriate selection of topic/subtopic keywords
   2. The use of a program subject heading thesaurus
   3. The use of a program index
   4. The use of a built-in cross reference mode
   5. The use of Boolean operators: *and, or, not*
   6. The use of the symbols which include root word variants.
C. You will request a specific format for output
D. You will activate the print button
E. At this moment, you are connected on-line.
F. Output will be forthcoming.
G. Analysis of results
H. Possibility of going back to search strategy because you are not satisfied with results; or,
I. Begin retrieval of source documents.

1. What is the purpose of the computer networking system known as on-line?
2. Why is it important that you make intelligent decisions in using the software package while readying your input before going on-line?
3. What is meant by the term "stringing" when it is used in regard to on-line data bases?
4. How might the library media specialist help you in structuring a retrieval strategy in locating needed sources such as books, magazines, journals, pamphlets, etc.?
5. Of what importance is the software thesaurus and the Boolean operators to the end result of your information search?
6. After analyzing the results of the information retrieved from going on-line, why might you go back to the software package to develop a different strategy?

Below is a diagram of a computer work-station in a media center. Draw your media center showing how the specific items connect.

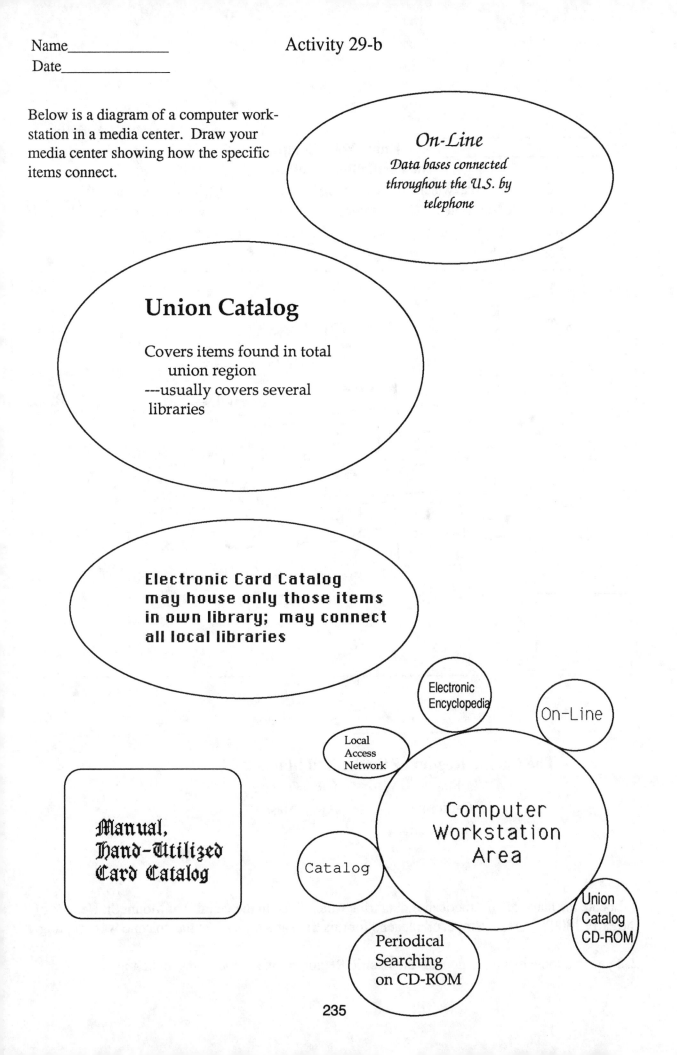

On-Line
Data bases connected throughout the U.S. by telephone

Union Catalog

Covers items found in total union region
---usually covers several libraries

Electronic Card Catalog may house only those items in own library; may connect all local libraries

Electronic Encyclopedia

On-Line

Local Access Network

Computer Workstation Area

Catalog

Union Catalog CD-ROM

Manual, Hand-Utilized Card Catalog

Periodical Searching on CD-ROM

Know Your Country:
The Pacific Region of the U. S.

Of this region, which two states are non-mainland? Which state is totally surrounded by water? Which three states share a border with another country? Which body of water forms boundaries for all five states? Use the map on Unit VII Activity to highlight these states.

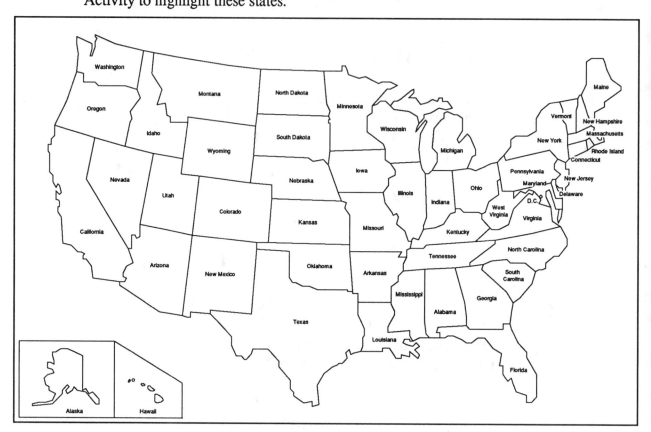

The Pacific Region of the United States

Washington = WA	OR = Oregon
California = CA	AK = Alaska
Hawaii = HI	

1. Locate the name of an American Indian tribe which lived in the vicinity of Mount St. Helen's in the early 1800's. Create a myth or a legend for this tribe at a time when the volcano was erupting.

2. Type in a topic having to do with the Pacific Region or one of the states in the region

on the Electronic Encyclopedia. List the number of citations. Do the same for union catalog and for on-line. Compare the numbers referenced. Make a generalization.

3. Choose one of the states from the Pacific Region. Construct a tourist commercial to be shown to other states enticing people to visit.

4. Create a flow chart for the Alaskan State Ferry System.

5. Chart the countries who have claimed any of the land of these Pacific states. Put this information on a time line.

6. Using electronic information on the current possibilities of productive gold panning and a regular map of the Pacific states area, chart on the map all the potential places for gold panning.

7. From any of the states in the Pacific states area, research and replicate an ancient tribal mask.

8. From any of the states in the Pacific states area, trace weapons and tools through the ages. Consider whether your information would educate your classmates better in a bulletin board design, a booklet of information, a timeline, or an audiovisual presentation.

9. Create a weather map showing seasonal precipitation for your chosen states from the Pacific region. Show averages for different areas.

10. Create an historical fiction story using an historical mode of transportation as the narrator for your story. Examples: Conestoga wagon, outrigger canoe.

11. Illustrate the produce grown in all the states in the region, using your choice of the method of presentation.

12. Using a map, trace the route of the Alaskan pipeline. Accompany the map with a chart of various kinds of information.

Unit VII The Aspects of Writing
    Lesson 30   One Research Process
    Unit Activity   Know Your Country: **Territories and Possessions**

One Research Process

FOCUS
This lesson focuses on teaching one type of research process.

TEACHER PREPARATION
1. Read thoroughly the material.
2. If your school has a required format for bibliography or footnotes, please include.
3. If your school has a requirement for a thesis sentence, please include. We allude to it, but do not teach what it is or how to write it.
4. If your school has a requirement for primary source material, please include.

BACKGROUND INFORMATION
1. Although teaching the research paper is enough to give you gray hair, you will be teaching a necessary skill.
2. The research process that we have put in here is the old tried and true way of note cards. It works because it organizes thoughts and information.
3. We have deliberately told the student that teacher and/or school requirements will differ from place to place and person to person. That, in itself, is always a good thing to know.
4. You can gauge your first requirements and whether you have to assign topics by how much experience the class has had.
5. You can do some oral exercises in limiting topics by throwing out to the class large topics and see if they can limit them.

CONCEPTS
- **The key to a good research paper is organization.**
- **Finding all the available sources is part of the research.**
- **Structuring the information is a necessary part.**
- **Outlining from note cards will make the paper original.**

VOCABULARY
format edit topic structure organization research requirement

OBJECTIVES
The student will:
1. Understand that finding all available sources is a part of research.
2. Understand the note card process.
3. Outline from the note cards.
4. Produce an original paper.

MATERIAL NEEDED
Activity Sheets 30-a.

ACTIVITIES
1. Read through the first activity. Reread those parts about note cards when you set the note cards up with the students.
2. Spend time limiting topics. Make sure that the student is not over-reaching. The process is primary; therefore, guide the students through the process. You can make it analogous to white-water rafting: you, as teacher, will be guiding and steering and the students should come out in the calm water richer for the experience.
3. Included in the Know Your Country activities are many topics conducive to practicing parts of the research process: writing different types of paragraphs, rough drafts, etc. Look them over and use some or all.

EXTENDED ACTIVITIES
1. It would add immeasurably if a research paper in another subject would be assigned shortly after the students completed this activity. If this might be the case, work cooperatively with your colleague and help guide the students through the second paper.
2. Perhaps some students could act as peer tutors.

One Research Process

One of the most difficult tasks that will be required of you during your days of schooling will be the meeting of the requirement of the Research Paper. It's capitalized because teachers tend to think of it in capital letters. A research paper is usually given as an independent assignment to an individual student. You must remember, to fulfill the requirements of the paper, the PROCESS, or the way in which you conduct your research, is even more important than the information that you collect. A student who takes the time to learn the research process correctly will provide him or herself with the opportunity to build the skills necessary to support a lifetime of research, or more to the point, a lifetime of learning. There are many ways in which the research process can be structured or organized. What will follow is just one idea that, of course, should be changed to meet the individual needs or requirements of your own personal assignment.

Remember: **Organization   =   Success**

TOPIC SELECTION

If you are not given a specific topic to research, you must then decide upon an area that you might find to be interesting. This is an important step because a topic of interest to you will be much easier to research because of the built-in motivation factor.

TOPIC: EXPANSION/LIMITATION

From your chosen general area, select a specific topic. You may find that you will have to expand or narrow your topic. This will be determined after you have gone to the library to examine the materials available on the subject. It is possible that you might have to write a thesis sentence, which will be the viewpoint of your topic and what you propose to prove about your topic. Your teacher will wish to check your thesis sentence.

DETERMINING AVAILABILITY OF SOURCE MATERIALS

After selecting a proposed topic, a trip to the library to check to see what is available in terms of information on your subject is a very important step in the research process. The following is only a suggested order.

1. Encyclopedia: Most encyclopedias will provide, through headings and subheadings, a good overview of a projected topic for research. It will provide information that may help you decide if your topic is too general and must be

limited. It will also help you to determine the subtopics of interest for your proposal. Through skimming and scanning, you will become acquainted with related key words or synonyms(cross reference terms) that will help you to find associated topic information through the use of the indexes in other reference sources. An encyclopedia should NEVER be the lone source for a research paper. **A Note:** Associated or related key words for the topic word can also be found through the direct use of a thesaurus or dictionary.

2. Card catalog: The card catalog, through the use of the developed list of keywords will help you to locate all the nonfiction materials located in your library on your proposed topic. Use of the narrative or summary part of the catalog card will help you to decide if the book's focus or main idea meets the purpose of your assignment. The copyright date will help you determine if the material is current enough to meet the requirements of your paper. And, of course, the tracings will provide still more key words by which you might continue research.
   A Note: The catalog of books in your library might not be on cards. It might be on CD-ROM or on-line. The same aids to research are available in the listings that you'll see on the screen.

3. Readers' Guide/Magazine Article Summaries: Next to a newspaper, the most current material available on any subject will be found in recent issues of magazines and periodicals. Be sure to check these sources when trying to determine availability of materials on a specific subject.

4. Library Indexes: National Geographic Index, American Heritage Index, are all indices to specific magazines. Be sure to check these sources.

5. Vertical file: The vertical file often contains information that is in pamphlet form on specific topics that will not be found on a shelf in a library. The vertical file is alphabetical by topic and easy to use.

If your library has transitioned into any of the following areas, easy access to available materials and locations will be quickly provided. (For a complete explanation of the purpose of these programs, see Lessons 28 & 29.)

COMPUTER ASSISTED RESEARCH WORKSTATIONS

1. CD-ROM: Many libraries have an electronic encyclopedia where the actual article on a subject can be found using the directions provided with the software. In addition to providing the entire article, the electronic encyclopedia will find where your topic word exists in all places in the encyclopedia. Magazine and periodical indexes and possibly the entire card catalog also can be found as part of this type of computer work station area.

2. <u>Union Catalog</u>: Available sources that can be found throughout the union regions can be located and citation and source location will be provided. The catalog will be available at one of the computer work stations.

3. <u>On-Line</u>: Through connections with available data bases throughout the country, on-line services will provide citations and abstracts and sometime full documents of the most current(within a week) articles written on any subject. Digests of on-line bases are available to determine the most appropriate data base before connection.

DETERMINING SUBTOPICS
AND
STRUCTURING A MAIN IDEA OUTLINE

Once you are satisfied with your topic, you must determine natural breaks or "chunks" of information. These "chunks" or aspects of the topic are, of course, subtopics. If you have a thesis sentence, these aspects will be a sequential way of proving your proposal. All of your pre-research work in the library should have paved the way for this to be an easy job for you to accomplish. You will then structure a main idea outline(without details) which should also be checked by your teacher. The codings from the main idea outline will become the basis by which you will code and organize your notecards. The codings are the Roman numerals for the outline subtopics along with other codes for sources. Without this type of organization, a report of this type would be almost impossible to write. With this type of organization, you will be surprised at how rapidly you will complete your report.

<u>Topic</u>
I.
II.
(Main idea outline   III.
without details)   IV.
V.

CODING NOTECARDS

Each source (book, magazine, encyclopedia, etc.) that you will be using for information will have an individual set of notecards coded by you according to your main idea outline.

<u>Topic</u>
I. - - - - - - -
II. x x x x x   Each Roman numeral represents a
III. / / / / / / /   subtopic of the topic
IV. o o o o o
V. \\\\\\\

(All notecards
are for one source.)

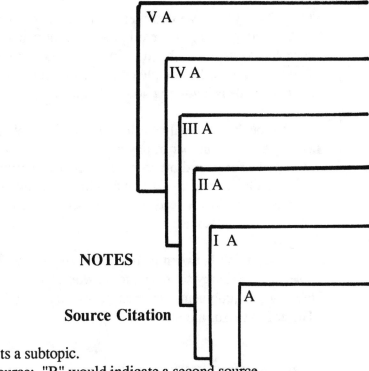

V A

IV A

III A

II A

I A

NOTES

A

Source Citation

Each Roman numeral represents a subtopic.
The Letter "A" indicates one source; "B" would indicate a second source.

Each source should be represented by one pack of notecards. Each card in the pack will contain the appropriate subtopic information as indicated on the above diagram. Therefore, all I's will have the same subtopic written on them. All first cards with just a letter on them, whether it's an A, B, C, or etc., will have the complete citation of the individual source. This will, in turn, enable you to complete a bibliography at the completion of your report. Also, if you are required to make footnotes, this will be the easy way to keep the information.

Notes are taken from the source on the front and back of the card. Your teacher might wish you to only use the front of the card, so you won't have to turn them back and forth when you are writing your report from them. If more room is needed, cards or papers should be stapled together. Care should be taken to place the correct notes under the proper subject heading which is the subtopic found at the top of each card. Remember to put down the page number or numbers you are using. Remember, also, you are taking notes. You are not copying verbatim from the source.

If you do intend to quote the source to make a point, remember to write down all the words exactly. You may quote a person who said something or you may quote a book that explains something. But you must always give credit for the quotation. All quotes should be indicated with page numbers and coding markings should be kept legible to complete footnote citations.

Once you have completed one or two sources and feel that you thoroughly understand the basic note card process, continue to take notes from the other sources to complete your research. It is important not to write the same detail over and over. Think of each of the completed packs of notecards as a screen to the next. Only write down new ideas involving your subtopics.

Although this is only a rule of thumb, you should compile as many pages of notes as the required number of pages for the paper. Otherwise you will risk running short of material for your draft copy of the paper. During notetaking you may find that you will want to replace a subtopic or add two or three others. This is fine. Be sure to go back over previously read sources to see if they also might provide added information on these new subtopics.

Distinguish between primary and secondary source material. Note that on your notecards. Primary source material would be the actual words of someone, the speech, the law, the judgment; whereas, secondary material would be someone reacting to it. The action versus the reaction.

ORGANIZING INFORMATION

Once all of the source cards are completed, it is time to reshuffle the cards to get them ready to support the writing of the first draft. First, all of the I's are piled together, then all the II's and so on. You will then have all the information on one subtopic in one pile from all your sources. You must then take one subtopic at a time and work on it individually. You must thoroughly read and reread all your notes on the subtopic. You are then ready to complete the second stage of outlining.

STRUCTURING THE DETAILED OUTLINE

In the second stage of outlining all details and subdetails are placed on the main idea outline. In this way, you will have completely organized your paper before you have begun to write. You will make changes where necessary. If you find that there is an imbalance in the material in your outline, there will also be an imbalance in your paper. Or you may find in your notes that you are straying from the focus of your thesis sentence. In either case, it may be necessary for you to go back and redevelop your notes and outline for that subtopic area. It is a good practice to balance your material before you begin to write. It would be a good idea, at this stage, to present your outline and ask your teacher for input.

THE FIRST DRAFT

Try to write your entire paper from the outline, referring back to your notes only when absolutely necessary, such as when you are in need of a quote or a footnote page number. Refer to the original source only to verify a fact if you become confused. In this way, you will be sure that the paper is truly yours, and not plagiarized. This will represent the body of your paper. You must rewrite and edit until you are completely satisfied. Is it logical? Is it sequentially organized? Have you kept the focus? Is the thesis sentence on target? Is it balanced? Have you made use of transitional devices that make the paragraphs flow naturally one to the other? Did you use primary source material? Did you give proper credit?

INTRODUCTION AND CONCLUSION

Once you are satisfied with the body of your report, it is time to concentrate on developing an introduction. An introduction can be a summary paragraph of what will be in the body of the report. It also can be a paragraph that indicates the basic structure of the information that will be presented. In other words, you might indicate that the paper consists of a comparison and contrast of a certain topic and your conclusion based on your study of the subject.

The conclusion of the paper should be a paragraph or two on your basic attitude toward the information contained in the paper with supportive detail pulled from the text. By the time you've finished your research and have written the paper, you find this quite easy to do.

EDIT/PROOF/FINAL COPY

After editing the entire paper, including the introduction and the conclusion, begin the final copy.

FORMAT REQUIREMENTS

Format requirements will basically depend on the length of the paper and your teacher's instructions. Some of the requirements might be the use of footnotes, citations, appendix, table of contents, and a title sheet. Sometimes graphs, charts or other visual aids are appropriate. Some teachers might request a continuous flow of text while another might insist that formal headings and subheadings be used to present a more structured written discussion of the subject.

Bibliographic and footnote or endnote sheets will be provided by your teacher. You should be aware that the bibliographic format is different for a book, encyclopedia, magazine, newspaper, etc. The more varied the types of sources used, the more individual will be the specific format for each source.

No matter what process or basic format used in fulfilling the requirements of a research paper, organization is the key to a successful completion of the task.

Congratulations are in order for you when you do successfully complete a paper!

Date_____   **Know Your Country:**
                                      Territories and Possessions of the U. S.

Which of these territories and possessions is on the mainland of the United States? Which three are in the Atlantic Ocean? Which are on the Pacific side of the United States?

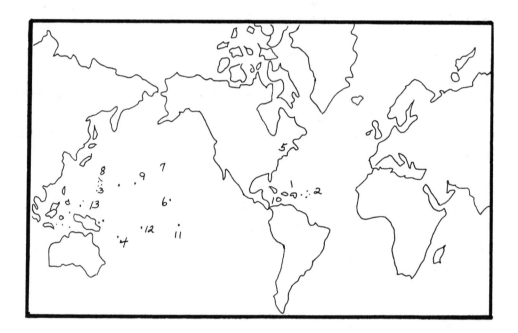

Territories and Possessions of the United States

1. Puerto Rico
2. Virgin Islands
3. Guam
4. American Samoa
5. District of Columbia
6. Johnston Island
7. Midway Island
8. Northern Marianas
9. Wake Island
10. Navassa Island
11. Kingman Reef and Palmyra Island
12. Baker, Howland and Jarvis Islands
13. Federated States of Micronesia, including the Marshall Islands and Palau

Unit VII Activity   Territories and Possessions of the U. S.

1.Make a globe or global map. Place flags for location on all territories and possessions.

2. Chart the governmental relationship of each territory and possession with the United States.

3. Look at the map. Write a paragraph stating conclusions about trade and transportation based on your understanding of the location of the individual territories and possessions.

4. Research the difference between American nationals and American citizens. Take notes. Submit note cards with sources.

5. Research the islands that are administered by branches of the United States military. Take notes and submit in outline form.

6. Research military history of Midway Island. Make bibliography including books, magazines, on-line and CD information, and any other media if applicable. List a minimum of 15 sources in correct bibliographic form.

7. Research the attempts at statehood for Puerto Rico. Take notes, write chronologically ordered outline. Write time-order paragraphs from outline.

8. Research the importance of the Arecibo Ionospheric Observatory in Puerto Rico. Develop one well-written paragraph from an intended report, showing evidence of proofing and editing before submitting draft.

9. Research the unique aspects of Buck Island Reef National Monument, off St. Croix. Develop an introductory paragraph for an intended report.

10. Research the origin of the brick in the building known as Fort Christansvaern on St. Croix. With an understanding of history, trade and transportation, what conclusions can you draw? Write them in paragraph form.

11. Research the District of Columbia. Complete the following sequence of instruction.
    a. Select a topic.
    b. Go to a library and, using appropriate material, expand or limit the topic.
    c. Generate approximately 5-6 subtopics.
    d. Develop thesis sentence, if required.
    e. Construct a main idea outline, using those subtopics.
    f. Construct note card packets on which notes will be taken.

Unit VII Activity   Territories and Possessions of the U. S.

g. Determine sources.

h. Analyze information to determine if subtopics must be expanded, more sources needed, or if some subtopics must be eliminated.

i. Finish note taking, making sure that sources are entered with complete bibliographic and footnoting information.

j. Reshuffle cards into subtopic areas.

k. Read through cards.

l. Use original main idea outline to construct final detailed outline.

m. Write draft version of the report directly from the outline.

n. Proof and edit.

o. Submit for interim approval.

p. Make necessary corrections.

q. Formulate introduction and conclusion.

r. Write final copy.

s. Build bibliography.

t. Create endnotes(footnotes on separate piece of paper), according to local standards.

u. Make title page in accordance with local standards.

v. Make table of contents, if required.

w. Make appendix, if necessary and/or required.

x. Submit.

Appendix Contents and Directions

Appendix A: **Rapid Study Technique**

Appendix A consists of factual bits of information that can be used with the students as self-testing devices. They can cut them apart; bend over the answers, test themselves or test a classmate. The first page serves as a model for a suggested print size, line delineation and spacing that would be considered appropriate for the age level.

Appendix B: **Simulation Card Catalog**

In Appendix B, catalog card clusters present a situation that students might encounter when searching for information. It provides practice in application of common rules as well as exceptions. There are three different sets of questions. A generic answer sheet is included. Question #1 solicits information from catalog card cluster #1 and this answer is placed on line #1 of the student answer sheet.

Appendix C: **Simulation Card Catalog Answer Key**

Appendix C includes answer keys for the three sets of questions located in Appendix B.

Appendix D: **Activities Answer Key**

Appendix D consists of individual answer keys for all the lesson activities. Each answer key is coded by a lesson number and a letter which corresponds to the activity.

Appendix E: **Discussion Question Answer Key**

Appendix E includes the answers to the student discussion questions which are interspersed throughout the student notes. Each lesson is indicated and all questions are numbered as they appear in the student text.

Appendix F: **Unit Tests**

Appendix F includes all seven unit tests and an answer key for each. All tests are clearly marked by unit number.

Appendix G: **Final Tests**

Appendix G includes a final test, an answer key, and a student answer sheet. Also, the test can be used as a pretest.

Appendix H: **"Did You Know?" Answer Key**

Appendix H includes the answer keys for the "Did You Know?" activities from Lesson 27. Each set of answers is alphabetically ordered by title.

Glossary

The glossary is for the student and is comprised of one hundred twenty-five common library terms.

Index

The index is for the teacher as it references both teacher and student notes.

NAME_____

DATE_____

Media Center

1. For what do the initials IMC stand?	Instructional Media Center
2. Literature can be broken into two parts. Name them.	A. Fiction B. Nonfiction
3. List the four basic sections of any library.	A. Fiction B. Nonfiction C. Reference D. Biography
4. Define fiction.	It provides information or plot sequence that is either totally or partially make-believe. It is written for entertainment value.
5. List the four types of fiction.	A. Historical fiction B. Modern realistic fiction C. Science fiction D. Fantasy

Media Center

6. In which type of fiction
    does the author break   Fantasy
    through the laws of nature?

7. In which type of fiction
    does the author create believable
    characters, a plausible plot,   Modern realistic fiction
    and a present day time
    setting?

8. In which type of fiction
    does the author create believable
    characters, yet also include   Historical fiction
    famous people? The time
    setting is in the past.

9. In which type of fiction
    does the author focus on the
    future but bases the conflict   Science fiction
    of the characters on knowledge
    of current technological
    advances?

10. Name the three types of
    fiction that are shelved   A. Myths
    in the nonfiction section   B. Legends
    because of their content.   C. Tales

11. Which main area of literature
    involves totally factual   Nonfiction
    information?

12. Which library area of factual
    information covers subjects   Nonfiction
    in an in-depth study?

13. Which library area of factual
    information covers subjects   Reference
    in a rapid review?

14. If you check an author's
    credentials or background is
    his/her field, you are   Expertise
    checking his/her _____.

15. If any author indicates
    through his/her writings
    that he/she is for or against   Bias
    a subject, that author is
    expressing a _____.

Appendix A   Rapid Study Technique

Media Center

16. Which two types of nonfiction books are interfiled in the biography section of the library?

A. Biography
B. Autobiography

17. What do you call a book written by one person about the life of another person?

Biography

18. What do you call a book written by a person about his/her own life?

Autobiography

19. List some instructional aids that might be found in an IMC?

records   Picture files   films kits   Sound filmstrips   tapes slides   newspapers   film loops transparencies   computer software vertical file   periodicals

20. List the four organizational systems that can be found in a library.

A. Chronological
B. Alphabetical
C. Topical
D. Numerical

21. In using the card catalog, which guides help you to locate the correct drawer?

Outside

22. In using the card catalog, which guides help you to locate the correct card?

Inside

23. The basic cards found in the card catalog are_____.

A. Author
B. Subject
C. Title

24. The cards that suggest other key words to help further research are_____.

The cross reference cards are:
   a. see
   b. see also

25. List the three added entry cards.

A. Joint author
B. Illustrator
C. Series

26. In which order would you find the inside guides for the drawer marked U. S. - History?

Chronologically placed
(By time period/era)

Media Center

27. What are the correct
    abbreviations for:
    a. Fiction?
    b. Reference?
    c. Biography?
    d. Record?

    a.   Fic
    b.   Ref
    c.   B
    d.   Rec

28. What are the correct
    abbreviations for:
    a. Sound filmstrip
    b. Map collections
    c. Film loop
    d. Transparencies

    a.   SFS
    b.   Map
    c.   MPL
    d.   Tra

29. What are the correct
    abbreviations for:
    a. Professional
    b. Picture file
    c. Vertical file
    d. Kit

    a.   Prof
    b.   PS/PA
    c.   vertical
    d.   Kit

30. What are the correct
    abbreviations for:
    a. Computer software
    b. Video tape

    a.   MRDF
    b.   VT

31. Simple   a, b, c,   order
    is known as_____.

    Alphabetical order

32. Order by simple number
    sequence is known
    as_____.

    Numerical order

33. Order by time period or
    time era is known
    as_____.

    Chronological Order

34. The order of the grouping
    of subjects in a content
    area book is known
    as_____.

    Topical Order

35. Name the four
    organizational systems
    as found in a library
    setting.

    A.   Alphabetical
    B.   Numerical
    C.   Chronological
    D.   Topical

36. Name the three basic card
    types found in the card
    catalog.

    A.   Subject
    B.   Title
    C.   Author

Media Center

37. Name the three card types
    known as the added
    entry cards.

    A. Joint Author
    B. Illustrator
    C. Series

38. Name the two types
    of cross reference
    cards.

    A. See
    B. See also

39. Explain the difference
    in the meanings of the
    terms: *see* and *see also*

    See: Indicates that subject word is
    not valid for the index; researcher
    must instead use one of the others
    provided.

    See also: Subject word valid, but use
    others if more information is
    needed.

40. What is the basic organization
    of the outside guides of the
    card catalog?

    Alphabetical

41. What is the rule regarding
    a, an, the, when using
    the card catalog?

    Drop at the beginning of
    a title; keep when
    within a title.

42. Under which word do you
    look when looking up a
    book title such as:
    Abraham Lincoln?

    First Name: Abraham

43. Under which word do you
    look to find an author or a
    subject such as John Kennedy?

    Last Name: Kennedy

44. How would you find a title
    card when the first word of
    the title is abbreviated?
    e.g. Dr.

    Spell out: Doctor

45. What is the rule regarding
    Mc/Mac in the card catalog?

    1. Mc/Mac are interfiled as
       though they are spelled the same.
    2. The Mc/Mac words are found in
       front of the words beginning with
       the letters "Ma"

Atlas

1. What is an atlas?	A collection of maps
2. Why is it important to read all the information at the beginning of the atlas that precedes the maps?	The information offers explanations of keys and abbreviations that are used in all the maps and are not necessarily explained as part of the map legend.
3. Why is it important to review the table of contents in an atlas?	It will give you a basic overview of the maps covered and will give you the atlas focus. This will help you decide if a particular map will be of use to you.
4. Why is it important to have a general knowledge of the information contained in an atlas?	Being geographically aware of the general and specific areas of the world will help you to become a more well-rounded student.
5. What part of the map will provide the map focus?	The title
6. What part of the map will define the individual symbols used on the map?	The legend
7. Why is it important to review all surrounding information offered on a map page before studying the map?	to decode the map
8. If you want to find the location of a specific area on a map, to what should you refer?	The index
9. What is the organization of an atlas index?	alphabetical
10. What type of information will an atlas index provide to help you locate a specific point on a map?	1. text page numbers 2. coordinates
11. What are coordinates?	Symbols used to establish a position of a map in grid format.
12. How might coordinates be represented?	By letter/number By longitude/latitude

Appendix A   Rapid Study Technique

Almanac

1. What is the purpose of an almanac?

   It is a book of facts whose focus is for one year.

2. To correctly and most efficiently use an almanac, to which section should you turn first?

   the index

3. How is an index usually organized?

   alphabetically

4. Name the parts of an index entry in an almanac.

   The parts are:
   topic; subtopic; detail; visual aid, if indicated; and specific page numbers corresponding to text.

5. What does a hyphen mean in an index?
   ex. 6-9

   A hyphen indicates that the two pages named and all the pages in between are included. Ex., 6,7,8,9

6. What does a comma mean when it separates two page numbers in an almanac index? ex. 7,10

   Pages indicated include those two specific pages before and after the comma.
   Pages 7 and 10.

7. List the specific type of information that you might obtain from an almanac

   1. A monthly review (chronological) overview of events or happenings during the year of focus.
   2. News stories of impact or importance
   3. A variety of specific information to be found through the use of the index.

Parts of a Book

1. What do you call credit given to original sources for material used?

   acknowledgement

2. Added material at the end of a book is called the_____.

   appendix

3. A person who writes original material based on sources is an _____.

   author

4. What do you call the main
   part of a book?   body/text

5. What do you call a person
   who gathers material into   editor, compiler
   book format that others
   have written?

6. What do you call a listing of
   sources of information that   bibliography
   comes at the end of a chapter
   or book?

7. What do you call the pages in
   a book that gives the dates of   copyright page
   publication of the book and is
   located on the back of the title
   page?

8. What do you call the front and
   back of the outer part of
   the book?   cover

9. What do you call the paper
   cover that protects the book?   dustcover, dustjacket

10. What do you call the
    illustration that is placed   frontispiece
    opposite the title page in
    some books?

11. What do you call a specialized
    dictionary that defines words   glossary
    according to subject areas and
    is found in a content area book?

12. Who draws the pictures for
    a book?   illustrator

13. What do you call an
    alphabetical listing by topic,
    then by subtopic of material   index
    or information covered in
    a book?

14. What do you call a city
    and/or state location of   place of publication
    a publishing company?

15. What is another word for
    an introduction to a book?   preface

Parts of a Book

16. What do you call the
    company that prints the book?   publisher

17. What do you call the
    listing of the major parts,
    units and chapters of a   table of contents
    book that is in page order?

18. What is the name of   title
    the book?

19. What is another name
    for the backbone of the
    book?   spine

Readers' Guide to Periodical Literature

1. What is the purpose   It is an index of articles in
   of the Readers' Guide?   magazines.

2. What is meant by an abridged   It is a shortened, concise form.
   version of a book?

3. Is Readers' Guide in book   No, it is also on the computer: on-line.
   format only?

4. What do the cross references   *See*: Indicates that subject word is
   see and *see also* mean?   not valid for the index; researcher
                                           must instead use one of the others
                                           provided.
                                    See also: Subject word valid, but use
                                           others if more information is
                                           needed.

5. What does an entry in   topic; subtopic, if given; detail, if given;
   Readers' Guide provide?   title of article; author of article, if given;
                                    indication if illustrated; volume number
                                    of magazine; page numbers; cross
                                    references; date of issue

6. For what words do the   a. portrait
   following abbreviations stand?   b. map
   a. por   c. bibliography
   b. map   d. illustration
   c. bibl
   d. il

7. Can you take the Readers'   No, it is an index that remains in the
   Guide home?   library at all times.

258

Readers' Guide to Periodical Literature

8. Why is it important to review the introductory materials that precede the index in Readers' Guide?

It will help in understanding how to use the guide, how to read the entries in the index, and to understand many of the common abbreviations used in the guide.

Magazine Article Summaries

1. How often are updates of Magazine Article Summaries published?

They are updated weekly.

2. How is Magazine Article divided?

MAS is divided into:
1. white pages of article summaries;
2. brown pages of index references.

3. How often is the index updated in Magazine Article Summaries?

The index is updated every two months and replaces all other indices published for that year.

4. What do the white pages contain?

Article summaries

5. What is the design of an MAS entry?

Topic, subtopic, detail

6. What type of a cross reference cue system does MAS use?

see/see also

7. What are the elements of an MAS index entry?

heading/subheading
column number
paragraph number
asterisk (indicates a cover story)

8. To what does an MAS index entry refer you?

To the appropriate article summary in the white pages by way of the elements of the MAS index entry.

9. What is the purpose of the article summary?

It offers the advantage of knowing the main idea or focus of the article before the article is taken from the periodical room shelf.

10. What is a cover story?

A very developed magazine article.

11. What is an inset?

A story within a story

Appendix A   Rapid Study Technique

Current Biography

1. What is the purpose of Current Biography?

Current Biography presents a concise but accurate, factual account of people who have achieved a leadership role in their associated field of expertise.

2. Does Current Biography give an explanation as to how information is gathered or collected?

Yes, a separate section in the book

The National Geographic Index

1. What type of entry can be used to retrieve information?

1. Subject by way of topic, subtopic and and detail;
2. Author, by last name
3. Title, of TV show, article, book or map
Subject, Author, Title: alphabetically organized.

2. Describe the cross reference cue system used in the National Geographic Index

See: Indicates that subject word is not valid for the index; researcher must instead use one of the others provided.
See also: Subject word valid, but use others if more information is needed.

3. How can the index user tell the difference among the TV shows, maps, magazine articles, and books?

By the color coding on the page.

4. Describe the elements of an entry in the National Geographic Index.

1. Indication as to whether the entry is of a book, magazine article, maps or TV show
2. Title, author, pages, visual aids, explanatory phrase, cross references.

5. How are acronyms handled in the National Geographic Index?

If an acronym appears in the entry, a cross reference of *see* will refer you to the original word upon which the acronym was based.

American Heritage Index

1. What is the purpose of the American Heritage Magazine?

The American Heritage magazine offers a broad overview of major events concerning America's past as well as her present.

2. What two type of indices does American Heritage Magazine publish?

1. Alphabetical index that covers many years of publication.
2. Chronological Index that is also topical.

3. Name entry types that can be utilized to retrieve information when using the American Heritage Index.

A. Subject
B. Author by last name
C. Article title

4. List the elements of an entry.

Subject in capital letters
Date of article
Volume number

Encyclopedia

1. Each book in a set of encyclopedia is called a:

volume

2. The information part of the book is called the:

body or text

3. When on the shelf, each book is identified by the number and letter markings on the _____ of the book.

spine

4. Encyclopedias can be in one of three orders and they are:

alphabetical
chronological
topical

5. The written compositions (in an encyclopedia) on the topics of people, places, and events are called_____:

articles or entries

6. Some articles give the name of the person who wrote it at the end and this is known as a _____ article.

signed

7. Words at the top of each encyclopedia page that indicate the first and last entries are called_____.

guide words

Encyclopedia

8. If the article or entry is long,
   it will be divided into parts
   by_____.

headings/subheadings
topics/subtopics

9. To help with research, the
   editors of an encyclopedia give
   alternative sources indicated
   by_____.

see/see also
(cross references)

10. To help you locate all the
    important information contained
    in an encyclopedia on a single
    topic, you should go to
    the _____, where
    you will find the appropriate
    volume numbers and page
    numbers.

index

11. Other articles do not have
    the author given and these
    are called _____ articles.

unsigned

12. At the end of each article, most
    encyclopedias give a listing of
    books that can be read to further
    knowledge on a subject. This
    list is called a _____.

bibliography

13. A summary listing of facts
    in an encyclopedia is called
    a _____.

fact summary

14. List at least six visual
    aids that can be found
    in an encyclopedia.

maps, graphs, charts, tables,
transparencies, illustrations,
diagrams

15. Under each visual aid will be
    a _____ to connect it to the
    body or text. The _____ is a
    written explanation of the aid.

legend

16. The _____ is found
    at the beginning of the book and
    gives the reader an overview of
    the ideas contained in the book.

table of contents

17. An _____ is a set of
    books found in the reference
    section of the library. It contains
    information about people, places,
    events.

encyclopedia

Name_____

Date_____

**Catalog Card Application
Form 1**

CATALOG SEARCH APPLICATION (Introductory Activity)

1. Who wrote *Ab to Zogg*?
2. How many book titles begin with the word "And"?
3. What is the call number for the book written by Walter Arm?
4. Is there a book about automobile racing on ice?
5. What type of books does Nina Brown Baker write?
6. What is the call number for a book by Bill Robinson entitled *Better Sailing for boys and girls*?
7. Who wrote *Bury my heart at Wounded Knee*?
8. Give the copyright for the only Fiction book.
9. What is the copyright date for Mary Lou Clark's book?
10. How big was *Colonel Meacham's Giant Cheese*?
11. In what year does *The Cornhusk Doll* take place?
12. In the category, DEAF - MEANS OF COMMUNICATION, what kind of language do all the books have in common?
13. Does the IMC have a fiction book about the city of Edinburgh?
14. What is the title of a book by Larry Engler?
15. Which biography book has a title card showing?
16. What is Admiral Farragut's middle name?
17. Is there a book with the subject heading, FOLKLORE - MAPS? If so, what is the title?
18. Did the same person write *Fun with crewel embroidery* and *Fun with mathematics*?
19. Under what subject heading would you look to find out about garbage?
20. Under what other library classification could Bettyanne Gray's book be put?
21. Under the HANDICRAFT subject heading, write down the title of a book about African handicraft.
22. Who wrote the book that Deanne Hollinger illustrated?
23. What is the call number for *Incredible but true*?
24. Does the IMC have a book on how to invent your own computer game? If so, what is the call number?
25. MacKinlay Kantor writes about a specific time in U.S. History. What is it?

Name_____

Date_____

Catalog Card Application
Form 2

CATALOG SEARCH APPLICATION - (Reinforcement Activity)

1. Name the library classification of all four cards.
2. Who wrote *And now Miguel*?
3. Who published *The arm of the starfish*?
4. Which book would tell you more about making a living from auto racing?
5. List the books in the order that they would appear on the biography shelf.
6,7,8. What subject card could be made for one of the books, and where did you find that information?
9. In which category is Margaret Clark's book classified?
10. What are the two series listed in this cluster?
11. How old is the child in this book?
12. How many subject heading groups are in this cluster?
13. Who is the illustrator of Sam Edge's book?
14. From the basic information given, what Dewey category would the On-Words Game fit?
15.What is the subtitle for the Silverstein book?
16. Who published the Farrand book?
17. Do all the books in this cluster have authors?
18. In this cluster, which author wrote the most books?
19. What is the subtitle?
20. Which of these might be historical fiction and why?
21. Which book might you use during your study of Early America?
22. List the order in which the two fiction books in this cluster would be shelved in the IMC.
23. Which card is for the non-book media?
24. Which two series are included in this cluster?
25. Who illustrated two of the books?

Name_____

Date_____

Catalog Card Application
Form 3

CATALOG SEARCH APPLICATION - (Evaluation)

1. Which book can tell you how to make and use an abacus?
2. Who wrote the book of which George Ancona is the joint author?
3. What is the name of the character who has a summer job as an assistant to a marine biologist?
4. In the book on the history of automobile racing, what year starts the history?
5. What are the years of Juarez's life?
6,7,8. Which book has a glossary?
9. What is the series of Margaret Clark's book?
10. What is the title of Mr. Fisher's book?
11. Who illustrated the book?
12. In what Dewey number would sign language be?
13. What is title of the fiction book about Edinburgh?
14. What is the series for Mr. Englebardt's book?
15. In the book about Ericsson, can you guess what the Monitor Ironclad was?
16. How would the title card to the Farr book be filed?
17. Who wrote the Mexican folklore book?
18. List the titles as they would appear on the shelf.
19. Who is the publisher?
20. What is the title for the non-book media?
21. Is there a bibliography is Cutler's book?
22. Which is the joint author card in this cluster?
23. Make an author card for the biography book.
24. What is the title on the only subject card in this cluster?
25. What is the series of two of these books?

The abacus: a pocket computer.
511 Dilson, Jesse
Dil   The abacus: a pocket computer; drawings by Angela
Pozzi. St. Martin's Press [©1968]
143p illus
Includes instructions for making and using the beaded counting frame which
originated in the Orient, with a discussion of the decimal system and the
binary system, which is used as a basis for the modern
electronic computer.

#1

ABACUS
511   Dilson, Jesse

Dil   The abacus; a pocket computer; drawings by Angela
Pozzi. St. Martin's Press [©1968]
143p illus
Includes instructions for making and using the beaded counting frame which
originated in the Orient, with a discussion of the decimal system and the binary
system, which is used as a basis for the modern electronic computer.

Ab to zogg
818 Merriam, Eve
Mer   Ab to zogg; a lexicon for science-
fiction and fantasy readers. Drawings
by Al Lorenz. Atheneum 1977
43p illus

A spoof of science fiction and fantasy
through a brief dictionary of new--but
recognizable--words and phrases.

1. Science fiction--anecdotes, facetiae,
satire, etc. I. Title

920 Aaseng, Nathan
Aas   World-class marathoners. (Sports
Heroes) Lerner Pub. Minneapolis,
©1982.
80p illus.

Summary: Outlines the history of
the marathon and the careers of
seven great marathon runners.

1. Runners (Sports)--Biography
2. Marathon running I. Title

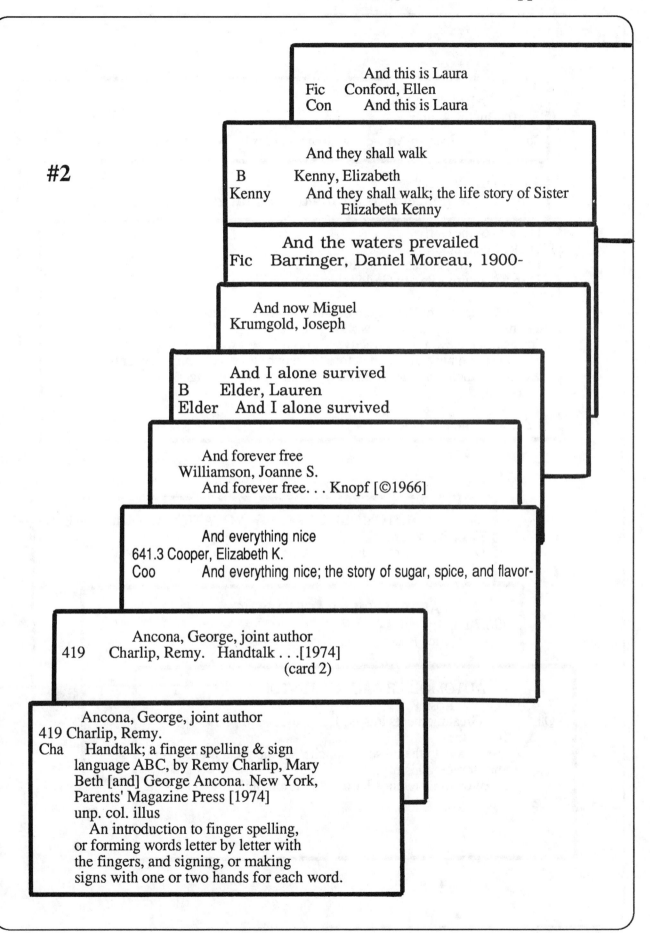

#2

And this is Laura
Fic   Conford, Ellen
Con   And this is Laura

And they shall walk
B   Kenny, Elizabeth
Kenny   And they shall walk; the life story of Sister
              Elizabeth Kenny

And the waters prevailed
Fic   Barringer, Daniel Moreau, 1900-

And now Miguel
Krumgold, Joseph

And I alone survived
B   Elder, Lauren
Elder   And I alone survived

And forever free
Williamson, Joanne S.
     And forever free. . . Knopf [©1966]

And everything nice
641.3 Cooper, Elizabeth K.
Coo   And everything nice; the story of sugar, spice, and flavor-

Ancona, George, joint author
419   Charlip, Remy.   Handtalk . . .[1974]
                    (card 2)

Ancona, George, joint author
419 Charlip, Remy.
Cha   Handtalk; a finger spelling & sign
     language ABC, by Remy Charlip, Mary
     Beth [and] George Ancona. New York,
     Parents' Magazine Press [1974]
     unp. col. illus
        An introduction to finger spelling,
     or forming words letter by letter with
     the fingers, and signing, or making
     signs with one or two hands for each word.

ARMADA, 1588
942.05 Buehr, Walter

Bue   The Spanish Armada; written and illus by Walter   **#3**

352 Arm, Walter
Arm   The policeman; an inside look at his role in a modern

The arm of the starfish
L'Engle, Madeleine
The arm of the starfish. Ariel Bks. 1965
243p (A Junior Literary Guild selection)

    Young Adam Eddington obtains a summer job as assistant to Dr. O'Keefe, the marine biologist, who is working on a small island off the coast of Portugal. In New York, attractive Carolyn Cutter warns him against two passengers on his plane, and before the day has passed ominous events take place, including the kidnapping of one of the passengers, a twelve-year-old girl.

1 Spies--Fiction I. Title

AUTOMOBILE RACING--VOCATIONAL GUIDANCE
796.7 Lerner, Mark
Ler   Careers in auto racing. Photos by

#4

AUTOMOBILE RACING ON ICE
796.7 Popp, Dennis
Pop   Ice Racing

AUTOMOBILE RACING--HISTORY
796.709 Olney, Ross R.
Oln   Great moments in speed. Prentice-Hall [©1970]
    146p illus
From 1894 to the present, sketches all the great moments in
  motor racing history..
1. Automobile racing--History 2 Automobile drivers I Title

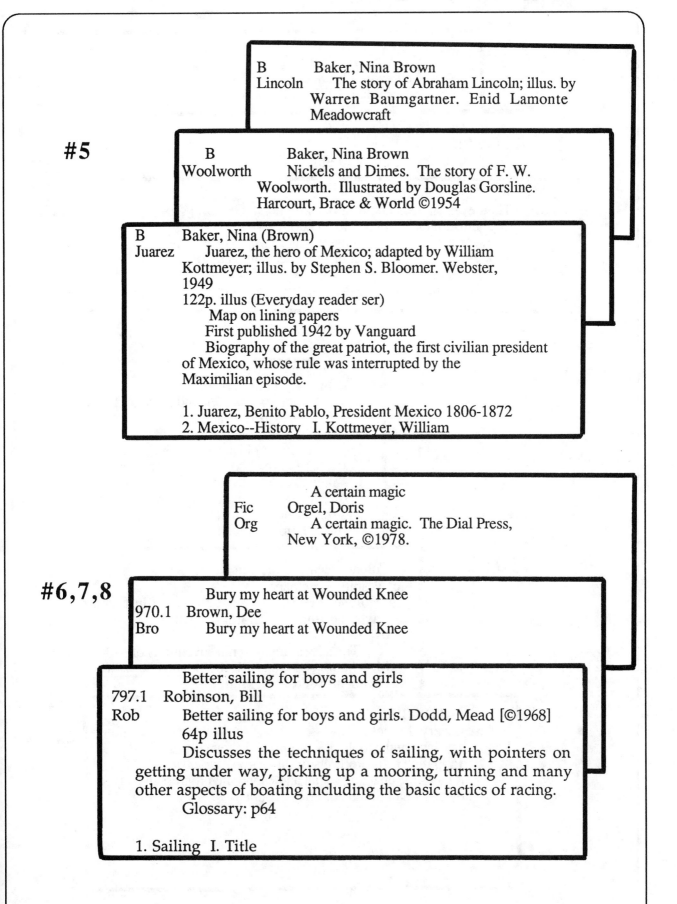

#5

B   Baker, Nina Brown
Lincoln   The story of Abraham Lincoln; illus. by
            Warren Baumgartner. Enid Lamonte
            Meadowcraft

B   Baker, Nina Brown
Woolworth   Nickels and Dimes. The story of F. W.
            Woolworth. Illustrated by Douglas Gorsline.
            Harcourt, Brace & World ©1954

B   Baker, Nina (Brown)
Juarez   Juarez, the hero of Mexico; adapted by William
Kottmeyer; illus. by Stephen S. Bloomer. Webster,
1949
122p. illus (Everyday reader ser)
     Map on lining papers
     First published 1942 by Vanguard
     Biography of the great patriot, the first civilian president
of Mexico, whose rule was interrupted by the
Maximilian episode.

1. Juarez, Benito Pablo, President Mexico 1806-1872
2. Mexico--History I. Kottmeyer, William

#6,7,8

            A certain magic
Fic   Orgel, Doris
Org   A certain magic. The Dial Press,
         New York, ©1978.

          Bury my heart at Wounded Knee
970.1   Brown, Dee
Bro   Bury my heart at Wounded Knee

          Better sailing for boys and girls
797.1   Robinson, Bill
Rob   Better sailing for boys and girls. Dodd, Mead [©1968]
          64p illus
          Discusses the techniques of sailing, with pointers on
getting under way, picking up a mooring, turning and many
other aspects of boating including the basic tactics of racing.
          Glossary: p64

1. Sailing I. Title

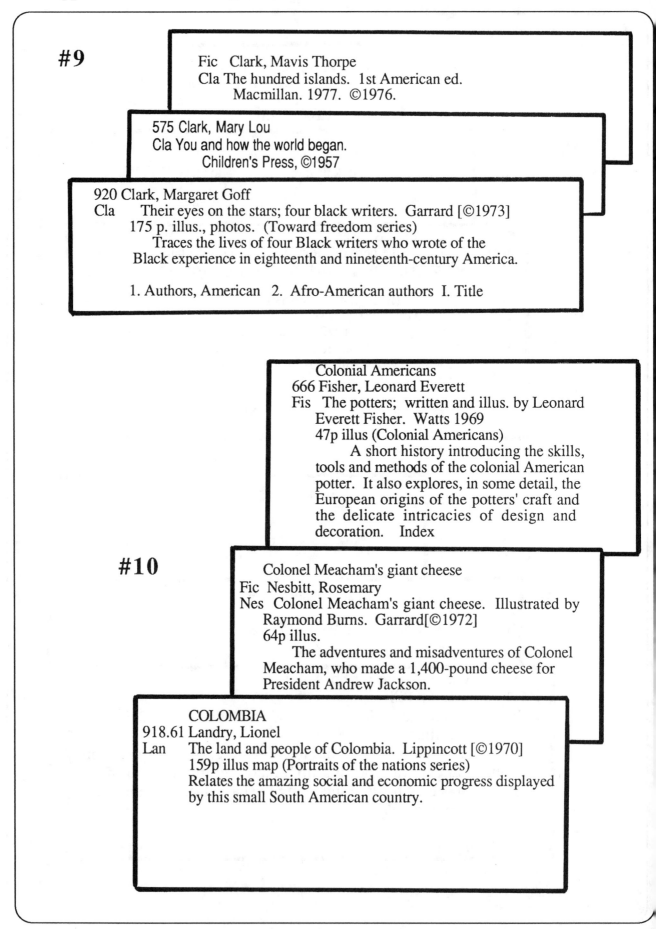

#9

Fic Clark, Mavis Thorpe
Cla The hundred islands. 1st American ed.
     Macmillan. 1977. ©1976.

575 Clark, Mary Lou
Cla You and how the world began.
     Children's Press, ©1957

920 Clark, Margaret Goff
Cla   Their eyes on the stars; four black writers. Garrard [©1973]
     175 p. illus., photos. (Toward freedom series)
          Traces the lives of four Black writers who wrote of the
     Black experience in eighteenth and nineteenth-century America.

     1. Authors, American 2. Afro-American authors I. Title

Colonial Americans
666 Fisher, Leonard Everett
Fis The potters; written and illus. by Leonard
     Everett Fisher. Watts 1969
     47p illus (Colonial Americans)
          A short history introducing the skills,
     tools and methods of the colonial American
     potter. It also explores, in some detail, the
     European origins of the potters' craft and
     the delicate intricacies of design and
     decoration.   Index

#10

Colonel Meacham's giant cheese
Fic Nesbitt, Rosemary
Nes Colonel Meacham's giant cheese. Illustrated by
     Raymond Burns. Garrard[©1972]
     64p illus.
          The adventures and misadventures of Colonel
     Meacham, who made a 1,400-pound cheese for
     President Andrew Jackson.

COLOMBIA
918.61 Landry, Lionel
Lan   The land and people of Colombia. Lippincott [©1970]
     159p illus map (Portraits of the nations series)
     Relates the amazing social and economic progress displayed
     by this small South American country.

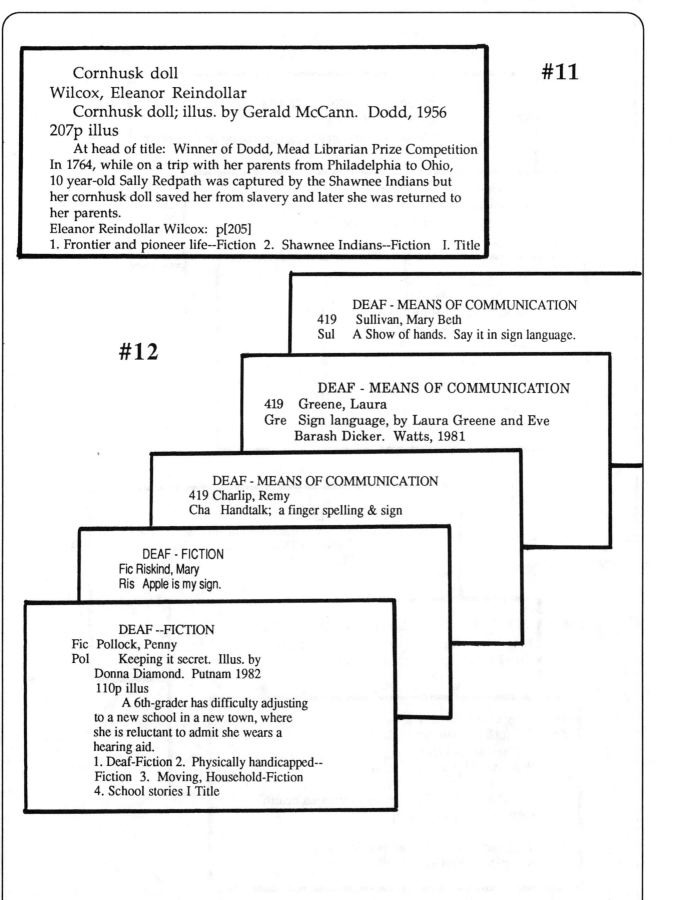

Cornhusk doll   **#11**
Wilcox, Eleanor Reindollar
    Cornhusk doll; illus. by Gerald McCann. Dodd, 1956
207p illus
    At head of title: Winner of Dodd, Mead Librarian Prize Competition
In 1764, while on a trip with her parents from Philadelphia to Ohio,
10 year-old Sally Redpath was captured by the Shawnee Indians but
her cornhusk doll saved her from slavery and later she was returned to
her parents.
Eleanor Reindollar Wilcox: p[205]
1. Frontier and pioneer life--Fiction 2. Shawnee Indians--Fiction   I. Title

#12

DEAF - MEANS OF COMMUNICATION
419   Sullivan, Mary Beth
Sul   A Show of hands. Say it in sign language.

DEAF - MEANS OF COMMUNICATION
419   Greene, Laura
Gre   Sign language, by Laura Greene and Eve
        Barash Dicker. Watts, 1981

DEAF - MEANS OF COMMUNICATION
419 Charlip, Remy
Cha   Handtalk; a finger spelling & sign

DEAF - FICTION
Fic Riskind, Mary
Ris Apple is my sign.

DEAF --FICTION
Fic Pollock, Penny
Pol   Keeping it secret. Illus. by
    Donna Diamond. Putnam 1982
    110p illus
        A 6th-grader has difficulty adjusting
to a new school in a new town, where
she is reluctant to admit she wears a
hearing aid.
1. Deaf-Fiction 2. Physically handicapped--
Fiction 3. Moving, Household-Fiction
4. School stories I Title

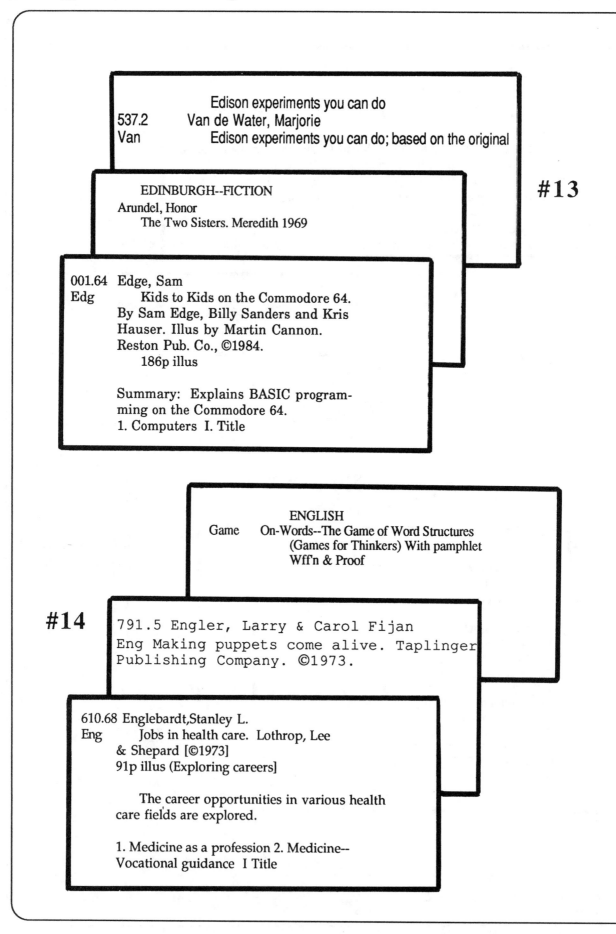

Edison experiments you can do
537.2   Van de Water, Marjorie
Van   Edison experiments you can do; based on the original

EDINBURGH--FICTION
Arundel, Honor
      The Two Sisters. Meredith 1969

#13

001.64 Edge, Sam
Edg   Kids to Kids on the Commodore 64.
By Sam Edge, Billy Sanders and Kris
Hauser. Illus by Martin Cannon.
Reston Pub. Co., ©1984.
      186p illus

Summary: Explains BASIC programming on the Commodore 64.
1. Computers I. Title

ENGLISH
Game   On-Words--The Game of Word Structures
        (Games for Thinkers) With pamphlet
        Wff'n & Proof

#14

791.5 Engler, Larry & Carol Fijan
Eng Making puppets come alive. Taplinger
Publishing Company. ©1973.

610.68 Englebardt,Stanley L.
Eng   Jobs in health care. Lothrop, Lee
      & Shepard [©1973]
      91p illus (Exploring careers]

      The career opportunities in various health
care fields are explored.

1. Medicine as a profession 2. Medicine--
Vocational guidance I Title

#15

Ernest Thompson Seton
B   Blassingame, Wyatt
Seton   Ernest Thompson Seton;
scout and naturalist. Illustrated by
Frank Vaughn. Garrard [©1971]
        80p illus. (Discovery books)
    A biography of one of the
founding fathers of the Boy Scouts,
whose nature stories and pictures
aided the cause of conservation and
the preservation of our wilderness
areas.

B   Erlanger, Ellen
Fonda   Jane Fonda, more than a movie star.
Lerner, 1984
56p. illus

    A biography of the actress whose
political activities and publishing
adventures have kept her constantly in the
public eye.

1. Fonda, Jane, 1937- 2. Actors and
actresses, American--Biography I. Title

        Erikson, Mel, illus
612   Silverstein, Alvin
Sil   The nervous system: the inner networks [by] Alvin Silverstein and Virginia
B. Silverstein. Illustrated by Mel
Erikson. Englewood Cliffs, NJ,
Prentice-Hall [1971]
64p. illus (part col.) 22cm
    Structure and function of the brain,
spinal cord, and nerve cells.

    ERIE CANAL
974.7 Adams, Samuel Hopkins
Ada   Erie Canal; illus by Leonard Vosburgh; Random
House, 1953
182p illus map (Landmark bks)
    Most likely the Erie Canal would never have been built but for
the strong-minded De Witt Clinton. On the Fourth of July, 1817,
digging for the canal was finally started at Rome, New York. How
it was carried through to success is told in this book.

    ERICSSON, JOHN
B   Latham, Jean Lee
Ericsson   Man of the Monitor; the story of John Ericsson;
pictures by Leonard Everett Fisher. Harper & Row [©1962]
231p illus map
    Life story of the Swedish-American who invented the ironclad
warship used in the naval battle against the
Merrimac during the U.S. Civil War.

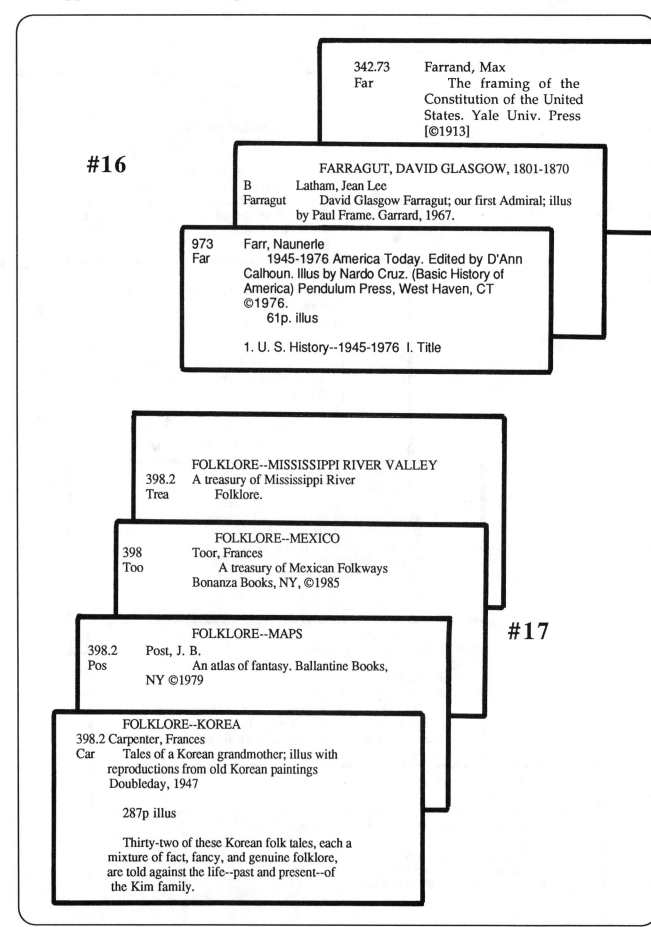

#16

342.73   Farrand, Max
Far   The framing of the Constitution of the United States. Yale Univ. Press [©1913]

FARRAGUT, DAVID GLASGOW, 1801-1870
B   Latham, Jean Lee
Farragut   David Glasgow Farragut; our first Admiral; illus by Paul Frame. Garrard, 1967.

973   Farr, Naunerle
Far   1945-1976 America Today. Edited by D'Ann Calhoun. Illus by Nardo Cruz. (Basic History of America) Pendulum Press, West Haven, CT ©1976.
              61p. illus

              1. U. S. History--1945-1976 I. Title

FOLKLORE--MISSISSIPPI RIVER VALLEY
398.2   A treasury of Mississippi River
Trea   Folklore.

FOLKLORE--MEXICO
398   Toor, Frances
Too   A treasury of Mexican Folkways
            Bonanza Books, NY, ©1985

FOLKLORE--MAPS
398.2   Post, J. B.
Pos   An atlas of fantasy. Ballantine Books, NY ©1979

#17

FOLKLORE--KOREA
398.2 Carpenter, Frances
Car   Tales of a Korean grandmother; illus with reproductions from old Korean paintings
            Doubleday, 1947

            287p illus

            Thirty-two of these Korean folk tales, each a mixture of fact, fancy, and genuine folklore, are told against the life--past and present--of the Kim family.

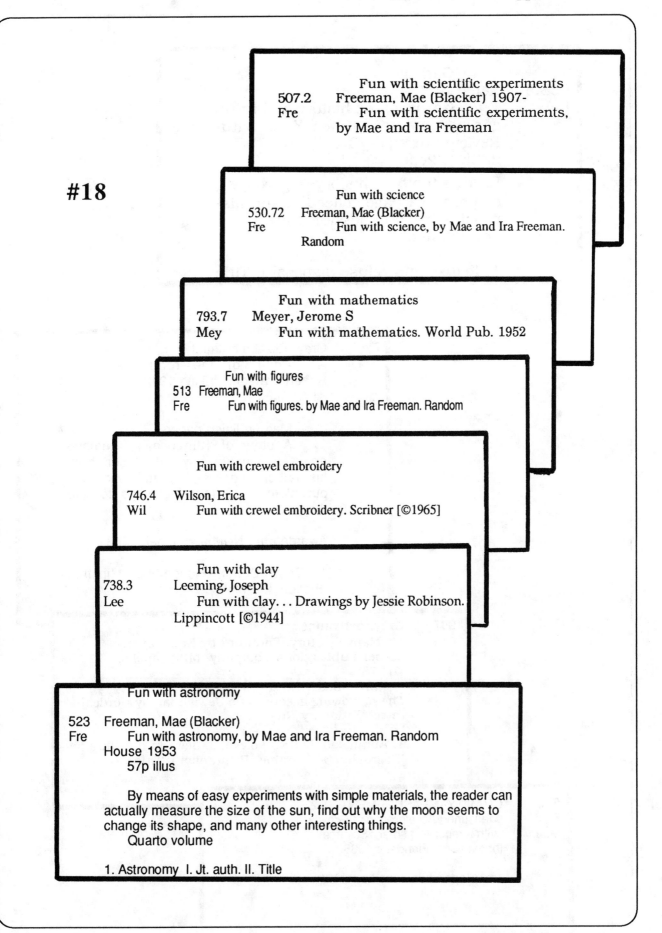

#18

Fun with scientific experiments
507.2   Freeman, Mae (Blacker) 1907-
Fre   Fun with scientific experiments,
by Mae and Ira Freeman

Fun with science
530.72   Freeman, Mae (Blacker)
Fre   Fun with science, by Mae and Ira Freeman.
Random

Fun with mathematics
793.7   Meyer, Jerome S
Mey   Fun with mathematics. World Pub. 1952

Fun with figures
513 Freeman, Mae
Fre   Fun with figures. by Mae and Ira Freeman. Random

Fun with crewel embroidery

746.4   Wilson, Erica
Wil   Fun with crewel embroidery. Scribner [©1965]

Fun with clay
738.3   Leeming, Joseph
Lee   Fun with clay. . . Drawings by Jessie Robinson.
Lippincott [©1944]

Fun with astronomy

523   Freeman, Mae (Blacker)
Fre   Fun with astronomy, by Mae and Ira Freeman. Random
House 1953
57p illus

By means of easy experiments with simple materials, the reader can
actually measure the size of the sun, find out why the moon seems to
change its shape, and many other interesting things.
Quarto volume

1. Astronomy I. Jt. auth. II. Title

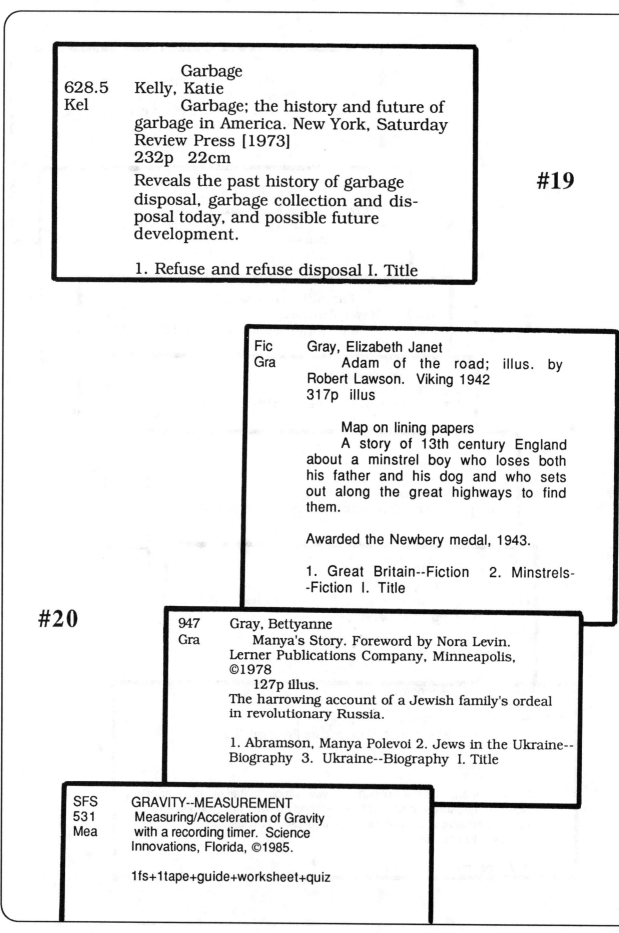

Garbage
628.5   Kelly, Katie
Kel   Garbage; the history and future of
garbage in America. New York, Saturday
Review Press [1973]
232p 22cm

Reveals the past history of garbage
disposal, garbage collection and disposal today, and possible future
development.

1. Refuse and refuse disposal I. Title

#19

Fic   Gray, Elizabeth Janet
Gra   Adam of the road; illus. by
Robert Lawson. Viking 1942
317p illus

Map on lining papers
A story of 13th century England
about a minstrel boy who loses both
his father and his dog and who sets
out along the great highways to find
them.

Awarded the Newbery medal, 1943.

1. Great Britain--Fiction   2. Minstrels-
-Fiction I. Title

#20

947   Gray, Bettyanne
Gra   Manya's Story. Foreword by Nora Levin.
Lerner Publications Company, Minneapolis,
©1978
127p illus.
The harrowing account of a Jewish family's ordeal
in revolutionary Russia.

1. Abramson, Manya Polevoi 2. Jews in the Ukraine--
Biography 3. Ukraine--Biography I. Title

SFS   GRAVITY--MEASUREMENT
531   Measuring/Acceleration of Gravity
Mea   with a recording timer. Science
Innovations, Florida, ©1985.

1fs+1tape+guide+worksheet+quiz

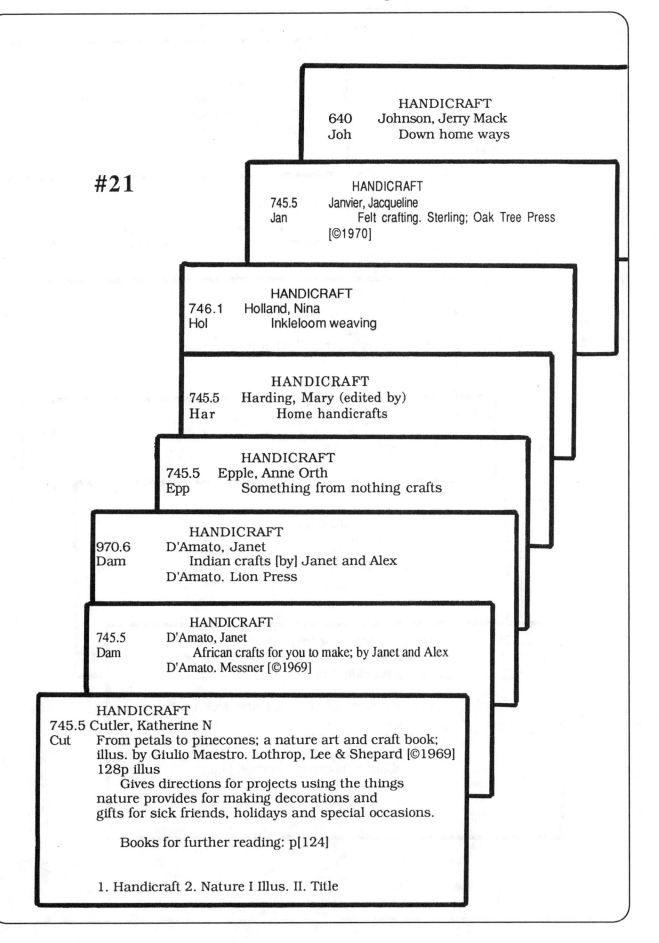

#21

HANDICRAFT
640   Johnson, Jerry Mack
Joh   Down home ways

HANDICRAFT
745.5   Janvier, Jacqueline
Jan   Felt crafting. Sterling; Oak Tree Press
[©1970]

HANDICRAFT
746.1   Holland, Nina
Hol   Inkleloom weaving

HANDICRAFT
745.5   Harding, Mary (edited by)
Har   Home handicrafts

HANDICRAFT
745.5   Epple, Anne Orth
Epp   Something from nothing crafts

HANDICRAFT
970.6   D'Amato, Janet
Dam   Indian crafts [by] Janet and Alex
D'Amato. Lion Press

HANDICRAFT
745.5   D'Amato, Janet
Dam   African crafts for you to make; by Janet and Alex
D'Amato. Messner [©1969]

HANDICRAFT
745.5 Cutler, Katherine N
Cut   From petals to pinecones; a nature art and craft book;
illus. by Giulio Maestro. Lothrop, Lee & Shepard [©1969]
128p illus
    Gives directions for projects using the things
nature provides for making decorations and
gifts for sick friends, holidays and special occasions.

    Books for further reading: p[124]

    1. Handicraft 2. Nature I Illus. II. Title

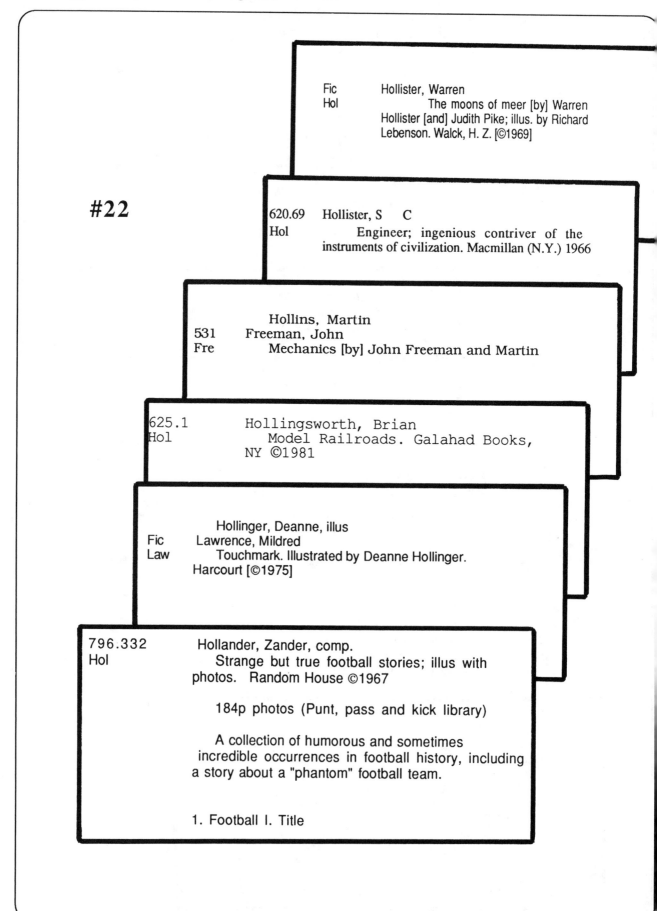

#22

Fic
Hol
Hollister, Warren
The moons of meer [by] Warren Hollister [and] Judith Pike; illus. by Richard Lebenson. Walck, H. Z. [©1969]

620.69
Hol
Hollister, S   C
Engineer; ingenious contriver of the instruments of civilization. Macmillan (N.Y.) 1966

531
Fre
Hollins, Martin
Freeman, John
Mechanics [by] John Freeman and Martin

625.1
Hol
Hollingsworth, Brian
Model Railroads. Galahad Books, NY ©1981

Fic
Law
Hollinger, Deanne, illus
Lawrence, Mildred
Touchmark. Illustrated by Deanne Hollinger. Harcourt [©1975]

796.332
Hol
Hollander, Zander, comp.
Strange but true football stories; illus with photos. Random House ©1967

184p photos (Punt, pass and kick library)

A collection of humorous and sometimes incredible occurrences in football history, including a story about a "phantom" football team.

1. Football I. Title

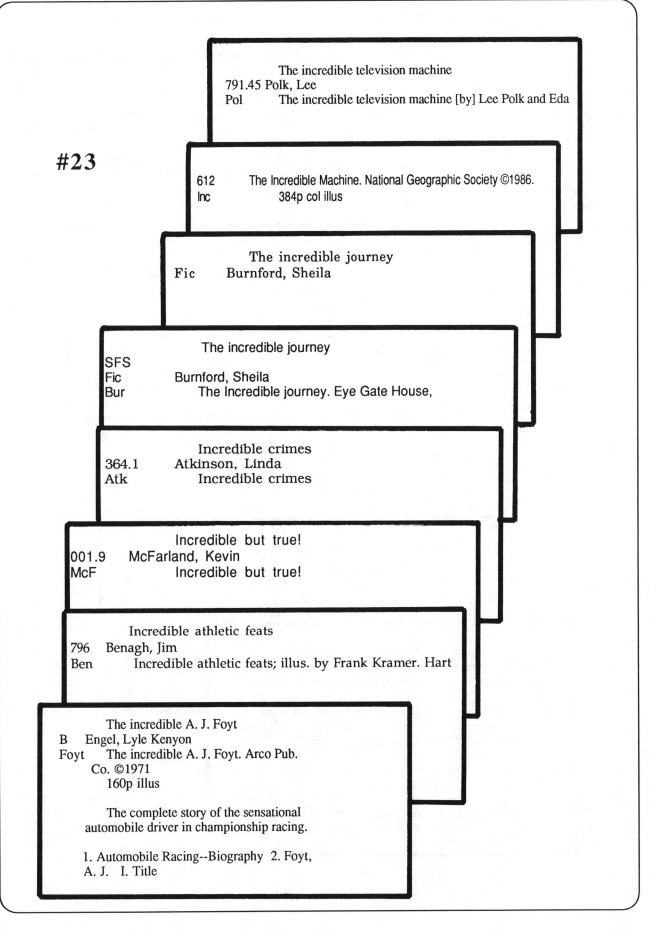

#23

The incredible television machine
791.45 Polk, Lee
Pol   The incredible television machine [by] Lee Polk and Eda

612   The Incredible Machine. National Geographic Society ©1986.
Inc   384p col illus

The incredible journey
Fic   Burnford, Sheila

The incredible journey
SFS
Fic   Burnford, Sheila
Bur   The Incredible journey. Eye Gate House,

Incredible crimes
364.1 Atkinson, Linda
Atk   Incredible crimes

Incredible but true!
001.9 McFarland, Kevin
McF   Incredible but true!

Incredible athletic feats
796   Benagh, Jim
Ben   Incredible athletic feats; illus. by Frank Kramer. Hart

The incredible A. J. Foyt
B   Engel, Lyle Kenyon
Foyt   The incredible A. J. Foyt. Arco Pub.
    Co. ©1971
        160p illus

    The complete story of the sensational
automobile driver in championship racing.

1. Automobile Racing--Biography 2. Foyt,
A. J.   I. Title

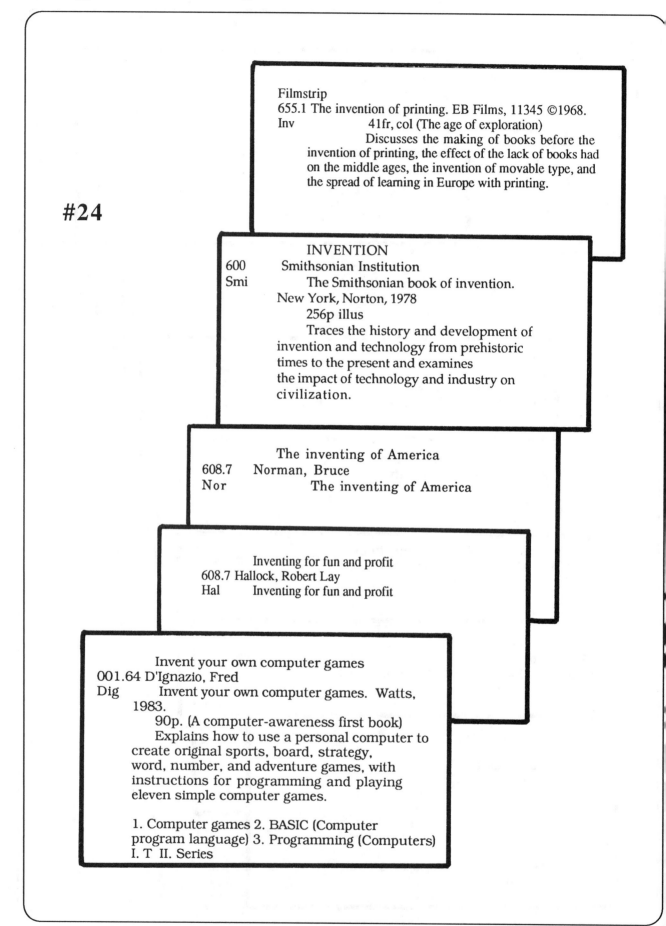

#24

Filmstrip
655.1 The invention of printing. EB Films, 11345 ©1968.
Inv   41fr, col (The age of exploration)
          Discusses the making of books before the
invention of printing, the effect of the lack of books had
on the middle ages, the invention of movable type, and
the spread of learning in Europe with printing.

INVENTION
600   Smithsonian Institution
Smi   The Smithsonian book of invention.
New York, Norton, 1978
          256p illus
          Traces the history and development of
invention and technology from prehistoric
times to the present and examines
the impact of technology and industry on
civilization.

          The inventing of America
608.7   Norman, Bruce
Nor   The inventing of America

          Inventing for fun and profit
608.7 Hallock, Robert Lay
Hal   Inventing for fun and profit

          Invent your own computer games
001.64 D'Ignazio, Fred
Dig   Invent your own computer games. Watts,
     1983.
          90p. (A computer-awareness first book)
          Explains how to use a personal computer to
create original sports, board, strategy,
word, number, and adventure games, with
instructions for programming and playing
eleven simple computer games.

          1. Computer games 2. BASIC (Computer
program language) 3. Programming (Computers)
I. T II. Series

#25

973.7   Kantor, MacKinlay
Kan   Lee and Grant at Appomattox; illus. by Donald
McKay. Random House 1950
            175p illus (Landmark bks)
            The story of Lee and Grant and the peace
negotiations at Appomattox. The author follows the
anxious exchange of early negotiations--Grant's repeated
demands for surrender, Lee's reluctant pleas for terms, a
last minute truce, and the final meeting at Appomattox.

1. Grant, Ulysses Simpson, President U.S. 2. Lee,
Robert Edward 3. U. S.--History--Civil War I. Title

Fic   Kantor, MacKinlay
Kan   If the South had won The Civil War
Bantam Books, NY ©1965
112p.

1. U. S.--History--Civil War--Fiction I. Title

973.73   Kantor, MacKinlay
Kan   Gettysburg; illus. by Donald McKay Random
House, ©1952.
            189p. illus. map (Landmark Bks)
            This account of the bloodiest battle of the Civil War,
which took place in quiet Pennsylvania, includes moving
stories of some brave leaders and men.

1. Gettysburg, Battle of, 1863 2. U. S.--History--Civil
War   I. Title

Appendix B   Catalog Simulation

Name_____
Date_____

Catalog Card Application
Form 1   2   3
Circle the correct form number, and place your answer on the correct line.

1._____
2._____
3._____
4._____
5._____
6._____
7._____
8._____
9._____
10._____
11._____
12._____
13._____
14._____
15._____
16._____
17._____
18._____
19._____
20._____
21._____
22._____
23._____
24._____
25._____

FORM _1_ 2 3

1. Eve Merriam

2. 7

3. 352/Arm

4. Yes

5. Biography

6. 797.1/Rob

7. Dee Brown

8. 1978

9. 1957

10. 1400 lbs.

11. 1764

12. sign language (hand talk, finger spelling)

13. Yes

14. Making puppets come alive

15. Ernest Thompson Seton

16. Glasgow

17. Yes; An atlas of fantasy

18. No

19. Refuse and Refuse Disposal

20. Biography

21. African Crafts for You to Make

22. Mildred Lawrence

23. 001.9/McF

24. yes; 001.64/Dig

25. Civil War

FORM 1 _2_ 3

1. Nonfiction

2. Joseph Krumgold

3. Ariel Books

4. Careers in Automobile Racing

5. JUAREZ, LINCOLN, WOOLWORTH

6, 7, 8. SAILING (In tracings)

9. 920 ——Nonfiction

10. Portraits of the Nations, Colonial Americans

11. 10 years old

12. 2

13. Martin Cannon

14. 400's or an indication of Dewey category: Language

15. The inner networks

16. Yale University Press

17. NO

18. Mae Blacker Freeman

19. the history and future of garbage in America

20. FIC/Gra *Adam of the Road* the only fiction and stated it in narrative

21. *Indian Crafts*; *Down home ways* If neither of these, accept another answer with a reasonable explanation

22. Fic/Hol *Moons of Meer* before Fic/Law *Touchmark*

23. SFS/Fic/Bur Incredible Journey (Sound filmstrip)

24. Computer-Awareness First Book; Age of Exploration

25. Donald McKay

FORM 1 2 _3_

1. 511/D; The Abacus

2. Remy Charlip

3. Adam Eddington

4. 1894

5. 1806 - 1872

6, 7, 8. 797.1/ Rob; Better Sailing for boys and girls

9. Toward freedom

10. The potters

11. Gerald McCann

12. 419

13. The two sisters

14. Exploring careers

15. Ironclad Warship

16. Nineteen

17. Frances Toor

18. *Fun with scientific experiments; Fun with figures; Fun with astronomy; Funwith science; Fun with clay; Fun with crewel embroidery; Fun with mathematics.* (By Dewey number)

19. Saturday Review Press

20. *Measuring/Acceleration of Gravity with a recording timer*

21. YES "Books for further reading: p 124"

22. Martin Freeman

23. Engel, Lyle Kenyon

24. *The Smithsonian book of inventions*

25. Landmark books

Lesson 1

Activity 1-b
Answers will vary according to student knowledge.

Activity 1-c
Answers will vary according to individual library design.

Activity 1-d
Answers will vary.

Lesson 2

Activity 2B
Answers will vary.

Activity 2C
Answer should indicate that all are totally or partially make-believe. The differences should include:
1. Modern realistic fiction: present day setting
2. Historical fiction: made up character; historically accurate; setting in the past
3. Science fiction: setting in future; believable for the future as based on technological advances of the present day

Activity 2D
Answers will vary.

Activity 2E
Placement of legends, fables and folktales is based upon the contents of the books which support a basic understanding of the thinking of the people living at the time in which they were written or were popular. The myths are placed in the 200 section because to the ancient people of Greece, Rome and other countries, mythology served as a religion. Common examples will vary.

Lesson 3

Activity 3B
Answers will vary.

Activity 3C
Answers will vary.

Lesson 4

Activity 4B
Answers will vary.

Activity 4C
Answers will vary.

Lesson 5

Activity 5B
Answers will vary.

Activity 5C
Answers will vary.

Lesson 6

Activity 6B
Answers will vary.

Activity 6C
Answers will vary.

Lesson 7

Activity 7B

Needlework see also Embroidery	Needlework see also Lace and Lace-making
Holland	Floods
see Netherlands	see also Natural disasters
National Songs	Near East
see also	see
Folk songs	Middle East

Lesson 8

Activity 8B
Outside guide is alphabetical
All inside guides are chronological
All card clusters in between inside guides are arranged alphabetically.

Lesson 9

Activity 9B
1. Nonfiction
2. Author
3. Athletes; physically handicapped
4. Summary: Brief Bio. . .
5. Winners never quit
6. not given
7. Lerner Publications
8. 1980
9. Nathan Aaseng
10. not given
11. 80 pages
12. illus
13. 920/Aas
14. Brief bios of athletes who overcame a handicap
15. Sports heroes library

Activity 9C
1. author
2. call number
3. publisher
4. illustrator
5. copyright
6. visual aids
7. tracings
8. title
9. page numbers
10. narrative
Card classification: nonfiction
Card type: subject

Activity 9D
1. subject
2. author
3. subject
4. author
5. subject
6. illustrator
7. title
8. title
9. joint author
10. joint author

Activity 9E
1. fiction
2. nonfiction
3. fiction
4. nonfiction
5. biography
6. fiction
7. nonfiction
8. fiction
9. reference
10. reference

Lesson 10

Lesson 10B
A. 6
B. 5
C. 3
D. 8
E. 1
F. 2
G. 4
H. 7
J. 10
K. 9

ACTIVITY 10 C
A. 4
B. 6
C. 5
D. 2
E. 3
F. 7
G. 8
H. 10
J. 9
K. 1

ACTIVITY 10 D
1. C
2. C
3. D, B
4. A, C, D
5. A
6. C
7. C
8. B, D
9. C
10. C
11. C, D
12. D, C
13. B, D
14. C
15. C
16. C, A, D

Activity 10 E
A. 10
B. 3
C. 7
D. 2
E. 9
F. 5
G. 8
H. 6
J. 1
K. 4

Activity 10F
1. Newark, Tim
2. NEWBERY AWARD BOOKS
3. NEW JERSEY-CIVIL WAR
4. NEW JERSEY-REV. WAR
5. New women in art and dance
6. New women in media
7. The new world
8. New worlds ahead
9. New year
10. NEW YORK STOCK EX-CHANGE

Activity 10G
1. Nervous system
2. Nesbit, E.
3. Nesbitt, Rosemary
4. Ness, Loch
5. Neuberger, Richard
6. New Family Cookbook
7. New Golden Book of Astronomy
8. New Guide to the Planets
9. New Hampshire Beautiful
10. New Jersey
11. New Jersey Almanac
12. New Jersey Almanac and Travel Guide

Lesson 11

Activity 11B
1. C
2. B
3. A
4. D
5. B
6. C
7. F
8. B
9. F
10. B
11. C
12. E
13. A
14. F
15. B

Activity 11C
INDIANS
INDIANS - FICTION
INDIANS - LEGENDS
INDIANS OF ANTIQUITIES
INDIANS OF MEXICO - ANTIQUI-TIES
INDIANS OF NEW JERSEY
INDIANS OF NORTH AMERICA
INDIANS OF NORTH AMERICA - ANTIQUITIES - COLLECTIONS
INDIANS OF NORTH AMERICA - ART
INDIANS OF NORTH AMERICA - BIOGRAPHY
INDIANS OF NORTH AMERICA - CAPTIVITIES - FICTION
INDIANS OF NORTH AMERICA - DICTIONARIES
INDIANS OF NORTH AMERICA - EDUCATION
INDIANS OF NORTH AMERICA - FICTION - CANADA

Activity 11 D
Circled:
1. Carver
2. George
3. Epstein
4. Cochise
5. Wyatt
6. Davis
7. Green
8. Charles
9. Dickens
10. Dickens
11. Mankowitz
12. Disney
13. Walter
14. Disney
15. Poe

Activity 11 E

A. 6 or 8	F. 10
B. 6 or 8	G. 1
C. 7	H. 5
D. 4	J. 9
E. 2	K. 3

Lesson 12

Activity 12B & 12C
Answers will vary.

Lesson 13

Activity 13B

001.4	002.06
001.43	002.6
014.6	124.008
014.63	134.08
123.8	246.12
123.84	246.121
463.03	359.06
463.3	359.6
848.07	684.7
848.7	684.73

Appendix D   Activities Answer Key

Lesson 14 Activites

14-c

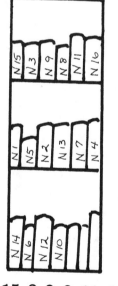

R 16-1-6-13-3-7
R 15-8-4-2-5-14
R 9-12-11-10

14-d

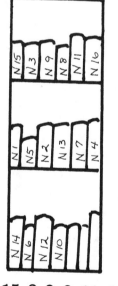

N 15-3-9-8-11-16
N 1-5-2-13-7-4
N 14-6-12-10

14-e

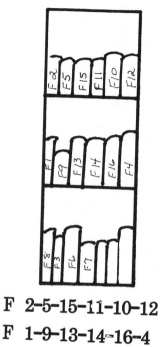

F 2-5-15-11-10-12
F 1-9-13-14-16-4
F 8-3-6-7

14-f

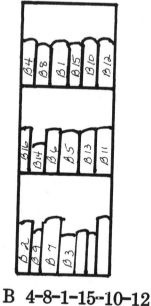

B 4-8-1-15-10-12
B 16-14-6-5-13-11
B 2-9-7-3

Lesson 15

Activity 15A
1. 32 p.
2. Elizabeth K. Cooper
3. 942.05/B

1. GANGS - FICTION
   NEW YORK (NY) - FICTION
2. Careers in a library
3. SPIES - FICTION

Activity 15B
1. 3
2. all nonfiction
3. Biography and nonfiction
4. The Lincoln Conspiracy
5. Native Americans of the desert
Southwest and history as they saw it.

Activity 15C
1. Delacorte
2. 913.38/B, Brumbaugh, Robert S.
3. Drake: the man they called a pirate
4. Ref/920/Bio, Biographical dictionary of scientists
5. Fantasy

Activity 15D
1. Bob Geldof
2. Warwick Press
3. Fic/L'En
4. Yes, "authorized"
5. REF/629.4/Bak

Lesson 16
Activity 16B
Answers will vary.

Activity 18-b
The World Book Encyclopedia Index

1. C:297
2. a. S:23
   b. F:152
3. Motion Pictures M:867
4. Nevada N:156
5. S:18
6. F: 27-28
7. F:585
8. glider G:228
9. Montreal M:779
10. C:1151

Activity 18-c
The Academic American Encyclopedia

1. Battle of the Little Big Horn, 12:372

2. 8:379 (illus)

3. 18:227

4. 8:219

5. bibliography = 3:210

6. a. 12:321

   b. 3:207-208

7. a. 4:314

   b. 15:410

   c. 14:435

8. 15:512

9. 15:534

10. 14:253

Activity 18-d
The World Book Encyclopedia Article

1. H. F. Alderfer
2. 1895
3. See also Basov, Nikolai; and Prokhorov, Alexander.
4. See City planning.
5. See Who, The.
6. Boom town, Borough, Local government, Town meeting, Township, Village
7. The author is the same.
8. See Revolutionary War in America (The Townshend Acts)
9. Robert J. Taylor
10. large scale communication into general use after 1750.
11. No unsigned articles; toxemia is continued on next page.

Activity 19-b
The World Almanac and Book of Facts
1. p. 310
2. pp. 103, 322, 323
3. a. p. 637
    b. p. 118
    c. pp. 537, 538, 571
4. a. p. 407
    b. pp. 400-402
    c. pp. 275-276, 285.
5. p. 432
6. a. pp. 449, 625
    b. pp. 438, 450
    c. p. 435
7. pp. 426, 758
8. pp. 335, 438
9. pp. 279, 288
10. pp. 740, 746
11. a. p. 809
    b. pp. 155, 156
    c. pp. 158-159
    d. see Income, salaries.

Activity 20-b
The Atlas

1. Rivers are indexed to their mouth or where they join another river.
       Symbol ⟶ follows name.
2. name of a country
3. first order administrative unit such as a state
4. counties in the United States
5. p. 192, 38° 7' N. Latitude, 46° 20' E. Longitude
6. p. 147, 46° 30' N., 8° 0' E. It is a country.
7. It is a river; p. 122; 11° 6' S., 67° 36' W.
8. p. 202; 17° 20' N., 96° 0' E.
9. It is a river; p. 84; 42° 33'N., 82° 25' W.
10. It is a first order administrative area; p. 216; 31° 0' N., 104° 0' E.
       It is also known as Sichuan.

The Readers' Guide to Periodical Literature
Activity 21-b

_____ #1
Limited Partnership
—

Hooking up to a cable TV limited partnership

M. Ivey
Business Week
il
—
152
June 8, 1987
Boston Ventures Mgt. Inc
Master limited partnership

———

_____ #2
Limited Partnership
Taxation
—
A PIG can help with tax shelter losses
B. Hitchings
Business Wek
—
—
94
April 20, 1987
Boston Ventures Mgt. Inc.
Master Limited Partnership
PIG= Passive income generators

_____ #3
Lightning
—
—
Whistling for Lightning's Rhythm
S. Weisburd
Science News
—
131
372
June 13, 1987
Space Flight
Lightning hazards
Research by William C. Armstrong

_____ #4
Lighthouses
Conservation and Restoration
—
The tide is turning for old beacons adrift at Land's End
D. G. Hanson
Smithsonian
il; bibl (145)
18
98-106+
August, 1987
—
cover story

Activity 21-c
The Readers' Guide to Periodical Literature
1.a. polo
   b. Multiple sclerosis victim who became a competitive equestrian
2. a. breeding, training, treatment
   b. horses, wild training
   c. D. Van Biema
3. 50 Plus; Volume 27, October, 1987
4. Entertaining, guests
5. Art News/ Vol 86/May, 1987
6. Motor Trend, Vol 39, Sept.,1987

Activity 22-b
The American Heritage Index

_____ #_1_
Suzanne Lenglen
_____
Aug, 1975; 1981
1975: 84,85; 1981: 68,69
Aug, 1981, p. 68

_____ #2_
Mexico Leon
_____
April, 1969
6
April, 1969:6

_____ #3_
Uriah Leonard
—
Dec, 1958
70,76
_____

_____ #4_
Leonardo da Vinci
Machine gun
Oct, 1957
48
—

_____ #5_
Bob Lemon
Baseball player
Aug, 1970
34
_____

_____ #6_
France LeMans
Flights, Wilbur Wright
Feb, 1960
107
_____

_____ #7_
William R. Leigh
—
Dec, 1954
41
_____

_____ #_8_
Leinster House
Prototype (White House)
Aug, 1964
6
—

Activity 22-c

A Chronological Subject Guide to American Heritage

_____ #1_
Emergence of Modern America, 1865-1914
Social and Cultural History
Mrs. Frank Leslie's Illustrated Newspaper
Lynne Vincent
American Heritage
Oct, 1975
42
Career of Miriam Follin, actress turned publisher

_____ #2_
Emergence of Modern America, 1865-1914
Foreign Affairs, 1867-1914
Seward's Wise Folly
Robert L. Reynolds
American Heritage
Dec, 1960
44
Purchase of Alaska, 1867

_____ #3_
Emergence of Modern America, 1865-1914
Social and Cultural History
How Mother Got her day

James P. Johnson
American Heritage
Apr, 1979
14
Anna Jarvis' campaign for a holiday celebrating mothers

_____ #4_
Emergence of Modern America, 1865-1914
Social and Cultural History
A Conquest of Solitude
Robert V. Bruce
American Heritage
Apr, 1973
28
Alexander G. Bell, Helen Keller

Activity 23-b
The National Geographic Index
_____ #1_
Northwest Territories
Television show
Journey to the High Arctic
not given
_____
April, 1971
590a-b
_____
Ellesmere Island; Nahanni National Park; Northwest Passage; Southampton Island

_____ #2_
Northwest
Map
Northwestern United States
_____
_____
April, 1960
_____
Atlas Series supplement
Idaho; Montana; Oregon; Washington

_____ #3_
Northwest
Book
America's Spectacular Northwest
_____
_____
1982
_____
Idaho; Montana; Oregon; Washing-

ton

_____ #4
North Slope
Article
Oil, the Dwindling Treasure
Noel Grove
Emory Kristof
June, 1974
792-825
—
—

_____ #5
Northwind
article
Our Navy Explores Antarctica
Richard E. Byrd
U. S. Navy official photos
October, 1947
429-522
[Coast Guard Icebreaker]

_____ #6
Northeast(region), U. S.
Map
Close-up: U. S. A., The Northeast,

January, 1978
-----
text on reverse; NJ, NY, PA included

Activity 23-c
The National Geographic Index

1. a. The Great Whales.
   b. Feb, 1978
   c. Namu
   d. The Great Whales: Migration and range, Dec., 1976
   e. Belugas; Blue Whales
   f. Hunting the Heartbeat of a whale, 49-64

2.   a. 1975
   b. Aug, 1975; 151
   c. Recreating Madagascar's Giant Extinct Bird

3. a. Explore a Spooky Swamp, 1978
   b. Corkscrew Swamp; Everglades; Okefenokee Swamp

4. a. Don Moser
   b. O. Louis Mazzatenta
   c. Peoples of the Arctic; Arctic Ocean
   d. Faeroe Islands; Nantucket; Western Australia

Activity 24-b
Magazine Article Summaries

1. See Boundaries

2. 406/2

3. *22/4(cover story); seed catalogs

4. 476/6; See also Helmut Kohl

5.   a. 361/6
   b. 362/1
   c. *190/4

6.   23/1 (Research)

7.   See also Mines and Mineral Resources

8.   243/6

9. 191/2

10.191/1; 362/2

Activity 24-c
Magazine Article Summaries

_____ #1
United Nations - Role of US
A majority of two
C. C. O'Brien
World Press Review
Oct, 88
15
2 p.
Yes
1 bw
Yes

_____ #2
Uniforms, Football
Do Black Shirts Make bad guys?
J. Horn

Psychology Today
November 1988
19
3 p.
Yes
4 color
No

_____ #3
Tournament of Roses Parade
1989 - Centennial
Rough Cut
B. Weber
NY Times Magazine
10/30/88
p. 102
1 p.
Yes
1 illus
no

_____ #4
United States. Postal Service —
Addresses & Essays
The United States Postal Service
Crisis
R. K. Brack, Jr.
Vital Speeches
10/15/88
p. 22
4 p.
no
—
no

Activity 25-b
The Statesman's Yearbook

1. NM, p. 1499

2. Spain, p. 1102

3. Bulgaria, pp. 240, 245

4. France, pp. 470-71, 483.

5. a. See Zimbabwe

   b. See Zambia

   c. See Zimbabwe

6. Kenya, p. 757-59

7. a. See Ronse

   b.Belgium, p. 195

8. p. 1522

9. p. 588

10. p. 1523

Activity 26-b
Current Biography Yearbook, 1987

#1
Patti Davis
Nov, 1986
——

#2
Samuel K. Doe
May, 1981
—

#3
Nathan Feinsinger
Jan, 1984
Yes

#4
Umberto Exo
Apr, 1985
——

#5
Garret FitzGerald
Aug, 1984
——

#6
David Dietz
Apr, 1985
Yes

#7
William DeVries
Jan, 1985
——

#8
Richard P. Feynman
Nov, 1986
——

#9
Raymond Donovan
Jan, 1982
——

#10
Elaine De Kooning
July, 1982

ANSWER KEYS TO DISCUSSION QUESTIONS IN TEXT

Lesson 1

1. The four library classifications are: fiction, nonfiction, reference, biography.
2. Some instructional aids are: records, films, sound filmstrips, filmstrips, slides, film loops, transparencies, picture files, kits, tapes, newspapers, periodicals, and vertical files.
3. The two main divisions of literature are fiction and nonfiction. Fiction is written to fulfill a general purpose of entertainment. The purpose of nonfiction is to present factual information.
4. It is important to be familiar with the areas and the materials in the IMC in order to acquire the necessary skills to become proficient in the area of information retrieval. This, in turn, hopefully will support a lifetime of continuous learning.

Lesson 2

1. In explaining the differences among historical fiction, modern realistic, and science fiction, one should compare time setting and believability of plots. In historical fiction, the time/place setting is in the past; in modern realistic fiction, the time/place setting is in the present; in science fiction, the focus concerns the future and the plot is based on knowledge of current technological advances as projected into the future.
2. Fantasy is a type of fiction that goes beyond the laws of nature in that certain aspects are not plausible.
3. In giving two examples of the fiction types, select from the following:

   A.) Historical fiction: *Johnny Tremain, Ivanhoe, Ghost Fox, The Master Puppeteer, My Brother Sam is Dead.*

   B.) Modern Realistic Fiction: *Ramona, Homecoming, Dicey's Song, The Great Gilly Hopkins, Friends Till the End.*

   C.) Science Fiction: *Children of the Dust, Star Trek, Dune, Stranger in a Strange Land, The White Mountains.*

   D.) Fantasy: *Wizard of Earth-Sea, Star Ka'at, The Dog Days of Arthur Cane, Below the Root, The Hobbit, The Blue Sword.*
4. Legends, fables, and folktales would be placed in the 300 section of nonfiction even though they are examples of fiction because the content of the book supports a basic understanding of the thinking of the people living at the time in which they were written or were popular.
5. The myth, although fiction, is placed in the library in the nonfiction 200's section because to the ancient people of Greece, Rome and other countries, mythology served as a religion, and thus provides understanding of the thinking of the people living at the time.

Lesson 3

6. It is important to check an author's credentials or expertise in his/her field to determine the accuracy of information.
7. There are two basic ways of checking the accuracy of information. One might use an index of field experts to check an author's credentials or possibly check that author's sources in terms of credentials. Verify the information by checking other sources.
8. Bias is prejudice for or against an idea, person, or thing.
9. A student might detect bias by determining if his/her attitude has changed about a subject after reading. If so, then the reader should take the time to try to understand why this has happened. The student should also have a good understanding of the ways in which an author might try to sway his/her reader such as name dropping, repetition, use of emotional words.

Lesson 4

10. The general purpose of the reference collection is to supply to the student a fast review of topical information on any subject. This is usually found in a multi-topic text.
11. In the nonfiction section a subject is usually covered in-depth through a book format. In a reference section a subject is usually covered in brief through a book involving a multisubject format such as an encyclopedia.
12. In order to be an efficient and effective researcher at the high school level, students must prepare in junior high by learning to use all the various types with which they will be confronted at the high school. Proficiency with the middle school materials will aid the students in mastering new resources.

Lesson 5

13. Biography is a book written about the life of someone by someone else. Autobiography is a book written about the life of someone by the subject of the book.
14. A biography that is well researched using the most appropriate sources and is completely true is a good example of nonfiction biography. In turn, a biography that is written by an unauthorized person (without permission) should not be considered totally factual or accurate because the most appropriate sources have not cooperated with the author of the text.
15. The two main divisions of literature are fiction and nonfiction. Fiction is written to fulfill a general purpose of entertainment. The purpose of nonfiction is to present factual information.
16. The four library classifications are: fiction, nonfiction, reference, biography.

Lesson 6

1. The card catalog is an index of all of the items in the library. Through its use, a student can access books or materials by subject or topic, by author or book title. (Also book access can be by series, illustrator, joint author as well as by multiple alternative key words as indicated by the cross reference cards. A detailed discussion in text will follow.)
2. The basic organization of the card catalog is alphabetical. (This is not true of the U.S. - HISTORY section which by inside guides is chronological. A detailed discussion in text will follow.)
3. Through the correct use of the outside guides, the student will locate alphabetically the correct drawer. The inside guides provide the alphabetical breakdown of the cards in the drawer and give the necessary information needed to locate a specific card.
4. The three basic types of cards found in the card catalog that correspond to a specific book located on a shelf in the library are known as the author, title, and subject cards.
5. One book might correspond to many subject cards in the card catalog because of the variety of subjects contained in the particular nonfiction book or because of the variety of synonyms that might be used for one subject. (e.g. garbage, refuse, pollution, waste, etc.) For these two reasons a great many subject cards might be generated for one book.

Lesson 7

6. In addition to the three basic types of cards, the researcher

might also encounter the added entry cards and the cross reference cards. The added entry cards are known as series, illustrator, and joint author cards. The cross reference cards will be indicated by the words *see* and *see also*.

7. The added entry cards are important in that they provide the researcher specific subject headings under which he might search to locate a specific book. A student might only know a book as part of a series or written by a joint author or as illustrated by a particular person.

8. The word *see* on a cross reference card indicates that the listed subject heading is not a valid one for this card catalog index and that there are no books referenced under that particular key word. The *see* card, therefore, supplies the more appropriate key words with which the student might continue his research.

9. The words *see also* on a cross reference card indicate that although the subject will offer some references under that topic, alternative key words are also provided to foster a more comprehensive research.

10. The term cross reference indicates the need for the researcher to search further than the first line subject provided on the card.

Lesson 8

11. The card clusters indicated by the inside guides located in the drawer marked U.S. - HISTORY will have a chronological organization in that they will be organized by time era/ time period or by year from earliest to most recent.

12. In developing a sequence to find a specific topic/subject in the U.S. - HISTORY drawer, it is important that the researcher first alphabetically locate U.S.-HISTORY by outside guides. Secondly, within the drawer, through the use of inside guides, chronologically locate the time period of the subject under research. Thirdly, within the indicated cluster of cards for the specific time period of research, alphabetically locate the appropriate card by subject. (Keeping in mind that all cards found in this drawer will be of the subject/topic card type.)

13. Answers will vary. Example:
I. United States
  A. History
    1. Colonial
      a. Costumes

14. All other corresponding catalog cards will be interfiled alphabetically throughout the card catalog.

15. All countries might be organized this way. It is left to the discretion of the library media specialist, based on curricular needs and volume of material located in the library on any given country.

Lesson 9

1. The different types of cards that can be found in the card catalog are the basic (subject, author, title), added entry (illustrator, series, joint author), and the cross reference (see, see also).

2. In explaining the similarities and differences of the basic and added entry cards, it must be remembered that all cards for one book will be exactly the same except for the first line which will indicate card type. For example, an author card will list the author on the first line, where a series card will list the series name on the first line.

3. The variety of the types of information that can be found on a catalog card are as follows: copyright date, title, call reference, pages, author, narrative, tracings, series indication, visual aids, publisher and sometimes bibliographic indication.

4. The importance of each section of the catalog card is listed below:

  A. <u>Copyright date:</u> Student must decide if book is current enough for use in topic under discussion. (Scientific topics will require a more current copyright than would a topic of 18th century inventors.)

  B. <u>Title:</u> Most descriptive book titles will indicate main idea or focus of book.

  C. <u>Call number:</u> Research must be based on nonfiction material. If call number indicates fiction then student will immediately realize that book is not suitable for purpose.

  D. <u>Author:</u> Name of author will help student in checking background or expertise of author in field.

  E. <u>Narrative:</u> This is basic focus of the book usually providing an indication of time and place setting.

  F. <u>Tracings:</u> This section gives alternative key words to be used by the researcher to help bring about a more comprehensive research.

  G. <u>Series:</u> It is important that the researcher realize that in a series there might be a separate volume index. Also, other books in the series might provide important information in regard to the topic under research and will be found only through use of an index.

  H. <u>Visual aids:</u> The researcher should realize that a visual aid such as an illustration or a chart visually depicts the information provided in print in the text and therefore provide another format of information to be used by the reader.

  I. <u>Publisher:</u> As the student progresses in school, it may be necessary to locate or purchase a particular book. Knowing the publisher's name will allow a student to check to see if a book is out of print or where it might be available.

5. Some of the common abbreviations that are used on the catalog cards are as follows: FIC (fiction); REF (reference); B(biography); REC (record); SFS (sound filmstrip); MAP (map); MPL (film loop); TRA(transparency); PROF(professional); PS/PA (picture file/art prints); KIT(kit with mixed media); MRDF (computer software); VT (video tape).

Lesson 10

1. To provide an easy method of book retrieval and information retrieval for the library patron or student is the most important objective of the librarian. Therefore, organizational systems that simplify this goal are important in the library setting.

2. The alphabetical organizational system is a simple a,b,c sequence. The system may be organized according to a letter-by-letter or word-by-word method. The library patron or student must be prepared to determine which method is employed to effectively use the card catalog, or the multiple indices found in the volumes located in the reference and nonfiction sections of the IMC. The alphabetical system is also used in the shelving of all fiction books, in the shelving of biography by subject and in the shelving of all reference and nonfiction books in terms of authors and titles once the Dewey number cluster has been located.

3. The chronological system is the placement by year, by time period or time era. It is used in the U.S. History cluster in the card catalog and it is also found in the organization of many of the books whose main content is the history of America (or

other nations).

4. The numerical organizational system employs simple number sequence and can be found in the Dewey Decimal System and the Library of Congress classification system.

5. Topical organization is also known as subject. It is used in most tables of contents of nonfiction and reference books. It can also be considered to be the basis of shelf placement of the biography section of the library in that the topics are the lives of people.

6. In a word-by-word system all of the same first words are clustered together and are alphabetically organized by the spelling of the second word. In a letter-by-letter system the spaces are ignored and the letters of all words are pushed together as though only one word exists.

Lesson 11

1. The articles *a, an, the* are dropped when they appear at the beginning of a title. Keep them when they are located within the title, though.

2. Be sure to differentiate between the article *an* and the conjunction *and*. *And* at the beginning of a title would definitely be used in alphabetizing while *an* would be dropped at the beginning.

3. You would look for the last name of a person when you know that person to be an author or if you are looking for that person as a subject. If you know a book to have as a title the person's full name, then that is the only time that you would look for the first name.

4. Abbreviations in a book title are filed alphabetically as if every abbreviation were spelled out. Sometimes, some abbreviations are filed just as they are, according to local custom.

5. Numbers are respelled in letters and filed alphabetically that way.

6. Go alphabetically to the author's last name in the card catalog, and you will find a complete alphabetical list of all the works(books and audiovisual items) written by that person alone. After the author's name alone, the author might be listed as being a joint author with someone else. If that is the case, more titles would need to be interfiled in your alphabetical list.

7. Mc and Mac are alphabetically filed as though they are spelled the same. Within the Mc/Mac cluster the names are alphabetized by the second syllable. Check to see how it is in your library.

8. Topics are also grouped alphabetically in the card catalog. Within this cluster the subtopic and details are also alphabetically grouped.

Lesson 12

1. With the topic key word selected, the next step is to generate other multiple key words associated with the original key word. You can list synonyms from your own knowledge, use a dictionary or thesaurus, use the tracings on catalog cards, or by using the cross references in a reference book index.

2. You might waste time and not be efficient. You might miss the most important books dealing with the topic because you might be in the reference section when, in fact, the book has been shelved in the nonfiction section. Or you might find the shelves empty and think that there are no books on the subject. In reality, they have been checked out; therefore, you could put a reserve request on them or request them through interlibrary loan.

3. Interlibrary loan is simply borrowing a book from another library. With today's new technology, the process is simpler and speedier and more comprehensive because more libraries are on the interlibrary loan system.

4. The likeness should indicate a similar pattern to that in 12-b.

Lesson 13

1. They structure a numerical system for the shelving of books. Those same numbers, in turn, represent a topic, subtopic and detail approach to classification.

2. It is a numerical coding by topic and subtopic of the factual information found in nonfiction and reference books. Dewey organized ten basic, general topics and assigned each topic a specific number. His numerical system of topics is in multiples of 10. Dewey then categorized each topic into a subtopic and each subtopic into details. The numbers reflect the general to specific in terms of breadth of information.

3. The books are already placed on the shelves according to a number=topic correspondence.

4. First line would be section location: reference, biography, fiction, nonfiction. [The reference book would also indicate nonfiction by the use of the Dewey Decimal System.] Then there would be an indication of author by the use of the first three letters of the last name. Biography would have the last name of the person about whom the book is written listed on the call number.

5. - 8. The steps are indicated in Activity 13-a.

Lesson 14

The answers to the activities are listed in the activities answer summary.

Lesson 15

1. 32 p.   2. Elizabeth K. Cooper   3. 942.05/Bue

1. GANGS - FICTION; and NEW YORK (N. Y.) - FICTION

2. Careers in a library   3. SPIES - FICTION

Lesson 16

1. The title page contains the title, author, illustrator(if given), publisher(company that prints the book), and place of publication of the book.

2. An author has written original material based on his/her personal research while an editor/compiler brings the written works of others into collected forms such as in an encyclopedia.

3. An illustrator is given credit for the drawings or illustrations in a book, a photographer is given credit for the photographs while a cartographer receives credit for the maps.

4. The acknowledgement page provides credits for those authors whose work is being used. Permissions from the holders of the copyrights had to be obtained for such use. A copyright is legal ownership of written material.

5. A descriptive title states the main idea of the book, the preface states the book's theme or purpose, and the text or body of the book is a written and detailed explanation of both theme and purpose.

6. It provides you with an overview of the general information as presented in the text.

7. It details in outline form the major topics and subtopics of the text through the headings and subheadings of the sections, units and chapters of the book. It also provides the corresponding page numbers, presented in number sequence. Also included in the table of contents will be the parts of the book other than the written text such as the glossary, atlas,

appendix and index listed by corresponding page numbers as they appear in the text.

8.   Very often the main idea or topics will be detailed by way of the headings of the sections, units or chapters: The bolder and larger the print, the more important the information.

9.   It is a specialized dictionary that presents a simplified entry in terms of definitions presented, focusing on understanding words as used in the context of the text.

10.   The purpose of the atlas is to provide important maps which are necessary visual aids that are supportive of the geographic concepts as presented in the text.

11.   The appendix will provide extra materials of interest and information that will supply you with a general background of knowledge.

12.   You will be able to pinpoint exact chapters or pages dealing with your research topic.

13.   The index is alphabetically organized first by topic then by subtopic. The topics are usually in bold print and are placed against the left margin. The cluster of subtopics are indented throughout the rest of the entry either in a vertical or horizontal pattern depending on the format of the index.

14.   In an index, a comma between numbers (6,8) indicates two separate pages where a hyphen between numbers (12-16) indicates that those two pages and all the pages in between the two numbers of 12 and 16 are included. In a horizontally structured entry a semicolon (;) separates topics while a colon (:) indicates a list or separates the entry from the rest of the entry.

15.   The purpose of the cross reference indicators are to support you in furthering your research in terms of providing you with other key words.

16.   The word *see* following an entry word indicates that the key word is not valid for the index. Others that are valid are provided for your use. The words *see also* indicate that while the located entry word is valid, if further information is required, other appropriate key words are also provided for your convenience.

17.   A bibliography is a listing books concerning a specific topic, subject or theme. It provides the necessary information in each bibliographic entry as to support the actual physical retrieval of the book represented by the entry. A bibliography also gives you an opportunity to check the author's sources in terms of expertise.

Lesson 17

1.   It contains information about people, places or events. It may include general topics from a wide field of knowledge or it may concentrate on reviewing one specific area in depth.

2.   They can by 1) alphabetically ordered (A-Z); 2) topically ordered (editor or author's chosen topic order); or 3) chronologically ordered (by time period, by year or time era).

3.   The various articles are written by a great many people who are considered experts in the specific field in which they are writing.

4.   The bibliographies will point you in the way of more information on the subject.

5.   The encyclopedia is a good starting point for research in that it will provide an overview of a topic and this, in turn, will help you to narrow or expand a chosen subject. It also will help you to generate other key words to help further your research.

Lesson 18

1.   The index is alphabetically ordered by entry word or key word.

2.   Each entry word begins a full entry which will provide volume numbers, page numbers, and cross references for each specific topic, subtopic or detail.

3.   The index can also be of a vertical or horizontal format.

4.   The importance of cross referencing and punctuation in an index has to do with the ability to retrieve as much information as possible.

5.   An alphabetization knowledge will permit effective retrieval of information.

6.   The main headings will be in bold dark print and the subheadings will be in a lighter print. In fact, the darker and bolder the print, the more important the information. The simple or descriptive title will be the largest in print size in the article.

7.   In some articles, at the end, the name of the article's author is given and this is known as a "signed" article. Where the name of the author does not appear, the article is considered unsigned.

8.   The guide words represent the first and last entries or article on a page or page spread. In an alphabetically organized encyclopedia, the guide words would be the same starting letters as on the spine of the volume.

9.   Maps, graphs, charts, tables, diagrams, time lines, fact summaries, transparencies, etc.

10.   Under each visual aid is a legend which is a word, phrase or sentence that connects or links the visual to the text.

11.   You, as a researcher, have more opportunities for research, for finding more information.

Lesson 19

1.   Its purpose is to present summaries of information on a variety of current topics of the day. It offers both a quick thumb index of topics as well as a quick reference index of a still more developed list of topics.

2.   Index use is of great importance as the text is topically organized and it would be impossible to retrieve all the possible information on a specific topic or division of the topic without its use.

3.   When the index page numbers are separated by a comma, two separate pages are indicated. Two pages separated by a hyphen, in turn, specify that those two pages and all the pages in between are included.

4.   Fact summaries are provided in the form of a selected top ten news stories of impact, and a chronological review of world events presented by month for an entire year (Nov-Oct) concerning the year prior to publication. It also contains a variety of lists, graphs, charts, and other visual aids presenting factual information.

Lesson 20

1.   Immediately become familiar with the map title to determine map focus and type (For example: North America - Climate). Also, read all concise fact summaries surrounding the map, and, of course, have a visual understanding of the individual map legend. Some atlases will indicate the area in relation to the globe. If the atlas does not do that, you should make a mental reference to a global area. It is also important to locate and understand the organization of the index.

2.   An atlas index will be alphabetical by topic, subtopic, and detail.

3.   Alphabetical by topic, then by subtopic and detail, the index provides the necessary information of page numbers and coordinates to be able to find a geographic place location

on a map in the atlas. Sometimes the coordinates are simply numbers on the top and side of a page. At other times the coordinates are the actual longitude and latitude readings of the place location.

Lesson 21

1. It is a subject index of articles found in magazines and periodicals in print.

2. It indexes only a selected number of magazines and periodicals.

3. The paperback editions are updates throughout the year.

4. All the information provided in the paperbacks is combined into one alphabet and in one hardcover volume.

5. Physically, each page of the index is divided into two columns creating two separate left margins. Topics, subjects or entry words are immediately recognizable in that they are in a bold print and are placed directly against the left margin of a column.

Subtopics are of a lighter and less bold print and are column-centered. A division of a subtopic would be a detail. The detail would be presented in italics and would be column-centered under the subtopic.

6. A special detail, *about,* which is always column-centered and in italics indicates that all entries that follow underneath are *about* a specific person.

7. The cue words *see* and *see also* will be found next to or below the corresponding topic, subtopic or detail. A *see* followed by a series of key words indicates that the original key word is not valid for the index and the other provided must be used to locate information on that specific topic. The words *see also* indicate that the original key word is valid and will provide some information through the entries but to find all the information as indexed in the volume, the new cross reference key words should also be utilized.

8. Specifically, each entry contains information in the following order: the entry word; complete magazine article title; the author's name, if given; indication of visual aids, if any; the abbreviated name of the magazine or periodical (more recently given in italics); the volume number of the magazine; the page numbers; indication of month, day, year of issue in abbreviated form.

9. por/portrait, map/map, bibl/bibliography, and il/illustration.

Lesson 22

1. It offers a broad overview of major events concerning America's past as well as her present.

2. It alphabetically references entries through subject, author and title.

3. You must list and use many key or entry words for topics or subtopic areas.

4. Structurally, each entry is offered on a three column page with the entry word placed against the left margin of each column with the rest of the entry indented. Each entry, in turn, contains the name of the author or illustrator, article title, issue by month, volume number and page. The volume number and pages are separated by a colon, the article title is in quotation marks but the title of any article or book from any source other than *American Heritage* will be indicated through italics.

5. Subject entries of people, places or things that are not immediately recognizable are often defined according to occupation or importance within the entry.

6. It is structured to focus on one general and ten chrono-

logically listed subject headings detailing America's growth. Each heading is divided into areas concerning the social, cultural, military, political and economic happenings of each time period.

7. The entry includes the title of the article as it appears in the *American Heritage Magazine*, the author, the date of the magazine issue, in parentheses will be the volume and number, the page or pages and a short summary statement of the focus of the article.

8. You would use this guide when you wanted a quick chronological reference that dealt with one of the specified subject headings.

9. Because the periodical deals with a broad overview of American history, you would benefit from the information contained therein. To access much of the information, you would use both the index and the guide.

Lesson 23

1. The entries are alphabetical.

2. The 1947-1983 index with the copyright of 1984 or any of the supplements.

3. All articles, books, television shows and maps are differentiated from one another through a coding system of figures and colors.

4. The physical presentation or format of a page in the index consists of a page divided into two or three columns, depending on the copyright of the index you have.

5. Subjects, topics, and names are placed in bold print two spaces to the left of the left margin of a column. All entries, in turn, are in line against the left margin under the corresponding subject. All subtopic entry words have a print lighter than the topic but darker than the entry. All subtopic entry words are in line and are indented 2(two) spaces to the right of the topic entry word.

6. The *see* entry is placed to the right of the invalid entry word and the replacement, valid entry words, will immediately follow. The *see also* cross reference, in turn, appears at the end of all the entries for a given topic or subtopic and will supply alternative entry words to help further research. Also cross referenced will be all acronyms by *see*. You then will be referred to the original words upon which the acronym was based.

7. An entry in *The National Geographic Index* will include the entry word or phrase, the complete article title, the author, the photographer or illustrator, number of illustrations in an article, indication if a map is included, pages, and issue date by month and year.

8. In a separate section, they are placed alphabetically by map title with a narrative description of the geographic content of each in the 1947-1969 edition, while they are interfiled with all entries in the 1947-1983 edition.

9. You will not find information on any other magazine except *National Geographic* .

Lesson 24

1. Its purpose is as a weekly index that references over 200 current magazines and periodicals.

2. MAS's contents are divided into white pages of article summaries and brown pages of index references.

3. It is alphabetically organized by heading, then by subheadings.

4. Each white page entry includes a heading, subheading, article, title, article summary comprised of up to 100 words, complete magazine title, cover date, number and type of

illustration, starting page of article and total number of pages covered in the article.

5.   Well-developed summaries offer the advantage of knowing the main idea or focus of the article before the magazine is taken from the shelf. This increases work and time efficiency.

6.   Insets, or short articles within an article, are also indicated with a one sentence focus.

Lesson 25

1.   It provides easy retrieval of information concerning international organizations, countries, and states of the world.

2.   A comprehensive table of contents offers you, the researcher, a total overview of the book.

3.   If you know how to use an index, you will be a step ahead in your research. The index of any book is like the key to any door: it helps you access the information.

4.   This book is about countries and states of the world with articles having the following format: history, area, population, climate, defense, international relations, economy, energy, natural resources, industry, trade, communication, justice, religion, education, and welfare.

Lesson 26

1.   Its purpose is to present a concise but accurate factual representation of people who have achieved a leadership role in their field of expertise.

2.   *Current Biography* offers a section of obituaries of subjects who have appeared in the Yearbooks previously. A listing of key abbreviations used is given in the front of the book. Other indices also included list the biographical references used and the periodicals and newspapers consulted and a listing by field classification of the people who appear in *Current Biography*.

3.   You might use this book if you want current biographical information on currently famous people.

Lesson 27 does not have discussion questions.

Lesson 28

1.   Through computer networking on local, regional, state and national levels, many libraries have garnered forces to interconnect through data bases to allow patrons to ascertain <u>what</u> is available on a subject, <u>where</u> it is available and <u>how</u> one would go about retrieving it.

2.   You will only be able to access what is on the disc.

3.   An encyclopedia, or a periodical index, or all the citations of books of one library or of a group of libraries, or summaries/abstracts of journals.

4.   All the citations of particular materials{books, magazines, etc.} from all the participating member libraries of a specific region.

5.   You would access the citation for the particular item you want through use of your union catalog, whether it is on paper, CD-ROM, or on-line. You would notify the holding library of your request and the book or journal would be sent by a delivery system or perhaps the article could be faxed.

Lesson 29

1.   On-line offers a national networking system to include multiple data bases throughout the country.

2.   So much will be available that you will want to make intelligent decisions about the source documents you will try to locate and retrieve.

3.   Stringing is networking multiple data bases at one time.

4.   On-line is a way in which the librarian can assist you in becoming aware of what is available on your chosen topic.

The librarian will be able to tell you what is available where.

5.   If you follow the instructions as given in the software package, these operators will help to narrow the field of citations to only those for which you are searching.

6.   You might go back to develop a different strategy because you are not satisfied with the results that you obtained.

Lesson 30 has no discussion questions.

Name_____Page 1 Unit I TEST
Date_____   The Instructional Media Center

I. Literary Types:
Circle the correct answer.
Multiple choice.

1. The subject of the book is the life of a person and it is written by someone else.
A. Historical fiction   B. Fantasy   C. Biography   D. Autobiography

2. A type of fiction which breaks through the laws of nature as we now know them.
A. Fantasy   B. Historical fiction   C. Modern Realistic   D. Science Fiction

3. Fiction which presents a believable set of characters and plot and whose time and place setting is in the present.
A.Science Fiction   B. Modern Realistic   C. Fantasy   D. Historical fiction

4. The subject of the book is the life of a person and is written by that same person.
A. Historical fiction   B. Fantasy   C. Biography   D. Autobiography

5. A type of fiction based on current technological advances as projected into a future time and place setting.
A. Historical fiction   B. Fantasy   C. Science Fiction   D. Modern Realistic

6. A type of fiction which presents a believable set of characters and plot and whose time and place setting accurately depict the past.
A. Historical fiction   B. Fantasy   C. Science Fiction   D. Modern Realistic

7. This type of literature is shelved in the 200 section because, to many ancient peoples, it served as religion.
A. Biography   B. Legend, Fable, Folktale C. Autobiography D. Mythology

8. Shelving is in the 300 section because the information or stories contained in these books are considered to support the basic thinking of the people living at the time in which the stories were first communicated.
A. Biography   B. Legend, Fable, Folktale C. Autobiography D. Mythology

Name_____Page 2 Unit I TEST

Date_____   **The Instructional Media Center**

II. Media Center
Match the letter next to the correct number.

A. Workstation   G. Readers' Guide
B. On-line   H. Newspaper
C. Circulation Desk   I. Atlas
D. Card catalog   J. Vertical file
E. Record bin   K. Magazine rack
F. Study carrels   L. Periodical room

_____1. Alphabetical file of materials that are of a pamphlet or single sheet format. They are materials that can not stand on a shelf.

_____2. A book of maps.

_____3. A room in which magazines are stored.

_____4. Storage area for records.

_____5. Storage area for current magazines.

_____6. Check out desk.

_____7. Desk for individual student study.

_____8. An index of magazines.

_____9. An index or catalog of all the materials stored in the IMC.

_____10. Current information circulated on a daily or weekly basis.

_____11. Computer area.

_____12. A computer hooked up to a telephone line.

Name_____Page 3

Date_____

Unit I TEST

The Instructional Media Center

III. The Media Abbreviations
Match letter to number.

1._____ B

2._____TRA

3._____Fic

4._____ MRDF

5._____ SFS

6._____ MPL

7._____ PS/PA

8._____ VT

9._____ REF

10._____ REC

A. Biography

B. Picture File

C. Film Loop

D. Fiction

E. Transparencies

F. Record

G. Reference

H. Video tape

I. Computer software

J. Sound filmstrips

IV. Media Specialist
List five (5) ways in which the Media Specialist might help you.

1.

2.

3.

4.

5.

Name_____Page 1   **Unit II TEST**
Date_____   **The Card and The Catalog**

1. List the three types of cards known as basic.
   A.
   B.
   C.

2. List the three types of cards known as added entry.
   A.
   B.
   C.

3. The words *see* or *see also* on a catalog card indicate that the card type is known as a _____.

4. All the basic cards and all the added entry cards for one book are exactly alike except for the _____line which indicates the card type.

5.   The   general   organization   of   the   card   catalog is_____.

6. The only topics that differ from the organization indicated in question five are the histories of countries such as the United States. Therefore, the organization of the drawer marked U.S. - HISTORY is

_____.

7. On the next page is an example of part of a drawer which is marked U.S. - HISTORY. Use your own key to indicate the two different organizations used in the set-up of the drawer.

KEY

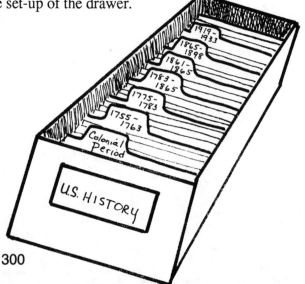

Name_____Page 2   **Unit II TEST**
Date_____   **The Card and The Catalog**

8. Look at this subject card and indicate the following:

A. Topic -
B. Subtopic -
C. Detail -
D. Subdetail -

U. S.- HISTORY - REVOLUTION - FICTION
Fic   Forman, James.
For   The Cow Neck Rebels. Farrar, Straus [©1969]
        [256p.]
        In 1776, his peaceful life shattered by the British
     siege of Long Island, Bruce Cameron reluctantly follows his
     militant grandfather and brother to soul-destroying defeat,
     returning home alone to wage his own nonviolent war.

        1. Long Island - History-Fiction. 2. U.S. -History-
     Revolution-Fiction. I. Title ○

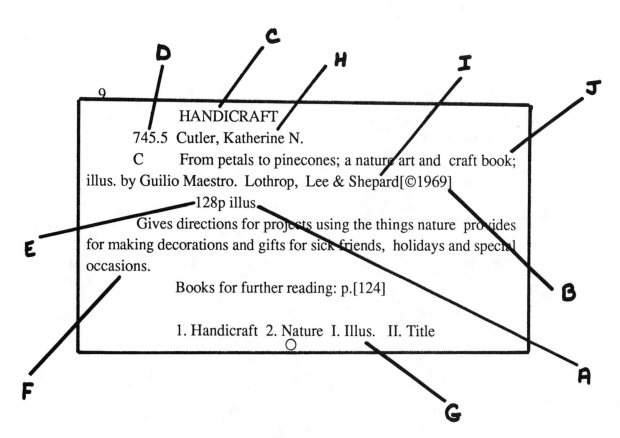

HANDICRAFT
745.5 Cutler, Katherine N.
   C   From petals to pinecones; a nature art and craft book;
illus. by Guilio Maestro. Lothrop, Lee & Shepard[©1969]
        128p illus.
    Gives directions for projects using the things nature provides
for making decorations and gifts for sick friends, holidays and special
occasions.

        Books for further reading: p.[124]

        1. Handicraft 2. Nature I. Illus. II. Title
                        ○

Name_____Page 3   **Unit II TEST**
Date_____   **The Card and The Catalog**

Identify the card parts:

A.   F.

B.   G.

C.   H.

D.   I.

E.   J.

10.   Explain the importance of the following to the researcher in terms of furthering research.

A. Call number:

B. Copyright date:

C. Series:

D. Narrative:

E. Tracings:

F. Visual aids:

11.

> Invent your own computer games
>
> 001.64   D'Ignazio, Fred
> Dig   Invent your own computer games. Watts, 1983.
>   90p. (A Computer-Awareness first book)
>   Explains how to use a personal computer to create
> original sports, board, strategy, word, number, and adventure games,
> with instructions for programming and playing eleven simple
> computer games.
>   1. Computer games. 2. Basic (Computer program
>   language). 3. Programming (Computers) I. T   II.
>   Series.

Indicate the specific information as asked:

A. Title:

B. Author:

C. Copyright:

D. Publisher:

E. Series:

F. Tracings:

G. Narrative (first three words):

H. Illustrator (if given):

I. Visual Aid types:

J. Pages:

K. Call number:

L. Card Type:

M. Classification:

N. Media Type:

Name_____Page 1   **Unit III TEST**
Date_____   **Understanding Organization**

DIRECTIONS:
I. Place the correct letter next to the appropriate definition.
      A = Alphabetical B=Numerical C=Chronological D=Topical

_____simple number sequence
_____simple a,b,c order
_____Placement by subject
_____Placement by year, time period, or time era

II.   The four organizational systems are indicated at the top of the page. Listed below
      are a variety of research sources or areas as well as the fiction section. Analyze
      each according to basic organization or organizations. Match the letter representing
      the organization to the source. (Some will have more than one letter.)

_____1. Encyclopedias' format   _____9. Atlas
_____2. Card Catalog   _____ 10. Table of contents
_____3. Nonfiction section   _____ 11. Current Biography
_____4. Book index   _____12. Fiction section
_____5. Biography section   _____ 13. Reference section
_____6. Dictionary   _____14. National Geographic Index
_____7. US History section of card   _____15. Reader's Guide
       catalog   _____ 16. American Heritage
_____8. Thesaurus

DIRECTIONS:
III.   Listed below are lists of words. Some are examples of word-by-word
      alphabetizing. Others are examples of letter-by-letter alphabetizing. Place an <u>A</u>
      next to the word-by-word. Place a <u>B</u> next to the letter-by-letter.

A = Word-by-word (Same first words are clustered.)
B = Letter-by-letter (Ignore spaces.)

_____ Newbery Library   _____ New Jersey Plan
      Newfoundland   New Sweden
      New Jersey Plan   New York City
      New Sweden   Newbery Library
      New York City   Newfoundland

Name_____Page 2   **Unit III TEST**
Date_____   **Understanding Organization**

___ North Dakota   _____ North Dakota
     North Pole   Northern Ireland
     North Star   North Pole
     Northern Ireland   Northrup, John Howard
     Northrup, John Howard   North Star

DIRECTIONS:

IV. Listed are the first lines of catalog cards. Next to each is a letter. Place this letter next to the arrow that indicates where the card would be placed alphabetically in the sample card catalog drawer.

A. . .Sarasas, Claude   E. . .S-51 Submarine
B. . .SIOUX INDIANS   F. . .SMALLPOX
C. . .Sugarman, Tracy, illus.   G. . .Seals, sea lions and walruses
D. . .Swift, Jonathan   H. . .SOCCER

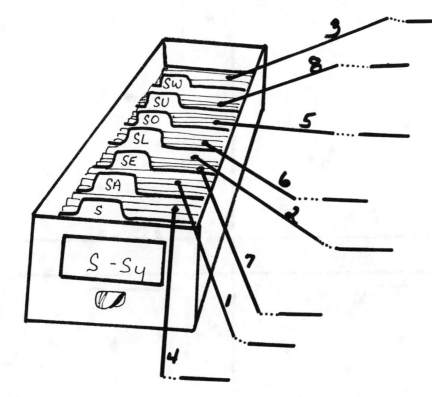

Appendix F   Unit Tests

Name_____Page 1   **Unit IV TEST**
Date_____   **Book and Information Retrieval**

I. Directions:

    1. In alphabetical order, list each of the four library classifications next to a number one.

    2. Then, under the corresponding classification, fill in an appropriate call number next to the correct number two.

    3. In order, write the book retrieval steps for the corresponding classification and call number, next to the correct number three.

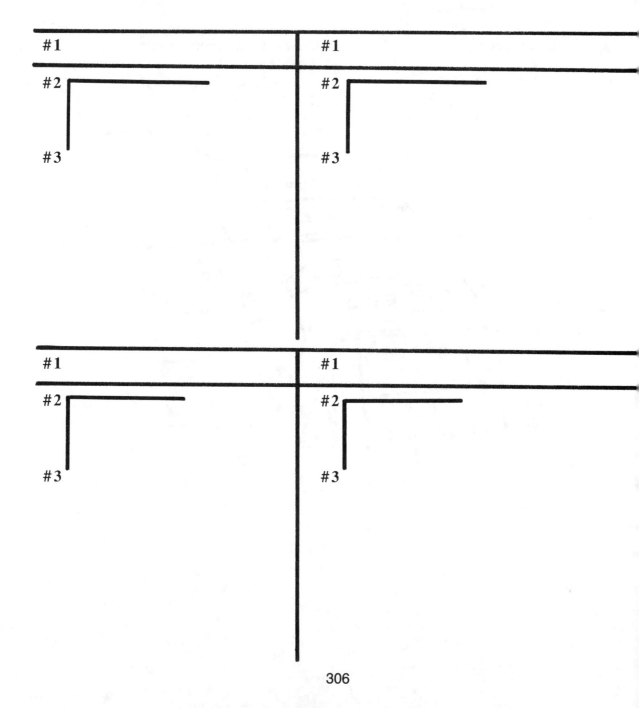

Name_____Page 2   **Unit IV TEST**
Date_____   **Book and Information Retrieval**

Card #1:

```
        U. S. - PUBLIC BUILDINGS

SFS   Washington, D. C. [Filmstrip]/National Geographic Society.-
917.53 Washington:  National Geographic, ©1980.
Was   2 filmstrips(approx. 48 fr. each): col.; 35mm. & 2 audio
      cassettes (2-track, 1 track for automatic operation, 1 track for
      manual operation. mono. 1 7/8 ips. approx. 14 min. each).
            With teacher's guide for each filmstrip, including script.
            SUMMARY:  Federal buildings and national monuments,
            museums, and parks in and around Washington, D. C.;
            history of the nation's capital.  For intermediate-adult.
            CONTENTS:  Visiting our government buildings. --Monuments
            and museums.
      1. U.S. - Public buildings.   2.   U.S. - Galleries and museums.
```

Card #2

```
        U.S. - HISTORY - WAR
SFS   Chevron, U.S.A., Inc.
973     War. (Filmstrip)Chevron School Broadcast.
        San Francisco. ©1983.
        (Images of America)
           Contents:  1 filmstrip (102 fr.) & audio-cassette (approx. 15 min.),
           teacher's guide and follow-up activities.
           Summary:  Illustrates how war as seen through fact and propaganda
           has been perceived by Americans since the Revolution.

           1. U. S. - History - War.  2. Series   I. Title
```

Card #3

```
          LAKES
551.48    Bramwell, Martyn
              Rivers and lakes. NY: Franklin Watts, ©1986.
          (Earth Science Library Series)
          32 p  col illus.,

          Explores the world of physical geography.  Explains
          the forces that shape the Earth.

             1. Lakes    I. Title  II. Series
```

II. Directions:
   1. Look at catalog card #1 and answer the following questions:
      a. publisher
      b. format of media
      c. copyright
      d. focus
      e. tracings
      f. call number
      g. card type

   2. Look at catalog card #2 and answer the following questions:
      a. call number
      b. format
      c. title
      d. series title
      e. copyright
      f. tracings

   3. Look at catalog card #3 and answer the following questions:
      a. call number
      b. format of media
      c. author
      d. series
      e. focus
      f. tracings
      g. number of pages
      h. publisher
      i. copyright

Name_____Page 1   **Unit V TEST**
Date_____   **Utilization of Sources/Parts of a Book**

I. Directions: Place the correct word on the line.

1._____A person who has gathered into book form material that others have written.

2._____A person who used reference sources but wrote original material.

3._____The name of the company that prints the book.

4._____The person who draws the pictures for a book.

5._____The front and back outer part of the book.

6._____The main part or body of the book.

7._____The listing of the major parts, units, and chapters of a book in page order. It gives a basic overview of the book's content.

8._____The introduction to the book.

9._____ __The cover that protects the book.

10._____The name of the book.

11._____City and/or state location of publishing company.

12._____Added material at the end of a book.

13._____A specialized dictionary defined according to subject area.

14._____Credit given to original sources for materials used.

15._____Binding of the book; the part that's seen on the shelf.

16._____An alphabetical listing by topic, then by subtopic of material or information covered in a book.

17._____Illustration placed opposite the title page.

Name_____Page 2   **Unit V TEST**
Date_____   **Utilization of Sources/Parts of a Book**

Fill in the correct word.

1. Each book in a set of encyclopedias is called a _____.

2. The information part of the book is called the _____.

3. An encyclopedia can be in one of three orders and they are:_____,

_____, and _____.

4. When on the shelf, each book is identified by the number and/or letter markings on

the _____of the book.

5. The written compositions on the topics of people, places and events are

called_____.

6. To help you locate all the important information contained in an encyclopedia on a

single topic, you should first check the _____where you will

find which books and pages to use.

7. Words at the top of each encyclopedia page that indicate the first and last entries are

called _____.

8. If the article is long, it will be divided into parts by _____ and

_____.

9. To help with research, the editors of an encyclopedia give alternative sources

indicated by the word and phrase_____and

_____.

10. Some articles give the name of the person who wrote it at the end of it and this is

called a _____article. Other articles do not have the source

offered and they are called _____.

Name_____**Page 3**   **Unit V TEST**
Date_____   **Utilization of Sources/Parts of a Book**

11. At the end of each article, most encyclopedias give a listing of books that can be

read to further knowledge of the subject under discussion. This is called a

_____.

12. Examples of visual aids used in an encyclopedia to help you to understand the

written information are: (List at least 5.)

_____   _____

_____   _____

_____   _____

13. Under each of these visual aids in an encyclopedia is a label

called_____. This is a word or phrase used to help your understanding of

the aid and its correspondence to the written text.

14. In an index, punctuation has meaning.
       6-10 =

       6, 10 =

III. Directions: Match letter to correct statement.

       A. Readers' Guide   E. Atlas
       B. National Geographic   F. Magazine Article Summaries
       C. Almanac   G. Current Biography
       D. The Statesman's Yearbook   H. American Heritage Index

_____1. Presents summaries of information on a variety of current topics.

_____2. A book of maps that present visual information concerning general and
              specific regions of the world.

_____3. Subject index to articles found in magazines and periodicals in print.

Name_____Page 4   Unit V TEST
Date_____   Utilization of Sources/Parts of a Book

_____ 4. A magazine that presents a broad overview of America's past as well as her present.

_____ 5. Indexes magazine articles, books, television shows and maps.

_____ 6. Provides easy retrieval of information concerning international organizations, countries, and states of the world.

_____ 7. Presents a concise but factual representation of people who have achieved a leadership role in their fields of expertise.

Name_____Page 1   **Unit VI TEST**
Date_____   **The Library Future**

Fill in the crossword puzzle using the clues listed.

ACROSS
1. Main idea of a subject
2. A thin, flat device that stores information
3. A network of data bases whose information can be commanded over a telephone line with modem and computer
4. A machine that prints out information as one connected to a computer
5. A code or a string of codes used to open an on-line computer system.
6. A single piece of media
7. The act of locating information
8. An arrangement of data bases
9. A bibliographic reference for a book, journal or magazine
10. A selection of choices presented on a computer screen
11. An arrangement of databases on on-line used at the same time in information retrieval
12. Final product of the interworkings of a database, software package, commands and keyboard
13. One example of a Boolean operator that limits citation retrieval
14. A plan of action specifically in conducting research.
15. A frame of information on a computer

DOWN
16. A work area for computers in a library
17. Means compact disc, read only memory
19. Copier that sends information and images across communication wires
20. The words and, or but as part of a software package
21. A drawing of a logical operation
22. Abbreviation for the Instructional Media Center
23. A dictionary of synonyms
24. Instructions punched into a computer
25. Information
26. A manual index of every item in the library
27. To retrieve on command or through a strategy

Name__________________Page 2 **Unit VI TEST**
Date___________________ **The Library Future**

The CROSSWORD:

COMPUTER • TECHNOLOGY

Name_____   **Unit VII TEST**
Date_____   **The Aspects of Writing**

Directions: Sequence the following clusters in the order in which each step would be completed when structuring a report.

I. Use numbers 1-4 to sequence:
_____Determining availability of source materials.
_____Determining subtopics.
_____Expansion/limitation of topic.
_____Topic selection.

II. Use numbers 5-8 to sequence:
_____Structure detailed outline.
_____Structure main idea outline.
_____Reshuffle notecards into subtopic area.
_____Code notecards.

III. Use numbers 9-13 to sequence:
_____Edit/proof draft.
_____Submit final copy.
_____Make sure all format requirements are included.
_____Write draft.
_____Add introduction and conclusion to body of paper.

IV. Directions: Answer the following questions in complete sentences.

1. Why is it important to write your report draft from a main idea outline rather than from your notecards?

2. Describe the information that should be included on your notecards to organize your notetaking.

3. Why is it important to proof not only your draft but also you final copy before you submit it to your teacher?

4. What type of information is included in a good introduction and conclusion?

5. What is the purpose of footnoting or developing a list of citations for a report?

Appendix F   Unit Tests

UNIT I TEST [ANSWER KEY]

I. Literary types
1. C. Biography
2. A. Fantasy
3. B. Modern Realistic Fiction
4. D. Autobiography
5. C. Science Fiction
6. A. Historical Fiction
7. D. Mythology
8. B. Legend, Fable, Folktale

II. Media Center
1. J. Vertical File
2. I. Atlas
3. L. Periodical Room
4. E. Record Bin
5. K. Magazine Rack
6. C. Circulation Desk
7. F. Study Carrels
8. G. Readers' Guide
9. D. Card Catalog
10. H. Newspaper
11. A. Workstation
12. B. On-line

III. Media Abbreviations
1. A. Biography
2. E. Transparencies
3. D. Fiction
4. I. Computer software
5. J. Sound filmstrip
6. C. Film loop
7. B. Picture file
8. H. Video tape
9. G. Reference
10. F. Record

IV. Media Specialist
(Answer examples; answers will vary.)
1. Help you locate materials.
2. Will suggest multiple sources for a topic.
3. Will help you expand or limit a topic.
4. Will locate materials constructed in a format other than a book.
5. Will help you check out materials.
6. Will introduce you to CD-ROM, on-line, if available.

UNIT II TEST [ANSWER KEY]
1. A, B, C: subject, author, title (In any order)
2. A, B, C: illustrator, series, joint author (In any order)
3. cross reference
4. first
5. alphabetical
6. chronological
7. Answer will vary, but should show differentiation of alphabetical and chronological organizations.
8. A. United States
   B. History
   C. Revolution
   D. Fiction
9. A. Indication of visual aids
   B. Copyright
   C. Subject
   D. Call number
   E. Indication of page numbers
   F. Narrative
   G. Tracings
   H. Author
   I. Publisher
   J. Title

10. A. Indicates if book is nonfiction and not fiction; gives book location.
    B. Tells if the book is current enough to use.
    C. Indicates if book might have a separate volume index.
    D. Gives a basic summary or focus of the book.
    E. Suggest alternative key words; suggests cross references
    F. Indicates visual aids in book in case a specific ty▮ is needed by research.

11. A. Invent your own computer games
    B. Fred D'Ignazio
    C. 1983
    D. Watts
    E. A Computer-Awareness First Book
    F. Computer Games; Basic, Programming; title; series
    G. Explains how to
    H. Not given
    I. Not given
    J. 90
    K. 001.64/D'Ig
    L. title
    M. nonfiction
    N. book

UNIT III TEST [ANSWER KEY]

I. B. Numerical
   A. Alphabetical
   D. Topical
   C. Chronological

II.
1. A, C, or D
2. A, C
3. A,B,D
4. A
5. A
6. A
7. C, A
8. A

316

9. A, D
10. D, B,C(sometimes)
11. A
12. A
13. B, D
14. A
15. A
16. A, C

II.
  1. B
  2. A
  3. A
  4. B

V. 1. A
  2. B or G
  3. D
  4. E
  5. H
  6. F
  7. B or G
  8. C

UNIT IV TEST   [ANSWER KEY]

I. 1. Biography
  2. B
    Edison
    Gra
  3. a.
    b.
    c.   [See pp 99-100]
    d.

  1. Fiction
  2. Fic
    Str

  3. a.
    b.
    c.
    d.   [See pp 99-100]
    e.

  1. Nonfiction
  2. 263.42
    Lew

  3. a.
    b.
    c.   [See pp 99-100]
    d.

  1. Reference
  2. REF

632.45
Mab
  3. a.
    b.
    c.   [See pp 99-100]
    d.

II. 1. a. National Geographic
    b. sound filmstrip
    c. 1980
    d. Government buildings, Wash., D.C.
    e. U. S.- PUBLIC BUILDINGS; U. S.-GALLERIES AND MUSEUMS
    f. SFS/917.53/Was
    g. Topic/subject

  2. a. SFS/973
    b. sound filmstrip
    c. War
    d. Images of America
    e. 1983
    f. U. S.-HISTORY - WAR; Series; title

  3. a. 551.48
    b. book
    c. Martyn Bramwell
    d. Earth Science Library Series
    e. Physical Geography
    f. LAKES; Tilte; series
    g. 32
    h. Franklin Watts
    i. 1986

UNIT V TEST   [ANSWER KEY]

I. 1. editor, compiler
  2. author
  3. publisher
  4. illustrator
  5. cover
  6. body, text
  7. table of contents
  8. preface
  9. dust cover, dust jacket
  10. title
  11. place of publication
  12. appendix
  13. glossary
  14. acknowledgement
  15. spine
  16. index
  17. frontispiece

II. 1. volume
  2. body, text
  3. alph., chrono., topical
  4. spine

5. articles
6. index
7. guide words
8. headings, subheadings
9. see, see also
10. signed, unsigned
11. bibliography
12. transparencies, illustrations, photos, charts, graphs, diagrams, timelines, tables, maps
13. legend
14. - = those 2 pages and all in between
   , = just the two pages listed

III. 1. C (almanac)
2. E (atlas)
3. A, F (Readers' Guide/ MAS
4. H. (American Heritage Index)
5. B. (National Geographic)
6. D. (The Statesman's Yearbook)
7. G. Current Biography

UNIT TEST VI [ANSWER KEY]
ACROSS
1. topic
2. disc
3. online
4. printer
5. password
6. item
7. retrieval
8. networking
9. citation
10. menu
11. string
12. output
13. and
14. strategy
15. screen

DOWN
16. station
17. CD ROM
18. computer technology
19. fax
20. operators
21. Venn
22. IMC
23. thesaurus
24. commands
25. data
26. catalog
27. access

UNIT VII TEST [ANSWER KEY]

I. 2, 4, 3, 1
II. 8, 5, 7, 6
III. 11, 13, 12, 9, 10
IV. 1. Helps to paraphrase ideas
2. All notecards should be separated into sources by packet and marked. All first cards for sources should include a complete citation. Each note card in packet should have subtopic marked on it, coded by a letter for easy reshuffling.
3. To catch any and all errors.
4. An introduction should include either a brief overview of the material in your report or an explanation as to the basic organization of the ideas presented.

A conclusion should include a summary of the most important ideas in your report with your conclusions and possibly recommendation based on your conclusions. A good conclusion is supported by the facts taken from the text of your paper.
5. The purpose of footnoting or developing a list of citations is to credit another author, maintain a list of sources consulted, and to allow review of your sources.

Stepping into Research

Name
Date

I. Multiple Choice; **Book Classifications/Organizations**

1. A book written about the life of a person by someone else is known as. . .
    A. Fiction   B. Nonfiction   C. Reference   D. Biography

2. A totally factual book dealing with an in-depth presentation of a topic . . .
    A. Fiction   B. Nonfiction   C. Reference   D. Biography

3. A book written for entertainment value and whose purpose is not to inform. . .
    A. Fiction   B. Nonfiction   C. Reference   D. Biography

4. A factual book, concerning multiple topics, whose purpose is to present a fast review of information . . .
    A. Fiction   B. Nonfiction   C. Reference   D. Biography

5. The organizational structure of the card catalog as a whole. . .
    A. Alphabetical B. Chronological   C. Numerical   D. Topical

6. The organizational structure of the section of the card catalog referred to as UNITED STATES - HISTORY . . .
    A. Alphabetical B. Chronological   C. Numerical   D. Topical

7. The Dewey Decimal System uses a _____system for the shelf organization of books. . .
    A. Alphabetical B. Chronological   C. Numerical   D. Topical

8. The numbers in the Dewey Decimal System classify the topic, subtopic and details of a book's content through a _____system.
    A. Alphabetical B. Chronological   C. Numerical   D. Topical

9. An indicator as to whether a catalog card is of a subject, author, or title type would be the . . .
    A. Narrative   B. Tracings   C. First line   D. Call Number

10. An example of an added entry card would <u>not</u> be a . . .
    A. Joint author   B. Illustrator   C. Title   D. Series

Stepping into Research

Name   **Page 2**   **Date**

II. Matching; **Literary Types**

_____1. Historical Fiction   _____5. Biography
_____2. Modern Realistic Fiction   _____6. Autobiography
_____3. Science Fiction   _____7. Legends/fables/folktales
_____4. Fantasy   _____8. Myths

A. Subject of the book is the life of a person written by someone else.
B. A type of fiction which breaks through the laws of nature.
C. Fiction which presents a believable set of characters and plot and whose time and place setting is in the present.
D. The subject of the book is the life of a person and is written by that same person.
E. A type of fiction based on current technological advances as projected into a future time and place setting.
F. A type of fiction which presents a believable set of characters and plot and whose time and place setting accurately depict the past.
G. This type of literature is shelved in the 200 section because, to many ancient peoples, it served as religion.
H. Shelving is in the 300 section because the information or stories contained in these books are considered to support the basic thinking of the people living at the time in which the stories were first communicated.

III. Fill-in; **Information: Bias, Expertise, Exceptions**

1. _____is prejudice for or against a subject and can be presented very subtly in nonfiction writings.

2. It is important to check an author's _____in his/her field when using his/her books as the basis of a report to determine accuracy of information.

3. The _____recognizes the purpose for which each book has been written, classifies it and places it on the shelf in the library.

4. The_____is an index of all the items in the library.

5. In the U.S. - HISTORY section of the card catalog, all the cards are _____ cards. All other card types are alphabetically placed throughout the card catalog.

6. All _____cards will have the first line in capital letters.

7. Cross reference cards are indicated in the card catalog by the word, phrase _____and_____.

Stepping into Research

8. The articles _____ are dropped when they appear at the beginning of a title in an alphabetical search for the card.

9. When alphabetically searching for a person's name in the card catalog, and the name is an author on an author card or a subject on a subject card, the student searches for the _____ name.

10. When alphabetically searching for a person's name in the card catalog and that name is the title of a book, the student looks under the _____ name.

11. When an abbreviation appears in a name, such as *Dr.*, the student looks under the word_____ in the card catalog.

12. In search of the title card for *101 Dalmations*, the student should look under _____ in the card catalog.

13. Topics first and then within the topic cluster, subtopics are grouped_____ in the card catalog except for the U. S.- HISTORY cluster.

IV. Matching; **Parts of a Catalog Card**

_____1. Call number   _____6. Series
_____2. Title   _____7. Narrative
_____3. Author   _____8. Tracings
_____4. Copyright Date   _____9. Visual Aids
_____5. Publisher   _____10. Bibliography

A. Main idea of the book.
B. Short summary of important information contained in the book.
C. Gives alternate key words to be used to further research.
D. Gives book classification or library address of the book.
E. Maps, graphs, illustrations, etc.
F. Name of the person who wrote the book.
G. Other sources used by the author in his/her research.
H. The year the book was published.
I. Might mean that a volume index is used.
J. Company that printed the book.

Stepping into Research

V. True/False; **Information**

_____1. Each book in the library is written to either fulfill a general purpose of entertainment known as fiction or for the purpose of supplying factual information known as nonfiction.

_____2. Classifications of books <u>never</u> overlap. One copy of a book may never be found in the nonfiction section and another copy found in the biography section.

_____3. In most reference books, there is a listing to check an author's credentials or expertise in his/her chosen field.

_____4. Everything in print is true and should therefore be believed.

_____5. Most reference and nonfiction book collections, as housed in a library, are developed in answer to the needs of the patrons.

_____6. If an unauthorized person writes a biography, it is always true.

_____7. Encyclopedias, atlases, and almanacs will always be found in the Biography section of any library.

_____8. A book format is the only one offered by most school libraries to provide factual information.

_____9. In the card catalog, the outside guide helps place the student at the correct drawer and the inside guide helps the student locate the correct card.

_____10. There is only one card per book in the card catalog index.

_____11. The student should start in the stacks in search of books for his/her topic.

_____12. There is only one system for alphabetizing in an index or in a catalog.

Stepping into Research

Name   **Page 5**   **Date**

VI. Matching; **The Catalog Abbreviations**

_____1. FIC   _____4. MRDF   _____7. PS/PA
_____2. SFS   _____5. MPL   _____8. TRA
_____3. B   _____6. REF   _____9. VT
                                           _____10. REC

A. Biography   B. Picture File   C. Film loop
D. Fiction   E. Transparencies   F. Record
G. Reference   H. Video Tape   I. Computer Software
J. Sound Filmstrip

VII. Fill-In; **Parts of a Book**

1._____A person who gather material into book form that others have
                   written.

2._____ A person who wrote his/her own original material but might have
                   used references.

3._____ The name of a company that prints a book.

4._____ The main part or the information part of the book.

5._____ A listing of the major parts, units, and chapters of a book in page
                  order.

6. _____ Page on which date of publication of the book is given.

7._____ A separate section containing added or extra materials usually
                  found at the end of a book.

8. _____ A specialized dictionary defined according to a subject or content
                   area.

9. _____An alphabetical listing by topic, then by subtopic of material or
                   information covered in a book.

10. _____The person who draws a picture for a book.

Stepping into Research

VIII. Fill-in; **The Encyclopedia**
Put correct letter next to statement.

A. articles, entries	F. signed
B. cross references	G. spine
C. guide words	H. text
D. headings, subheadings	I. visual aids
E. organizations	J. volume

_____1. Alphabetical, chronological and topical are _____ that can be found in all encyclopedias.

_____2. Words at the top of each encyclopedia page that indicate the first and last entries are called _____.

_____3. The written compositions in an encyclopedia on the topics of people, places and events are called_____.

_____4. The information part of an encyclopedia is called the _____.

_____5. Each book in a set of encyclopedia is called a _____.

_____6. In an encyclopedia, some articles give the name of the author at the end of the entry. When this occurs the entry is known as_____.

_____7.Maps, graphs, charts, transparencies, illustrations, diagrams, and tables can all be categorized as _____.

_____8. If an article is long in an encyclopedia, it will be divided into topics and subtopics by _____.

_____9. When on a library shelf, each book in a set of encyclopedias is identified by the number and letter markings on the _____of the book.

_____10. To help the researcher, the editors of an encyclopedia give alternative sources through the use of the words *see* and *see also* which are known as _____.

Stepping into Research

Name   **Page 7**   **Date**

IX. True/False;   **Search Strategies**
Indicate whether statement is true or false.

_____1. A student must use multiple sources when collecting information for a report.

_____2. To find all the information contained in a set of encyclopedia on a single subject, the student should turn to the table of contents of the set.

_____3. In an index, all the information contained in a book is divided into topics, subtopics, and details.

_____4. The information on a CD-ROM is contained on a disc.

_____5. Union catalog expands the research base of a library to all that is included in the union catalog region.

_____6. All libraries are computerized.

_____7. On-line is connected to cablevision.

_____8. CD-ROM, On-line, and union catalog output only one type or format of information.

_____9. When collecting information, a student should take notes and then outline the data gathered from all sources.

_____10. Multiple sources, CD-ROM, union catalog, and on-line can all be used as part of a student's search strategy when conducting research.

Stepping into Research

X. Matching; **Multiple Sources**
A. almanac   D. Magazine Article Summaries   G. Readers' Guide
B. atlas   E. National Geographic   H. Statesman's Yearbook
C. Current Biography   F. American Heritage   I. encyclopedia

If you wanted to locate information on a specific topic or subtopic, which of the above would you use?

_____1. If you wanted to locate information about the life of a person who is living?

_____2. If you wanted information about a subject that is current within the last six months?

_____3. If you wanted information about a country in South America?

_____4. If you wanted information concerning map studies?

_____5. If you wanted information about the American Revolution?

_____6. If you wanted to check a specific fact?

_____7. If you wanted a listing of motion pictures that won Academy Awards?

Stepping into Research Answer Sheet

Name
Date

I. Multiple Choice; **Book Classifications/Organizations**

1.	6.
2.	7.
3.	8.
4.	9.
5.	10.

II. Matching; **Literary Types**

1.	5.
2.	6.
3.	7.
4.	8.

III. Fill-in; **Information: Bias, Expertise, Exceptions**

1.	5.	9.
2.	6.	10.
3.	7.	11.
4.	8.	12.
		13.

IV. Matching; **Parts of a Catalog Card**

1.	6.
2.	7.
3.	8.
4.	9.
5.	10.

V. True/False; **Information**

1.	7.
2.	8.
3.	9.
4.	10.
5.	11.
6.	12.

Stepping into Research Answer Sheet, page 2

VI. Matching; **The Catalog Abbreviations**

1.   6.
2.   7.
3.   8.
4.   9.
5.   10.

VII. Fill-In; **Parts of a Book**

1.   6.
2.   7.
3.   8.
4.   9.
5.   10.

VIII. Fill-in; **The Encyclopedia**

1.   6.
2.   7.
3.   8.
4.   9.
5.   10.

IX. True/False; **Search Strategies**

1.   6.
2.   7.
3.   8.
4.   9.
5.   10.

X. Matching; **Multiple Sources**

1.   5.
2.   6.
3.   7.
4.

Stepping into Research Answer Key

Name
Date

I. Multiple Choice; **Book Classifications/Organizations**

1.D	6.B
2.B	7.C
3.A	8.D
4.C	9.C
5.A	10.C

II. Matching; **Literary Types**

1.F	5.A
2.C	6.D
3.E	7.H
4.B	8.G

III. Fill-in; **Information: Bias, Expertise, Exceptions**

1.bias	5.subject	9.last
2.expertise	6.subject	10.first
3.librarian(media specialist	7.see, see also	11.doctor
4.card catalog	8.a, an, the	12.one
		13.alphabetically

IV. Matching; **Parts of a Catalog Card**

1.D	6.I
2.A	7.B
3.F	8.C
4.H	9.E
5.J	10.G

V. True/False; **Information**

1.TRUE	7.FALSE
2.FALSE	8.FALSE
3.TRUE	9.TRUE
4.FALSE	10.FALSE
5.TRUE	11.FALSE
6.FALSE	12.FALSE

Stepping into Research Answer Key Sheet, page 2

VI. Matching; **The Catalog Abbreviations**

1.D	6.G
2.J	7.B
3.A	8.E
4.I	9.H
5.C	10.F

VII. Fill-In; **Parts of a Book**

1.editor, compiler	6.copyright
2.author	7.appendix
3.publisher	8.glossary
4.text, body	9.index
5.table of contents	10.illustrator

VIII. Fill-in; **The Encyclopedia**

1.organizations	6.signed
2.guide words	7.visual aids
3.articles, entries	8.headings, subheadings
4.text	9.spine
5.volume	10.cross reference

IX. True/False;   **Search Strategies**

1. TRUE	6.FALSE
2.FALSE	7.FALSE
3.TRUE	8.FALSE
4.TRUE	9.TRUE
5.TRUE	10.TRUE

X. Matching; **Multiple Sources**

1.C,D	5.F,I,G
2.D,G	6.A,I
3.B,H,E	7.A
4.B	

Annals of America
1. Volume 4, page 142.
2. Volume 1, page 154 and Conspectus II, page 423-424.
3. Volume 13, page 559; William Jennings Bryan; Secretary of State to President Wilson.
4. 304-309; Transcript of presidential news conference. (President Reagan, reporters, Attorney General, Secretary of Transportation participating in a news conference.)

Atlas of the Third World
1. pages 218, 219.
2. Gatun Lake
3. pages 134, 135; Burma.
4. 520 +/square mile.

Atlas of the United States, Rand McNally
1. p. 88; New Mexico.
2. Kansas City, St. Louis, Springfield.
3. 3
4. 9.

Bartlett's Familiar Quotations
1. Page 975a.
2. 1725-1780, p. 445
3. p. 1061; He was born in 1902; she, in 1907. Book is chronological in that fashion.
4. p. 1270; p. 1050b; Langston Hughes, *The Black Men Speak*.

Bulfinch's Mythology
1. p. 435; a knight of King Arthur's Round Table
2. p. 367
3. p. 8; daughters of Jupiter and Mnemosyne. They were goddesses of memory and later of the Arts and Sciences.
4. On p. 8: Calliope, epic poetry; Clio, history; Euterpe, lyric poetry; Melpomene, tragedy; Terpsichore, choral dance, song; Erato, love poetry; Polyhymnia, sacred poetry; Urania, astronomy; Thalia, comedy.

Encyclopedia of American History
1. p. 763.
2. p. 1054; Salem, Indiana; October 12, 1838.
3. 777; 1790-91, Samuel Slater, reproduced Arkwright machinery, employing water power at Pawtucket, Rhode Island.
4. Yes, page 1152; Biography of Samuel Slater.

Encyclopedia of Black America
1. p. 820; zoologist, educator.
2. p. ix.
3. 2
4. p. 669; Mildred E. Phillips, 1928.

Encyclopedia of the Third World
1. 1599
2. World Bank, 1818 H Street, NW, Washington, DC 20433
3. 199
4. Bhutan

Encyclopedia of Visual Art
1. Volume VII, page 328, Volume IX, page 683.
2. Volume 9, page 743-768; Thread stretched on a loom for weaving, through which the weft threads are passed.
3. Volume 10, page 163. Archaeological Museum.
4. Volumes 6, 7, 8.

Encyclopedia of World Biography, McGraw-Hill
1. Afro-American champion cowboy. Volume 6, page 596-597.
2. Chiaranalle, Italy; August 31, 1870.
3. A. Oakley; Volume 8, pages 167-168.
4. Annie Oakley was Phoebe Anne Oakley Mozee.

Lands and Peoples
1. Vol. 5, page 347.
2. 191; Burkina Faso; The White Volta, The Red Volta, the Black Volta.
3. 431.
4. all year.

New Book of Popular Science
1. Volume 5, page 26.
2. p. 330; Another table of contents; p. 414.
3. Volume 6, page 299-315.
4. Volume 3, page 384; *Micrographia*.

Occupational Outlook Handbook, 1986-87
1. Biological scientists, p. 88
2. p. 13
3. Electrical Design Engineer, p. 65.
4. Institute of Electrical and Electronics Engineers/United States Activities Board, 1111 19th Street, NW, Suite 698, Washington, DC 20036

Past Worlds; The Times Atlas of Archaeology
1. p.211; early public building in E. Peru
2. p. 76
3. pp. 40, 41; Archaemenid empire, p. 159.
4. cotton, flax, wool, silk

Readers Encyclopedia, Benet's, either edition
1. Epic poets.
2. Elizabeth Barrett Browning, English child labor in mines and factories.
3. Henry Wadsworth Longfellow and Henry Rowe Schoolcraft.
4. Schoolcraft was the first to translate Indian poetry; he discovered the source of the Mississippi River, and he confused the Iroquois Hiawatha with the Chippewa young man. Longfellow repeated the error.

Roget's Thesaurus
Not all versions of Roget's will have all the same words. The following answers are a representation of several different versions:
1. nudge, thrust, jostle, assume, bear, carry, sustain, maintain, support, poke

2.   inn, hostelry, tavern
3.   adjective
4.   Just one of following: overdo, hyperbolize, exaggerate,
overdraw

Science and Technology Illustrated, Encyclopedia Britannica
1.   Volume 23, page 2880.
2.   p. 1942, 1943; precision balance(scale)
3.   Volume 10, page 1182.
4.   Etching and engraving.

United States Energy Atlas
1.   pp. 128, 131
2.   p. 389
3.   pp. 174, 179.
4.   Picture of Three Mile Island.

What's What
1.   pp. 464-465.
2.   stagecoach and hansom cab
3.   p. 381
4.   gnomon

Who was Who, Who is Who in America
1.   H for Historical
2.   congressman
3.   Mary Eno, 1864.
4. a. First treasurer and member of executive committee of
Bartholdi Statue of Liberty
     b. One of early subscribers to Metropolitan Museum of
Art.
     c. One of the founders of Yale Forest School, New
Haven, CT.
     d. Founder of Yale Summer School of Forestry, Milford,
PA.
     e. Vice-president, American Forestry Association.

World Book Encyclopedia of Science
1.   p. 49.
2.   The topmost layer of the Moon and Earth-like planets,
which has been broken up by meteoric bombardment.
3.   p. 131
4.   Charles Macintosh (1766-1843) Scottish chemist who
invented a method of waterproofing fabric. Raincoats using
that fabric were named for him.

Worldmark Encyclopedia of the States
1.   page 619
2.   page 689.   A public official empowered to hear and
investigate complaints by private citizens about government
agencies.
3.   pages 13-20.
4.   Sheldon Jackson, 1834-1909: Presbyterian missionary,
introduced reindeer to region and founded Alaska's first
college in Sitka.

abbreviations - a shortened form of a word or phrase

abstract - a summary or a brief statement of the important ideas of a book or magazine article

access - to retrieve on command or through a strategy

acknowledgement - a page recognizing original sources of visual materials

acronym - a word formed from the first letters of more than one word

added entry cards - a card catalog entry card such as joint author, series, or illustrator card

almanac - a book of facts whose focus is one specific year

alphabetical order - regular order of the letters of the alphabet

appendix - additional material usually added to the end of a book

atlas - a book or section of maps. Often includes tables, charts and illustrations concerning geographic information

author - a person who writes original material

autobiography - a book written about the life of a person by the subject of the book; written in the first person

basic cards - author, subject, and title cards for one book

bias - positive or negative attitude for or against a subject

bibliography - a listing of sources on which a work is based

binding - the hard covering of a book; the spine is the part that faces you on the shelf and protects all the signatures making up the book. The spine of the book usually has information on it indicating classification, author, and shelf location.

biography - a book written about the life of a person by another who has researched and reported

boolean operators - the words: *and, or, but*, added to topic keywords during use of software package to limit citation/abstract retrieval from on-line databases.

call number - the number in the upper left hand side of the catalog card used to identify classification and shelf location of item; a combination of letters and numbers

card catalog - a catalog of every item in the library organized through the use of multiple cards or entries for each item

cartographer - a map maker

catalog card - a card in a card file whose basic organization is alphabetical; contains standard information about one item in the library.

CD-ROM - compact disc, read only memory; informational data base for a computer, information is limited to that specific disc.

chronological order - sequence by year, time period or time era

circulation desk - check-out desk

citation - a bibliographic reference for a book, journal, magazine, etc.

classification - a system of grouping by like characteristics. The four basic library classifications are: fiction, nonfiction, biography, reference

commands - instructions punched into a computer

copyright date - date of publication

cover story - a comprehensive written discussion on a specific topic

credentials - a certificate, diploma or wide experience in an area to expertise in a field

cross reference - referrals from key words not used in a specific catalog or index to those that are

333

Glossary

cumulative index - an index that includes all citations from the first date of publication

data base - a compact store of information; also written as one word: database

detail - an aspect of a subtopic

Dewey Decimal System - a cataloging system used by most schools and public libraries to catalog all the items in the library. Main classes are shown by a three digit number and subdivisions are indicated by numbers after a decimal point.

disc - a thin, flat circular format that contains information and is read by a laser

edit - proof

encyclopedia - one book, or a set of books that provide information of a specific area or on multiple topics

exceptions - items that do not follow the usual rules as stated

expertise - expert knowledge in a particular field of study

fable - a short story that usually involves animals and teaches a lesson

fantasy - a short story that is usually make-believe and breaks through the laws of nature as we now know them

fax(facsimile machine) - copier that sends images and information across communication wires

fiction - a story that is not true whether in whole or in part

film loop - very short informational film on a specific subject

folktale - an oral tale without time or place setting circulated among a group of people becoming part of their tradition

format - arrangement

frontispiece - a picture facing the first page or tit. page of a book

glossary - a specialized dictionary that direct] relates to the word meanings or definitions of th field or area or topic about which the book wa written

historical fiction - a short story or novel wit believable characters and plot set in the past wit accurate time and place setting. It often reference people or events that are historically correct but th main characters are fictitious

illustrator - an artist who draws pictures or illus trations for a book

IMC - instructional media center; multi-medi format approach to informational access

index - found as part of a book or as a separat volume in a set of books. It alphabetically list topic, subtopic and details giving appropriate pag numbers

informational retrieval - the accessing of infor mation to fulfill a specific purpose

inset - a brief story or picture within a longer articl in a magazine

inside guides - tabs found inside the catalog draw ers separating the cards alphabetically except i drawers housing countries' histories; the tabs ar then chronologically ordered.

interlibrary loan - exchange of materials betwee libraries

keywords - main words or synonyms that repre sent key thoughts or concepts

kits - multi-media items

legend - a story passed down through many gen erations, believed to have an historic basis, but no based on total fact; the key to a map, usually foun in a corner of the map or adjacent to it

letter-by-letter - alphabetical filing that does no observe the spaces at the end of the words

library media specialist - a person who organizes a library for efficient information selection and retrieval process and offers support in all areas of the research process

Library of Congress - an alpha-numeric cataloging system used by most academic libraries to categorize all the items housed in the library

literature - all writings

media - the formats by which ideas are expressed(media is plural; medium is the singular form)

menu - a selection of choices presented on a computer screen

microfiche - a flat 4 x 6 film format of pages of a magazine or journal to be read using a special machine

microfilm - sequential photographs of magazine pages and newspaper pages on a long continuous strip of 35mm film to be read using a special machine

modern realistic fiction - a short story or novel with believable characters and plot, accurate current time and place setting but is not based on fact

mythology - served as primitive science and as a religion to the people of the time. It is a traditional story often explaining natural events through the super human efforts of the characters

narrative - a summary of a book, often including time and place setting, main characters and the basic purpose for which the book was written

networking - an arrangement of data bases. Can be used to refer to libraries working together; can be used to mean on-line databases that can be used individually or simultaneously(at the same time) to retrieve requested information by command through a software package

nonfiction - prose writing that focuses on factual information and on true events and subjects

numerical order - number sequence to include decimals and whole numbers from lowest to highest

on-line - a network of data bases whose information can be commanded through one or all bases according to a specific set of keywords or combinations of keywords over a telephone line modem and computer.

organizational exceptions - cases to which the generally accepted rule does not apply

organizational systems - four general organizational systems are alphabetical, chronological, numerical, and topical

output - final product of interworkings of database, software package, commands and keywords

password - code or string of codes used by a librarian to open an on-line computer system

periodical - magazine or journal that is published at intervals of more than one day

photographer - a person who takes pictures

picture file - separate file or catalog of pictures of specific subjects

preface - introduction

printer - a machine that prints out information as one connected to a computer

process - a method to accomplish a task

publisher - a company that prints the book, the name and address of the publisher found on the title page of the book

reference - section of the library that houses books of factual information whose focus present short, concise articles on a topic

retrieval - to find information and bring it to you

science fiction - the focus concerns the future and is based on knowledge of current technological advances as projected into the future

screens - a series of frames of information on a

Glossary

computer

search strategy - a method devised to use for information retrieval

see - refers reader from an unusual keyword to others that are used in a catalog or index

see also - refers readers to other keywords that are related to the original keyword

series - a collection of books arranged in an order that indicates progression

setting - time frame or place of location in a story

shelving - object specifically built and placed to hold items such as books in a library

slides - photographic transparencies arranged for projection

software package - the programmed material devised to help the user in information retrieval

source material - all nonfiction materials in a library which can be used for research
   [primary] - those source materials that contain original documents from which history has been made; includes speeches, laws, minutes of convening bodies.
   [secondary]- what other people have to say about primary source materials; in other words, what was and is being written about the events themselves.

spine - that part of the binding of a book on which specific shelf placement information can be found

stacks - a structure of bookshelves designed for the compact storage of books

strategy - a plan of action specifically in conducting research

string - an arrangement of databases on on-line used simultaneously(at the same time) in information retrieval

study carrels - individual areas set aside in the library to enhance independent study

subtopic - the first specific delineation of a topic and offers supportive information concerning the topic

summary - basic ideas presented in brief form

supplement-a new issue of something, such as an index that adds additional or newer information

table of contents - an overview of a book through its sections, units, and chapter arrangements in page order

thesaurus - a synonym dictionary

title - the main idea of a book

topic - the main idea of a subject

topical order - subject order

tracings - the subject headings and other items at the bottom of a catalog card for which other cards are made

transparencies - visual materials to be shown on an overhead projector

union catalog - a alphabetical listing of the holdings of all the libraries in a region.

Venn diagram - a drawing of a logical operation that expresses the limiting or expansion of a topic through the Boolean operators when working on-line

vertical file - contains alphabetically organized selected materials that cannot be placed on the library shelves due to the physical limitation of the materials.

visual aids - materials that reexplain the author's factual statements in graphic form to include: maps graphs, charts, pictures, illustrations, tables, diagrams, etc.

word-by-word alphabetical order - alphabetical filing that observes the spaces at the end of each word

work station - an area in a library of computers each of which has a different purpose

Index